Alabama's State & Local Governments

DAVID L. MARTIN

Alabama's

STATE & LOCAL

GOVERNMENTS

THIRD EDITION

THE UNIVERSITY OF ALABAMA PRESS
TUSCALOOSA & LONDON

Copyright © 1994
The University of Alabama Press
Tuscaloosa, Alabama 35487-0380
All rights reserved
Manufactured in the United States of America

designed by zig zeigler

∞

The paper on which this book is printed meets the minimum
requirements of American National Standard for Information
Science-Permanence of Paper for Printed Library Materials,
ANSI Z39.48-1984.

Library of Congress Cataloging-in-Publication Data

Martin, David L.
    Alabama's state and local governments / David L. Martin. — 3rd
ed.
        p.   cm.
    Includes bibliographical references and index.
    ISBN 0-8173-0738-9 (alk. paper)
    1. Local government—Alabama.   2. Alabama—Politics and
government.   I. Title.
JK4516.M33   1994
320.4761—dc20   94-3923

British Library Cataloguing-in-Publication Data available

To the memory of my mother . . .
who suspected all politicians

Contents

Preface ■ xiii

1. Alabama's Heritage and People ■ 1

2. Constitutional Development ■ 17

3. Voters, Nominations, and Elections ■ 43

4. Politics in Alabama ■ 57

5. The Legislature: Your Representatives in Action ■ 87

6. Elected State Officials: Leadership Has Many Faces ■ 117

7. State Administration:
Services and Selected Agencies ■ 141

8. Alabama's Judicial System ■ 183

9. Alabama Local Government ■ 217

10. Challenges for Alabama's Citizens ■ 243

Appendixes ■ 253

Index ■ 269

Illustrations

Figures

1.1	English Colony of West Florida, 1763–1783	3
1.2	Alabama at Statehood in 1819	4
1.3	Alabama's Rivers and Regions	6
1.4	Alabama's Forests	9
1.5	Alabama Median Income by County	11
1.6	Metropolitan Statistical Areas	13
2.1	Steamboat at Montgomery	18
2.2	Alabama State House, 1861	20
2.3	Constitutional Convention, 1875	24
2.4	Alabama Councils of Governments	36
3.1	Notice to Voters	44
3.2	Alabama Voter Registration Application	45
3.3	Absentee Voting Affidavit	47
3.4	Challenge Oath	48
3.5	Sample Ballot with Party Emblems	50
4.1	Appointment of Principal Campaign Committee	61
4.2	Summary of Contributions and Expenditures	63
4.3	Fair Campaign Practices Act: Cash Contributions	64
4.4	In-Kind Contributions	65
4.5	Receipts from Other Sources	66
4.6	Fair Campaign Practices Act: Expenditures	67
4.7	Statement of Economic Interests	68

4.8 Lobbyists in the Capitol   76
4.9 Lobbyist's Registration Statement   77
4.10 Principal's Registration Statement   80
4.11 State Ethics Commission Complaint Form   82
4.12 Alabama Council of Association Executives   83
5.1 The Alabama Legislature Meets in the Statehouse   89
5.2 The Senate Presiding Officer and Secretary   92
5.3 A Joint Legislative Committee Meeting   98
5.4 Alabama House of Representatives in Floor Session   105
5.5 House Member Using the Electronic Voting System   106
5.6 A Citizen Petitions for Redress of Grievances   111
5.7 State Senate Lobbyist Registration Form   113
6.1 The Governor's Mansion, Montgomery   118
6.2 Governor "Big Jim" Folsom on the Campaign Trail   124
6.3 Governor Wallace Addresses the Legislature   127
6.4 Media Coverage at Governor Hunt's Conviction   131
7.1 State Government of Alabama Organizational
     Chart   142
7.2 Higher Education Institutions in Alabama   150
7.3 Population Vital Statistics   154
7.4 AIDS in Alabama, 1982–92   155
7.5 State Highway Construction and Maintenance   161
7.6 Alabama State Docks and Inland Ports   163
7.7 "Wet" and "Dry" Counties and Cities   165
7.8 Offenders on Parole and Probation   170
7.9 Alabama National Guard Disaster Assistance   172
7.10 State Position Announcement   174
7.11 Application for Civil Service Examination   176
7.12 Alabama's State Capitol Complex   179
7.13 Persons State Office Building   180
8.1 Alabama Judicial System   186
8.2 Municipal and District Courts   192
8.3 A Courtroom View   194
8.4 Alabama's Judicial Circuits   196
8.5 Anatomy of a Jury Trial   198

8.6	State Felony Case Process	200
8.7	Alabama Search Warrant	201
8.8	Grand Jury Indictment	208
8.9	Juror Qualifications	211
9.1	Alabama County Seats	218
9.2	Incorporated Places in Alabama	229
9.3	Environmental Testing Near Residences	230
9.4	The Mayor-Council Form of Municipal Government	232
10.1	Alabama's State Budget	244
10.2	The Tax Collecting Process	246
10.3	State Government Bond Offering	249

Tables

1.1	Alabama's Population	7
1.2	Distribution of Alabama Household Incomes, 1990	8
1.3	Types of Alabama Employment, 1990	10
2.1	Amendments to the Alabama Constitution of 1901	28
5.1	Alabama Legislative Committees	94
5.2	ALERT: the Alabama Legislative Computer	101
7.1	Alabama's Largest State Agencies	143
7.2	Leading Alabama Crops and Livestock	144
7.3	Occupational Licensing in Alabama	147
7.4	Primary Reason for Substance Abuse Treatment	156
7.5	Public Welfare in Alabama	158
7.6	Medicaid in Alabama	159
7.7	Worker's Compensation in Alabama	160
7.8	Crime in Alabama	167
7.9	Alabama's State Prison Population	168
8.1	The Alabama Supreme Court	187
8.2	Alabama Court of Civil Appeals	189
8.3	Alabama Court of Criminal Appeals	190
8.4	Alabama's Trial Courts: Record Caseloads	195

9.1   Alabama County Commissions   220
9.2   Methods of Electing County Commissions   222
9.3   Minimum Salaries for County Officials   224
10.1 Alabama Appropriations by Purpose   245

Preface

The purpose of this book, now in its third edition, continues to be to give Alabama's citizens an understanding of the structure and operations of their government. This comprehensive yet concise reference is needed since the state's *Official and Statistical Register* has not appeared in many years due to fiscal limitations, and even annual legislative directories are published by private interest groups. The suggestions for further reading at the end of each chapter give more specialized sources of information.

A second distinguishing characteristic of this text is that it is written for students. It defines terms, explains concepts, and is illustrated with examples to facilitate study in political science. Where practices and procedures vary in Alabama, these differences are pointed out.

Most important, this book discusses policies of interest to all Alabamians as citizens, taxpayers, and voters. Arguments for and against are given on major issues, for politics is inherently controversial, which explains why politics is Alabama's favorite event after football. The operations of our state and local governments affect our daily lives in a multitude of ways. The choices made in the past affect our quality of life today, and the decisions made by our governments will extend far into the future.

Many people contribute to the composition of a book. Comments by readers and teachers have been used in preparing this third edition, as have responses of my own students, who simply ask "why?" in class. Officials too numerous to mention generously provided information and illustrations, but any errors are the responsibility of the author, and any corrections or suggestions would be appreciated.

David L. Martin

O N E

Alabama's Heritage
and People

Alabama became the twenty-second of the United States in 1819, covering some 50,750 square miles (28th in area), and its present population of slightly over four million ranks it twenty-second among the states. The name *Alabama* is derived from an indigenous tribe and was first written in three of the chronicles of the De Soto expedition of 1540.

Discovery

The Spanish were the first Europeans to explore the land of the Alabamians. De Soto's expedition moved south along the Coosa River, across the center of the fertile Black Belt near present-day Selma, and then southward to the native village of Maubila, located somewhere between the Alabama and Tombigbee rivers. Here the 500 explorers fought a pitched battle with the Native Americans under Chief Tuscaloosa ("Black Warrior") in which at least twenty Spaniards and 2,500 Maubilians were killed. Licking its wounds and unwilling to admit defeat, the De Soto expedition turned away from a Spanish fleet waiting in the Gulf and moved up the Tombigbee Valley into what is presently Mississippi. An attempt by Tristan de Luna in 1559 to found a colony on the Gulf Coast was frustrated by a hurricane and the hostility of the inhabitants inland, when the survivors sent food-gathering expeditions up the Alabama and Coosa rivers.

Thus it was the French who founded the first permanent settlement in 1702 on Mobile Bay, under Jean Baptiste Le-Moyne, Sieur (Lord) de Bienville. Mobile was established at its present site in 1711, and the French heritage is indicated by some of the original street names—St. Louis, Royal, Dauphin, and Conti—and by the annual Mardi Gras celebration.

From Frontier to Statehood

Alabama remained part of the Louisiana Territory until the French and Indian War (Seven Years War, 1754–1763) when victorious England acquired the land east of the Mississippi and created the colony of West Florida below latitude 32°28′ (a line running from where the Yazoo River flows into the Mississippi to a point just south of the present city of Columbus, Georgia, on the Chattahoochee) and reserved the country northward for the Indians.

At the conclusion of the American Revolution in 1783, Spain received both west and east Florida below the 31st parallel, so that by 1798 all of what is now Alabama and Mississippi except a thirty-mile-deep strip of the Gulf Coast was in American hands. Pressure from settlers coming from Georgia led to conflict with the tribes, and Tennessee General Andrew Jackson defeated the militant "Red Stick" Creeks at the Battle of Horseshoe Bend (of the Tallapoosa River) in 1813 on his way to victory over the British at New Orleans. This accelerated a series of Indian land cessions (see Figure 1.2) opening additional areas for settlement by Tennesseans, Georgians, and Napoleonic exiles (the "Vine and Olive colony" of Demopolis). The Indian removal acts of the 1830s under President Jackson forced the remaining tribes on "the trail of tears" to Indian Territory, now Oklahoma. While some 16,000 Alabamians reported themselves to be Native Americans in the 1990 census, not until 1984 was the Poarch band of Creeks

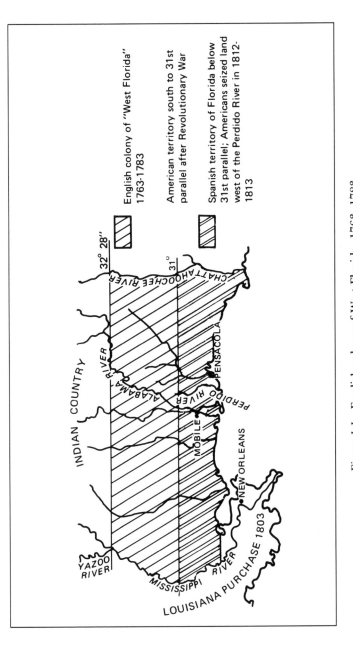

Figure 1.1 English colony of West Florida, 1763–1783.

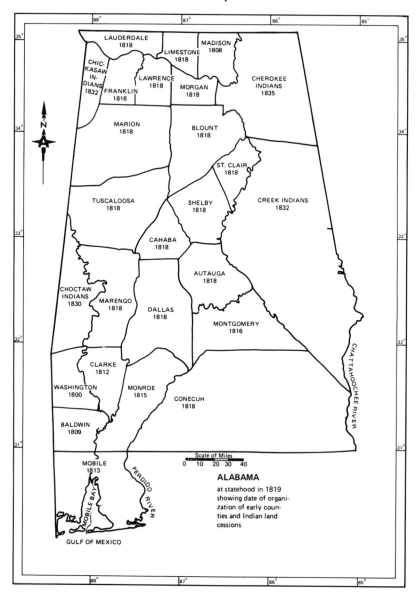

Figure 1.2 Alabama at statehood in 1819.

again recognized by the federal government. Other tribes are seeking recognition.

Originally part of the Mississippi Territory created in 1798, the Alabama Territory was organized in 1817 along the present state boundaries. William Wyatt Bibb of Georgia was appointed territorial governor and then elected as the state's first governor in 1819. Early Alabama politics was a contest between the "Georgia faction" and the "North Carolina machine," composed of settlers from those regions. Alabama's politics soon became intrastate, as the following chapter on constitutional development relates. By the 1900s political pundits characterized the state as divided among the "hillbillies" of north Alabama, the "ginseng diggers" along the Coosa River, the "rosin chawers" of the piney woods, the "Wiregrass braves" of the southeast, the "sorghum soppers" in the west, and the "Black Belt princes" of the central plantations. A defeated politician is said to be "sent to Buck's Pocket" in northeastern Alabama (Figure 1.3). This humorous classification illustrates the state's political diversity.

Population Growth and Patterns

Collection of vital statistics is a necessary function of state government for computing population change, labor supply, economic dependency, and other factors in formulating public policies. Table 1.1 shows Alabama's population change in recent censuses and the percentage in each age group. Such statistics are reflected in government programs. For example, the increase in the elderly led to introduction of senior citizen programs which had not existed earlier.

Alabama's 3.8% population increase during the 1980s was the state's lowest growth rate reported by the census this century. During the decade 1980–1990, over half of Alabama's sixty-seven counties lost population, more counties than during the 1970s. Population change has an important impact

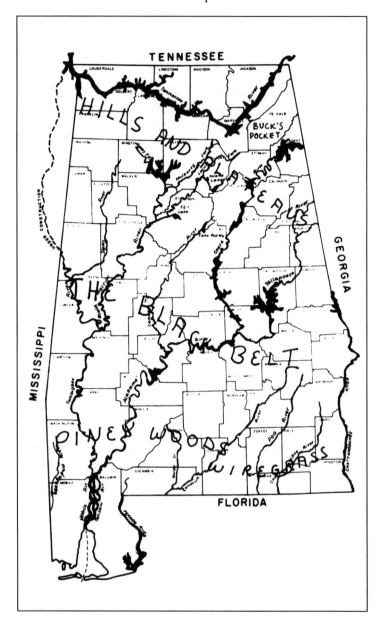

Figure 1.3 Alabama's rivers and regions.

Table 1.1
Alabama's Population

Census	Total	% under 16	% 16–44	% 45–64	% 65+
1940	2,832,961	33	48	15	4
1950	3,061,743	32	45	16	7
1960	3,266,740	34	39	19	8
1970	3,444,165	29	41	20	10
1980	3,893,888	23	46	19	12
1990	4,040,587	23	45	19	13

upon local government revenues and services and the apportionment of legislative seats.

Demographically, the 1990 census reported that 74% of Alabamians were white, 25% black, and 1% American Indian, Asian, or other races. Women outnumbered men 52% to 48%.

Population change is affected by the three factors of migration, fertility, and mortality. Alabama experienced heavy net migration losses during each decade from 1930 to 1970, with a consequent loss of congressional seats to other states. During the 1970s there was a population migration to the sun belt states, but there was a decline in migration to Alabama during the 1980s. Alabama's fertility and mortality rates have both declined although both are above the national average.

In 1960, for the first time, a majority of Alabamians lived in urban areas (designated by the census as places of over 2,500 people). Today 60% of Alabamians live in urban areas, compared to 75% of all Americans. The effect of these population factors will be examined in a following section on priorities and problems facing the state.

The Economy: Wealth and Resources

Alabama remains one of the poorer states in terms of personal income, even within the southeastern region. Table 1.2 shows the range of Alabama household incomes compared with those of its neighbors. Alabama's considerable natural resources and enormous energy supplies from natural gas, hydroelectricity, three nuclear power plants, and coal combine to form industrial potential. In the 1970s, forest products surpassed iron and steel as the state's largest industry, and Alabama now ranks third among the states as a wood supplier. In agriculture, Alabama raises poultry, cattle, hogs, soybeans, and peanuts (Dothan claims to be the "peanut capital of the world"), but cotton is no longer king. Besides iron and coal, Alabama mines marble (used in many government buildings in Washington and elsewhere), limestone, gravel, salt, and oil. Seafood (shrimp, oysters, crabs, red snapper, mullet, and flounder) is landed at Alabama's gulf ports, and there is commercial aquaculture in many inland fish ponds.

Alabama has a "right to work law" (legislation barring union membership as a condition for employment), and only one tenth of the state's two million workers are unionized. Periodic recessions have often pushed Alabama's unemployment rates above the national average as orders for raw materials are cut

Table 1.2
Distribution of Alabama Household Incomes, 1990

Income	AL	FL	GA	MS	TN	U.S.
under $15,000	33%	25%	25%	39%	31%	24%
$15,000–24,999	19%	20%	18%	20%	20%	18%
$25,000–49,999	31%	34%	34%	29%	33%	34%
$50,000–99,999	14%	17%	19%	11%	14%	20%
$100,000 or more	3%	4%	4%	1%	2%	4%

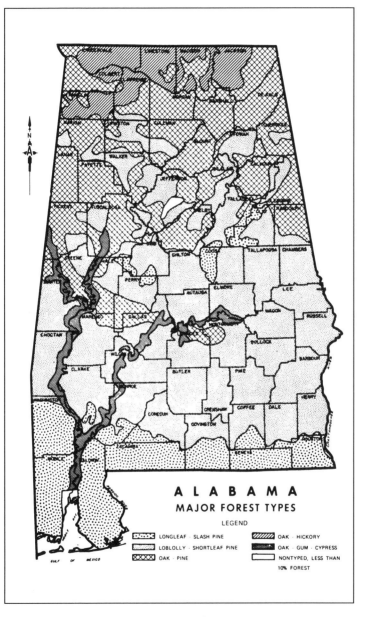

Figure 1.4 Alabama's forests. (Source: U.S. Forest Service)

Table 1.3
Types of Alabama Employment, 1990

Services	29%
Manufacturing	23%
Trade	20%
Government	15%
Agriculture	3%
Other	10%

back or lower-skilled workers laid off. Rural counties with smaller work forces tend to have the highest unemployment, sometimes exceeding 10%.

To interest companies in locating or expanding their operations in Alabama, the Alabama Development Office matches by computer a list of suitable locations with an industry's specific needs for a plant site. The Alabama Industrial Development Training Program recruits potential employees and trains them as required at no cost to the company. Such incentives are part of the government's efforts to diversify Alabama's economic base.

Priorities and Problems

■ *Personal income* means the current income of persons or households from all sources, and it measures the collective wealth of a community or state. While Alabama has tried to improve its relative standing, the 1990 census showed that nearly one in six Alabama families had incomes below the poverty level defined by the government. There are also great disparities in wealth among Alabama's sixty-seven counties, as shown in Figure 1.5. Measurements of income are an important indicator of a state's level of prosperity and potential for further development.

	Median Income[1]			Percent of Families[2] With Income Less Than		
	1990 $	1980 $	1970 $	Poverty 1990	Poverty 1980	Poverty 1970
AUTAUGA	32,240	18,433	7,530	12.0	13.5	19.6
BALDWIN	30,199	16,917	7,338	10.4	13.2	17.9
BARBOUR	23,838	11,952	5,133	20.0	24.5	55.9
BIBB	23,714	14,709	5,559	17.3	17.5	29.8
BLOUNT	26,323	14,701	6,170	11.4	15.3	22.2
BULLOCK	17,796	10,623	3,737	31.4	28.4	46.7
BUTLER	21,499	12,385	5,331	24.6	20.3	31.1
CALHOUN	28,340	16,131	7,401	11.7	12.6	16.6
CHAMBERS	26,331	15,336	7,106	13.4	13.2	19.9
CHEROKEE	24,932	14,036	6,137	14.2	15.1	21.1
CHILTON	26,203	14,206	5,691	13.1	15.6	24.8
CHOCTAW	23,609	12,277	5,319	23.8	27.6	35.4
CLARKE	23,080	14,815	5,900	19.5	20.3	29.8
CLAY	24,145	13,360	5,756	14.0	16.8	28.8
CLEBURNE	25,900	14,642	6,448	11.4	13.8	22.3
COFFEE	27,653	16,292	6,776	11.7	14.1	19.9
COLBERT	27,862	17,664	7,735	11.1	11.1	18.7
CONECUH	21,231	11,880	4,729	22.8	24.3	35.5
COOSA	23,472	12,654	6,238	15.3	20.6	23.6
COVINGTON	23,257	13,791	5,930	16.5	15.5	24.5
CRENSHAW	21,368	11,021	4,527	19.9	24.8	38.3
CULLMAN	25,856	14,161	6,207	12.1	15.5	21.3
DALE	27,585	14,176	7,401	10.9	14.1	14.8
DALLAS	20,517	12,817	5,828	31.4	25.4	31.5
DEKALB	24,836	13,901	5,316	14.2	16.4	29.4
ELMORE	30,853	17,510	6,891	11.1	13.2	21.9
ESCAMBIA	22,858	14,113	6,321	21.9	16.4	25.1
ETOWAH	27,071	16,275	7,645	13.2	12.9	17.4
FAYETTE	26,002	14,802	5,501	15.4	15.3	24.6
FRANKLIN	22,755	14,783	6,049	17.2	14.4	23.5
GENEVA	24,989	13,105	5,787	15.6	17.4	25.4
GREENE	15,663	9,917	3,034	39.2	36.1	53.6
HALE	18,272	10,368	3,852	28.7	33.0	44.7
HENRY	27,554	13,952	5,139	13.1	17.7	31.6
HOUSTON	29,818	16,327	7,376	12.8	13.5	19.9
JACKSON	25,772	15,706	6,372	12.6	13.7	22.1
JEFFERSON	31,609	18,880	8,562	12.7	12.0	14.5
LAMAR	25,506	14,958	5,247	14.4	14.3	34.4
LAUDERDALE	29,589	17,585	7,608	11.3	11.4	18.8
LAWRENCE	25,478	14,689	6,083	16.5	19.4	27.3
LEE	32,596	17,176	7,593	13.2	13.9	17.9
LIMESTONE	31,739	16,303	6,820	11.2	14.0	21.7
LOWNDES	18,535	9,766	3,823	31.7	36.7	50.5
MACON	20,096	11,454	5,058	28.1	28.4	37.4
MADISON	39,264	19,350	10,439	8.4	10.8	11.6
MARENGO	23,015	13,356	4,309	24.3	25.5	20.2
MARION	22,394	14,228	5,964	15.6	13.7	22.5
MARSHALL	26,135	14,757	6,596	14.5	13.9	20.8
MOBILE	27,601	17,359	7,811	17.5	15.4	18.7
MONROE	26,413	14,585	5,442	18.0	19.3	34.3
MONTGOMERY	32,351	17,990	8,220	14.1	14.7	18.7
MORGAN	32,912	18,276	8,360	9.4	10.8	16.2
PERRY	16,404	9,983	4,258	36.8	32.8	41.1
PICKENS	22,474	12,735	5,293	23.3	22.6	32.5
PIKE	23,735	12,766	5,644	20.6	20.1	29.8
RANDOLPH	23,994	12,614	5,800	14.6	18.2	27.4
RUSSELL	24,642	13,821	5,996	16.8	19.6	28.2
ST. CLAIR	27,388	16,374	6,461	12.1	12.6	21.8
SHELBY	42,549	20,514	7,155	7.1	9.9	18.7
SUMTER	17,881	12,106	3,938	32.9	28.7	44.9
TALLADEGA	25,225	14,806	7,071	16.3	16.3	20.8
TALLAPOOSA	27,247	14,905	6,591	13.1	13.3	20.3
TUSCALOOSA	30,135	17,166	7,435	13.5	14.6	19.9
WALKER	25,322	15,831	6,317	14.2	13.8	23.6
WASHINGTON	23,818	15,623	6,041	21.4	19.4	31.5
WILCOX	15,306	10,679	3,917	39.3	36.2	46.4
WINSTON	22,023	13,679	6,268	15.7	15.6	22.7
ALABAMA	28,688	16,353	7,266	14.3	14.8	20.7

[1]The median is the midpoint. Example - in Jackson County, 1970, half the families had an income less than $6,372 and half had an income greater than $6,372.

[2]The 1970 poverty level varied by size of family, head of household and urban-rural residence.

Figure 1.5 Alabama median income by county. (Source: U.S. Bureau of the Census, courtesy of the Alabama Department of Economic and Community Affairs)

■ *Economic development* is thus a major priority for Alabama. Historically the state has encouraged immigration, and the growth philosophy continues to be actively promoted today. The generative cycle of income and investment creates demand for new jobs, more production, and ultimately a greater tax base. Alabama happened to develop first in agriculture and then extractive industries adversely affected by recessions, showing the importance of economic diversification, not simply growth. A jurisdiction's wealth, the political willingness to tax it, and the purposes for which government will spend its resources are what make politics controversial.

■ *Urban Growth.* The United States Census Bureau defines metropolitan growth in terms of Metropolitan Statistical Areas (MSAs), consisting of a county or group of contiguous counties that include a central city (or adjacent "twin cities") with a population of at least 50,000 or an urbanized area with a total population of at least 100,000. MSAs are named after their largest city or cities, and Alabama's counties presently so defined are shown in Figure 1.6. Additional MSAs may be designated if there is future urban growth. The political significance of MSAs is that these areas are eligible to receive federal aid targeted to metropolitan areas.

■ *Responsible Political Leadership.* Such growth brings pressure for political change. Chapter 2 discusses traditional rivalries between parts of Alabama, Chapter 4 covers increasing political participation by African Americans, and Chapter 5, reapportionment of the state legislature. To maximize Alabama's growth, government policies ought to be wisely considered by elected officials who are responsive to state and local needs. Recent political campaigns have thus focused on the need for "leadership" for long-term development. Origination of policy alternatives often occurs in a competitive, two-

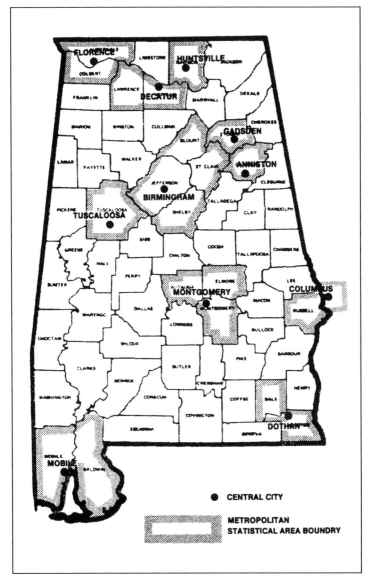

Figure 1.6 Metropolitan Statistical Areas. (Source: U.S. Bureau of the Census, courtesy of the Alabama Department of Economic and Community Affairs)

party system. While Democrats have dominated election to state offices, Republicans have consistently won congressional seats since 1964, and the GOP carried the state for president in 1964, 1972, 1980, 1984, 1988, and 1992. The increasing diversity of Alabama's economy and voters guarantees contests in the political arena.

■ *Education.* In the 1990 census, two-thirds of adult Alabamians reported that they were high school graduates, 16% had earned bachelor's degrees from college, and 6% held graduate or professional degrees. These percentages are far below those of other states. Education is the most important determinant of lifetime income, but in the early 1990s, Alabama spent $3,000 per pupil in public schools, among the lowest of American states. Yet the State of Alabama during the same period devoted half of all its funds appropriated to the schools. Migration of young people educated at Alabama's expense to other states in search of better-paying jobs is a source of serious concern. Governmental priorities are decided not only by voting, but also by individual actions, which collectively determine the future of the state.

For Further Reading

Alabama Department of Economic and Community Affairs. *Alabama County Data Book.* Montgomery: issued annually.

Alabama Department of Industrial Relations. *Alabama Labor Market News.* Montgomery: issued monthly.

Alabama Department of Public Health. *[Year] Alabama Vital Events.* Montgomery: Center for Health Statistics: issued annually.

The De Soto Chronicles, Lawrence A. Clayton, Vernon James Knight, Jr., and Edward C. Moore, eds. 2 vols. Tuscaloosa: University of Alabama Press, 1993.

Dodd, Donald B. *Historical Atlas of Alabama.* University: University of Alabama Press, 1974.

United States Bureau of the Census. *1990 Census of Population, Summary Tape File 3A.* Washington, D.C.: Government Printing Office. Also available on CD-ROM in many public libraries.

Videotape: "Now Let Us Praise Famous Men—Revisited," Public Broadcasting System, "The American Experience" series, 1988. (Alabama sharecroppers—and their descendants.)

TWO

Constitutional Development

Many historical factors are manifested in constitutional development. Constitutions not only set up the basic framework of government, but also represent the prevalent political forces in society.

Alabama's Constitutions

Alabama, like many other states, has written several state constitutions at various periods in its history. Each of Alabama's six constitutions has been a statement of views about the purpose of state government when it was adopted.

The *Constitution of 1819* is often called the "frontier constitution" because it was adopted when Alabama was admitted to the Union as a state and lasted until secession in 1861. The enabling act passed by Congress allowing the Alabama Territory to write a constitution authorized the calling of a convention to meet in Huntsville. Forty-four delegates were elected to the convention, many of whom became state political leaders. Sectional rivalry was shown between the twenty-eight delegates elected from north Alabama and the sixteen from the southern half of the state, which had a smaller but wealthier population. John W. Walker of Huntsville, northern Alabama's candidate, was elected the convention's president. In apportioning representation in the state legislature, south Alabama wanted to use the United States Constitution formula of counting five black slaves as three white persons, or repre-

sentation by counties, but north Alabama successfully demanded a white population basis only, which favored that section. Negotiations provided that the first legislature meet in
Huntsville, but that subsequent sessions convene at Cahaba
along the southern Alabama River until a permanent capital
was to be decided by 1825. The regional struggle moved the
state capital from Huntsville (1819–1820), to Cahaba
(1821–1825) which flooded, to Tuscaloosa (1826–1846) which
burned, and finally to Montgomery, which was centrally located for steamboat and railroad transportation. Montgomery's selection indicated the growing political power of the fertile Black Belt plantation economy, and the city's businessmen
raised money for a new capitol building. The sobriquet "Goat

Figure 2.1 The location of Montgomery was determined by how far
up the river steamboats could go without grounding. (Courtesy of
the Alabama Film Commission. Used by permission)

Hill" derives from the animals used for lawn mowing or possibly legislative greed.

A drafting committee of fifteen, chaired by Clement C. Clay, composed what has been considered a liberal document for its time. The 1819 constitution provided for universal white male suffrage without property qualifications for voting or holding office. Slaves accused of more than petty crimes had the right of an "impartial trial" by jury, and maltreatment of a slave was punishable (except in case of insurrection) as if "the like offense had been committed on a free white person." Passage of the strict State Slave Code by the legislature in 1852 meant the constitutional provisions were rarely enforced.

The legislature was the strongest branch of government, consisting originally of representatives elected for one year and senators elected for three years, terms lengthened by popular amendment to two years for representatives in 1846 and four years for senators in 1850. The legislature appointed a secretary of state, a state treasurer, and a comptroller of public accounts. Judges were elected for life by the legislature until 1830, when they were appointed for six-year terms, and lower court judges were elected by the people beginning in 1850. The governor was elected by all white males over twenty-one for a two-year term and could succeed himself except that he could not serve more than four years in any six-year period. A sheriff was elected in each county by the voters for a three-year term.

The constitution allowed creation of a state bank, which was established following the Panic of 1819, since credit was scarce on the frontier. Initially the bank was profitable enough to cover the expenses of state government without taxation. Unfortunately, the bank was subjected to political manipulation and made unsound loans to legislators, resulting in bankruptcy after the Panic of 1837. The failure of the bank not only wiped out the educational trust funds for the public schools and the university, but saddled the state with debt and destroyed public confidence in government. The restrictive nature of subsequent constitutions was affected by the conservative attitudes toward government as a result of this scandal.

Alabama's first constitution was not ratified by the people, but was accepted by Congress as the "republican form of government" required by the federal Constitution, so the territory became a state on December 14, 1819, "Alabama Day."

The *Constitution of 1861* is known as the "secession constitution" because it separated Alabama "from the government known as the United States of America." Except for the explanatory provisions stressing the state's "sovereign and independent character" and more restrictive regulations on banking, the 1861 constitution retained intact the basic sections of the 1819 document. After the presidential election of 1860,

Figure 2.2 Alabama Statehouse, 1861. (Courtesy of the Alabama Department of Archives and History. Used by permission)

the state was divided over what should be done, so one hundred delegates were elected to a secession convention meeting in Montgomery in March 1861. Most of the fifty-four delegates from south Alabama wanted to secede immediately, while the forty-six delegates from north Alabama, the "cooperationists," favored efforts at reconciliation. North Alabama's demand that the eighty-seven to five decision for secession be submitted to a vote for the people was turned down, so the popular will was uncertain. After divisive procedural votes, the convention unanimously adopted the 1861 constitution. Several northern counties had Unionist sentiments, and one reputedly declared independence as "the Free State of Winston" after Alabama seceded. While Alabama served as the "Cradle of the Confederacy" since its first seat of government was Montgomery, the state was divided (as was said, "Rich man's war, but a poor man's fight") on the secession issue.

The *Constitution of 1865* was termed "the reorganization constitution" following the defeat of the Confederacy. President Andrew Johnson appointed Lewis E. Parsons of Talladega as provisional governor until such time as a loyalist constitution be written and a legislature elected by voters who would swear allegiance to the federal Union. The ninety-nine elected convention delegates who met in Montgomery in September 1865 largely consisted of those who had opposed secession in 1861 and the anti-Confederates of north Alabama. Fewer prominent figures were in evidence, since most public leaders had held Confederate positions. The convention was headed by former United States Senator Benjamin Fitzpatrick who, because of his Unionist sentiments, had reluctantly left Congress in 1861 and retired to his Wetumpka plantation during the war. The convention declared secession null and void, repudiated Alabama's war debts of over $20 million, abolished slavery in Alabama, and instructed the first legislature to ratify the Thirteenth Amendment, a condition for reentering the Union. However, the first legislature under the

1865 constitution was also instructed to prohibit racial inter-marriage, and state office was still restricted to white males. The legislature now elected not only the state executive officers, but the attorney general and prosecuting attorneys in each judicial circuit as well. The 1865 constitution could be summed up by its provision regarding the newly freed slaves: "Guard them and the state against any evils that may arise from their sudden emancipation." African-American suffrage was not contemplated.

These provisions were unacceptable to the radicals in Congress, who refused to seat the Alabama delegation. The Reconstruction Acts were passed over President Andrew Johnson's vetoes, and the state was placed under the military governorship of Major General Wager Swayne during 1867 and 1868.

The *Constitution of 1868* is thus called the "reconstruction" or "radical" constitution, since it was designed to get Alabama readmitted to the Union on the radicals' terms. Of the one hundred delegates, ninety-seven were Republicans (called "scalawags" by other southerners), nineteen blacks, and about twenty-six northerners ("carpetbaggers") who came south at Reconstruction and were elected by constituencies composed of blacks and the few whites who were not disenfranchised by Confederate affiliations. The Reconstruction Acts made black male suffrage a condition of readmission to the Union, disenfranchised erstwhile Confederates, and provided that the new constitution be popularly ratified by those voters taking a loyalty oath, so that the suffrage issue became a bitter dispute in the convention. North Alabamians of Unionist sentiments who had suffered persecution under the Confederacy wished to bar their political opponents. The 1868 constitution provided for the election of all state officers by the people, based legislative apportionment on the entire population rather than whites alone, and created several new offices, such as lieutenant governor, commissioner of industrial resources, and a state board of education, all of which could be filled by the carpetbaggers. Indeed, whole sections of the 1868 constitution were copied from those of midwestern states. Increased support for public education was pledged, although much of the money was stolen or misused, and whites demanded separate schools. Public office was no longer restricted to white males, and residency requirements were reduced. For the first time, a limit on taxation was put in the state's constitution. The legal rights of women were enhanced, the poor were protected by personal property exemptions and homesteading of land, and imprisonment for debt was absolutely prohibited.

The 1868 document was the first Alabama constitution to be submitted to the people for ratification. The Reconstruction Acts required that a majority of all electors approve a constitution by referendum, and many whites registered their protest by staying home. Amid charges of widespread election irregularities, the measure passed overwhelmingly, but not quite by a majority of all registered voters. The Alabama constitution became part of the Reconstruction battle between President Andrew Johnson and the radicals in Congress. The president objected to forcing upon the state a constitution supported by less than half the electorate, but the radicals in Congress overrode his veto and Alabama was readmitted to the Union in June of 1868.

The *Constitution of 1875* is known as the "redeemer" or "Bourbon" constitution because it marked regained control by the white conservatives after Reconstruction. Of the hundred delegates elected, a majority were lawyers, many were ex-Confederates, and only a few were Republicans, including four blacks. The conservative delegates intended to restore white supremacy, reduce the state's debt, abolish the "unnecessary carpetbag offices" (such as lieutenant governor, commissioner of industrial resources, and the board of education), and promote honesty and economy in government by reducing all state executives' salaries and limiting sessions of

Figure 2.3 Constitutional convention, 1875. (Courtesy of the Alabama Department of Archives and History. Used by permission)

the legislature to fifty days every two years. Abuse of the state's power to issue development bonds by railroad promoters had quadrupled the state's indebtedness and led to the constitutional prohibition against public credit being extended to any corporation or association. The state, counties, and cities were restricted in the amounts they could tax. These limitations favored by the agrarian conservatives made the 1875 document much longer than previous Alabama constitutions and also hampered the state's subsequent expansion, since constitutions are more difficult to amend than legislative enactments.

A state debt commission was subsequently appointed, and it repudiated many of the unconstitutional and fraudulent bonds issued under the carpetbaggers and reduced the amount of valid debts to fit the state's ability to pay. This impaired the state's ability to borrow, and money could be obtained only at high interest rates, since Alabama had become a poor risk for lenders. The conservatives' image of integrity was also tarnished in the 1880s by the state treasurer (reelected under the nickname "Honest Ike"), who absconded to Mexico with $230,000 in state funds. However, an asset in Alabama politics from 1874 to the end of the century was a Confederate war record. So many gray veterans were elected that the era has been called the "rule of the brigadier generals."

The Republican Party's remaining strength after the defeat of 1874 was in the Black Belt counties, but their legislative representation was reduced by the 1875 convention, and local elective offices were made appointive by the governor (controlled by the conservatives) so that the party declined as the carpetbaggers left until the Black Belt became synonymous with Bourbon plantations. Most voters joined the Democratic Party, whose nomination label, the rooster and banner of "white supremacy," virtually assured election. The usual compromises under this one-party system were an unwritten two-term limit on the governorship (formalized by a 1968 amendment) and a tacit agreement that one United States senator come from north Alabama and the other from the southern part of the state.

The *Constitution of 1901*, Alabama's present constitution, has been called the "disenfranchising constitution" because it effectively kept African Americans from voting until the civil rights acts of the 1960s. Blacks had been progressively disenfranchised by complicated election laws and gerrymandering (drawing election districts so as to exclude voters), as well as by intimidation and violence. Both the Bourbons and the reformers of increasingly industrialized north Alabama had engaged in election fraud and the manipulation of voters to attain victory. The Populist revolt of the 1890s, composed of poor farmers and laborers, convinced the Bourbon leaders and the industrial magnates that the ballot should be kept from the hands of the masses, both black and white.

The 155 delegates to the 1901 convention enacted the most restrictive qualifications for voting: lengthy residency requirements in the state and election districts; good character as defined by lawful occupation and by never having been convicted of any of thirty specified crimes (including wife beating); and ability to read and write the United States Constitution, expanded by the 1946 Boswell amendment to an "understanding" test, meaning complicated questions which could be administered in a discriminatory manner. To be eligible to vote involved paying a poll tax of $1.50 (a laborer's half-day's pay at that time), which became accumulative until age forty-five if not paid each year nine months before the November election. It has been estimated that by the 1940s more whites (600,000) were disenfranchised by the poll tax than blacks (520,000). With over a million adults excluded, there were only 440,000 registered voters.

To ensure ratification of the constitution there was a "grandfather clause" which until 1903 allowed the educational and property qualifications to be waived if a man's ancestors had fought in any American war. One had only to be twenty-one years of age and pay the poll tax. (In contrast to some western states, in Alabama women were not allowed to vote until the federal Nineteenth Amendment was ratified in 1920.) The popular vote on the 1901 constitution again showed sectionalism: north Alabama and the Wiregrass, where Populism had been strong, were against it, fearing disenfranchisement of poor whites. Southern and Black Belt Alabama, which had favored secession and exclusion of African Americans, overwhelmingly approved, and the 1901 constitution was adopted 108,613 to 81,734.

The conservative attitude of the delegates was also reflected by other restrictions placed upon the government. The legislature was to meet only once every four years for fifty days, the most infrequent regular session of any American state. So many special sessions had to be called to transact business that a 1939 amendment adopted biennial sessions of thirty-six legislative days each. Executive leadership was diffused by the creation of the offices of lieutenant governor and commissioner of agriculture and industries. The governor's term was lengthened along with those of other state executives from two to four years, but the officials were forbidden successive terms until a 1968 amendment allowed two consecutive terms in office. Counties and municipalities were restricted on the taxes they could levy and the amounts they could borrow. The state was more severely restrained than before on the amounts it could tax and new state debt was limited. Legislators and judges were prohibited from accepting free railroad passes, an admonition illustrating distrust of corporations. The education article specified separate school systems; no child of either race would be permitted to attend a school of the other race. Section 102 prohibited the legalizing of marriage between whites and blacks. Many sections of the 1901 constitution have now been held unconstitutional by federal or state courts.[1] The legislature was restricted from enacting local, special, or private legislation upon thirty-one subjects in the notorious Section 104.

Alabama's Constitution Today: How Much Longer?

Alabama's 1901 constitution is now the longest in the nation, since Georgians voted in 1982 to adopt an entirely new state constitution. By the 1990s, some 550 constitutional amendments had been adopted (many others have been submitted to the voters and failed), producing an Alabama constitution hundreds of thousands of words long, compared to only 5,700 words in the United States Constitution with twenty-seven amendments made over 200 years. Only about one-fourth of the Alabama amendments are general, applying statewide; the rest (containing two-thirds of the words) are local, having limited applicability. This is because the 1901 restrictions on local legislation meant that any city or county wanting a change had to submit a constitutional amendment to be voted on by the people of the entire state, who were often unfamiliar with the local issues. Amendment No. 425, passed in 1982, provided that amendments affecting only one county would no longer have to be voted on statewide, but bond counsel have long memories (to the earlier defaults) and have advised statewide ratification, so local amendments continue to baffle all Alabamians and proliferate constitutional length.

The amount of statutory material contained in the state constitution has made it longer and more rigid than any in Alabama's history. Length is not necessarily bad, but the detailed 1901 document encumbered by amendments creates the following problems:

1. Inflexibility cripples governmental operations. The Alabama constitutional prohibition against state debt has been circumvented by judicial interpretations allowing borrowing by some two dozen public corporations and authorities whose officers are state officials, such as the governor.

Table 2.1
Amendments to the Alabama Constitution of 1901

Decade	Amendments	Decade	Amendments
1901–09	1	1950–59	81 to 140
1910–19	2 to 7	1960–69	141 to 311
1920–29	8 to 22	1970–79	312 to 381
1930–39	23 to 41	1980–89	382 to 505
1940–49	42 to 80	1990–	506 to ?

2. The specifics of the past are included, even though many of the restrictive provisions, such as racially separate school systems (Sec. 256), have been declared unconstitutional.
3. It is a complex document to understand, as new material has been inserted. For example, Amendment No. 394, creating the Alabama Heritage Trust Fund from petroleum royalties, is longer than the entire United States Constitution.
4. Conflicts arise because of contradictory amendments, requiring legislative interpretation or expensive litigation in the courts. Many amendments are no longer in force, having been superseded by later ones.

The constitution of 1901 can be amended by two processes: a majority vote of the legislature can call a constitutional convention if a majority of voters agree, or three-fifths of each house can submit a proposed amendment that is ratified by a majority of the people voting on it at an election. Governor "Fob" James campaigned for office in 1978 supporting a new constitution, but his proposal to hold a constitutional convention was defeated, the governor charged, by special interests benefiting from present arrangements. In 1983 the legislature passed a revised constitution, but the Alabama Supreme Court ruled six to three that it could not appear on the November 1983 ballot because the entire document was improperly submitted by the legislature as an amendment, rather than being drafted by a constitutional convention. The political challenge remains of drafting a state constitution that can serve as a framework of principles for the three branches of government, distribute responsibilities between state and local jurisdictions, and safeguard individual liberties without putting government in a legalistic straitjacket. The citizens of Alabama will have a continuing opportunity to participate in the process of constitutional revision during the years ahead.

State Governmental Structure:
Privileges and Obligations

"The United States shall guarantee to every State in this Union a Republican Form of Government," which means an elected legislature and a nonhereditary executive. Article IV of the United States Constitution also lists several responsibilities states have toward each other:

■ *Privileges and Immunities.* "The citizens of each State shall be entitled to all the privileges and immunities of citizens in the several states." The Fourteenth Amendment adds: "No state shall make or enforce any law which shall abridge the privileges or immunities of the citizens of the United States." Thus citizens from out of state must be treated the same as Alabamians, such as in a recent case where the courts ruled that the state could not tax pensions from out of state differently from those of Alabama government retirees.[2] However, if services are involved, nonresidents can be charged more, such as out-of-state tuition for students, or visitors' hunting or fishing licenses, to substitute for the taxes paid by state citizens. Americans have freedom to travel among the states, and the courts ruled that the legislature could not charge more for toxic waste from other states coming into Alabama for disposal.[3]

■ *"Full Faith and Credit* shall be given in each State to the public acts, records, and judicial proceedings of every other State." In such civil (as opposed to criminal) matters as laws, corporate charters, deeds, vital records, and judicial decisions, one state will honor the documents of another. Alabama will accept your Mississippi birth certificate showing you were born on a certain day, or let you drive your car on Alabama highways if you are from Georgia because that state has licensed you as being qualified to operate a motor vehicle. This obligation does not imply automatic enforcement of one state's judicial decision by another. Suppose you did not pay your rent in Florida, and a civil judgment was rendered against you. Your former landlord would have to seek an Alabama court order requiring collection from you. Another area in which this clause has been contested is divorce. While one state must recognize another's decree, valid residence in the granting state must have been established; it is not possible simply to go to another state for a "quickie divorce."

■ *Extradition.* "A person charged in any State with Treason, Felony, or other Crime, who shall flee from Justice, and be found in another State, shall on demand of the executive authority of the state from which he fled, be delivered up, to be removed to the State having jurisdiction of the crime." A law enforcement officer of one state can chase a fleeing criminal into another under the doctrine of "hot pursuit," but if a person is later apprehended in another state, the governor of the state where the crime occurred must ask for return of the suspect. Extradition is a courtesy imposed by reciprocity, although in rare circumstances Alabama governors have not acted upon a request for humanitarian reasons. Interstate rendition of fugitives is almost routine, since no governor wants to be accused of harboring criminals in the state.

The Place of Local Governments

What constitutes an independent unit of government is difficult to define. To be counted as a government by the United States Bureau of the Census, the following characteristics are used:

1. Existence as an organized entity. A government is usually conceived as possessing some type of authority over a defined territory, although it may exercise power outside its

boundaries, such as Alabama cities' "police jurisdiction" (see Chapter 9). It is a public body possessing such corporate powers as a name, perpetual succession (a continuing organization with officials, although incumbents change), and a separate legal existence with the right to sue and be sued, to make contracts, and to acquire and dispose of property. When a unit has ceased to operate (when it collects no revenue, conducts no activities, and has no current officeholders), the census bureau does not count it as an existing government.

2. Governmental character. Presumably a public body was created by consent of the people and/or the state legislature, which sets minimum requirements for territory and population. The government's officers are popularly elected or are appointed by public officials. A basic characteristic of a government is its power to collect taxes, and interest paid on its debts is exempt from federal taxation. Responsibility is enforced by requirements for accessibility of its records to public inspection and reporting. In performing functions regarded as governmental in nature, it incurs accountability to the public.

3. Substantial autonomy, subject to state limitations and supervision, of fiscal and administrative affairs. Financially, this means an ability to raise revenues on its own, not being dependent upon appropriations from elsewhere. It can determine its own budget without approval or modification by other governments, set tax levies, fix and collect charges for its services, and borrow money on its own authority. An independent unit is not simply a spending agency; it is politically responsible for its finances. Administrative independence is measured by having a popularly elected governing body, or if it is appointed, on the basis that the unit performs different functions from those of its creating government(s). Conversely, an agency is not autonomous if the creating government's officials must ap-

prove all proposals, or if the agency's responsibilities and property will revert to the parent government after debts are repaid. The idea is that a governmental entity has discretion in a certain area and has at least one function to perform on its own.

By these criteria, the 1990 census counted in Alabama 67 counties, 439 municipalities, 129 school districts, and over 400 special districts performing other functions.

Local governments, such as those of cities or counties, are legally viewed as creations or instrumentalities of the state government for better local administration. Alabama law adheres to the famous Dillon's Rule, which states that a municipal corporation possesses and can exercise only the following powers: "First, those granted in express words; second, those necessarily or fairly implied or incident to the powers expressly granted; third, those essential to the accomplishment of the declared objects and purposes of the corporation—not simply convenient, but indispensable."[4] The local government must prove that the activity it wishes to pursue is within this definition; otherwise the power will be denied by the courts.

Local governments are thus the agents of the states; while states have a constitutional position in the federal government, local governments do not. Counties are legally regarded as subdivisions of the state more than are municipalities, which are incorporated at the initiative of a community. Local governments can be created, abolished, or have their powers changed by the state. For example, during the civil rights struggle, the Alabama legislature passed a bill redrawing Tuskegee's city limits so as to eliminate all but a handful of registered black voters. This decision was not reversed until the United States Supreme Court in *Gomillion v. Lightfoot* (1960) ruled that such a discriminatory act was racially motivated and violated the Fifteenth Amendment to the United States Constitution. (Participating in the unanimous decision was one of the court's most distinguished justices, Hugo Black of Alabama.) The bill abolishing Macon County was not implemented because surrounding counties did not want its black voting population.

Provided that it does not violate constitutional guarantees, the state government retains ultimate control over local governments. Many states (such as Florida and Georgia) have granted "home rule," or the delegation of authority to local governments to run their own affairs. This does not exist in Alabama, which means counties and cities must go to the state legislature for specific permission. Thus the Alabama legislature passes annexation measures changing municipal boundaries, amends cities' forms of government, gives permission for some counties to levy certain taxes, and passed Act 84-59, "to permit flea markets to remain open on Sunday in Cullman County." Proponents of home rule would argue that Cullman County is perfectly competent to decide when its flea markets should be open and that the state legislature has more important things to do.

The 1901 constitution, Section 104, prohibits local or special legislation upon thirty-one specified subjects. To give local communities what they desire, the technique of "classification" is used. This means general laws (theoretically applicable to the whole state) are passed that apply to only certain-sized jurisdictions. In 1978, the Alabama Supreme Court refused to allow increasingly narrow "bracket bills," prompting Constitutional Amendment No. 375, which provided that the legislature establish not more than eight classes of municipalities based on population size.

Besides constitutional restrictions, state influence over local governments is exercised in the following ways:

1. Legislative oversight. The Alabama legislature has several standing committees on local government and special committees that have examined certain problem issues for local

units. For example, there is the Senate Committee on Governmental Affairs, or the House Local Legislation No. 1, which considers the "general bills of local application" just discussed. Local Legislation No. 2, composed of the legislative delegation from Jefferson County, considers only measures applying to that county, and similarly other local legislation committees have a defined focus.

2. State administrative supervision can range from the following mildest to strongest measures: require reports, authorize state inspections (e.g., of schools), give advice, provide financial grants-in-aid for programs, bestow state approval for projects, review activities, order something to be done, remove local officials (as for corruption), appoint local officials, and finally, substitute administration (as happened during the vice cleanup of Phenix City during the 1950s).

3. Judicial actions are important, since local law is subordinate to national and state statutes. So that laws can be fairly enforced, courts may grant such remedial writs as an *injunction*, a restraining order that something not be done until there is judicial determination of the issue; *mandamus*, which compels an action; and *certiorari*, which calls a lower court judgment up for review by a higher court on appeal. The courts may also decide that a local ordinance is in conflict with or not applicable under "state preemption" because state law already covers the subject.

Interlocal relationships can take several forms. *Inter-jurisdictional agreements* can be either formal or informal cooperative arrangements between local governments. Nearby cities usually have mutual aid pacts to lend personnel and equipment during emergencies, such as fires or floods. *Contracts* are written agreements to provide services on a continuing basis, as between a city and a county. Contracts can also be used to prevent duplicate investment. An example was the agreement between the City of Huntsville, which had street-painting equipment, and Madison County, which had money but no crew or equipment. One summer the county contracted with the city for its crew to paint county road stripes, thus offering employment to a number of students. *Regional cooperation* is promoted by councils of government and regional planning commissions. Councils of government (COGs), in which both counties and cities are members, function in Alabama primarily to coordinate local government planning activities, although some provide services. They are financed by an assessment on each participating jurisdiction according to population. These twelve districts (Figure 2.4) established by

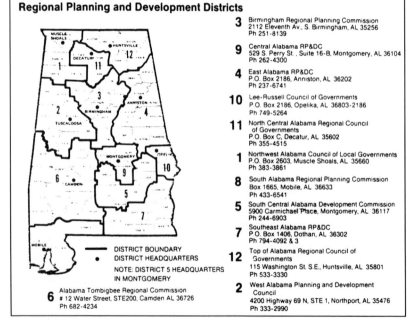

Regional Planning and Development Districts

3 Birmingham Regional Planning Commission
2112 Eleventh Av., S. Birmingham, AL 35256
Ph 251-8139

9 Central Alabama RP&DC
529 S. Perry St., Suite 16-B, Montgomery, AL 36104
Ph 262-4300

4 East Alabama RP&DC
P.O. Box 2186, Anniston, AL 36202
Ph 237-6741

10 Lee-Russell Council of Governments
P.O. Box 2186, Opelika, AL 36803-2186
Ph 749-5264

11 North Central Alabama Regional Council
of Governments
P.O. Box C, Decatur, AL 35602
Ph 355-4515

1 Northwest Alabama Council of Local Governments
P.O. Box 2603, Muscle Shoals, AL 35660
Ph 383-3861

8 South Alabama Regional Planning Commission
Box 1665, Mobile, AL 36633
Ph 433-6541

5 South Central Alabama Development Commission
5900 Carmichael Place, Montgomery, AL 36117
Ph 244-6903

7 Southeast Alabama RP&DC
P.O. Box 1406, Dothan, AL 36302
Ph 794-4092 & 3

12 Top of Alabama Regional Council of
Governments
115 Washington St. S.E., Huntsville, AL 35801
Ph 533-3330

2 West Alabama Planning and Development
Council
4200 Highway 69 N, STE 1, Northport, AL 35476
Ph 333-2990

─── DISTRICT BOUNDARY
● DISTRICT HEADQUARTERS
NOTE: DISTRICT 5 HEADQUARTERS
IN MONTGOMERY

6 Alabama Tombigbee Regional Commission
12 Water Street, STE200, Camden AL 36726
Ph 682-4234

Figure 2.4 Alabama councils of governments. (Courtesy of the Alabama Department of Economic and Community Affairs)

the Alabama legislature must review local applications for federal programs to ensure that the federal funding is being put to planned and coordinated projects. Thus while these regional bodies are not "supergovernments," they make the local units cooperate in order to receive federal assistance.

Powers and Limits on Governments

American government is a federal system. Federalism is distinguished by at least two levels of government (the nation and the states) ruling the same territory and people, each level having at least one domain for discretionary action, and there is some guarantee (usually a federal constitution) of autonomy. Alabama Governor George Wallace made a national reputation campaigning on the issue of "states' rights." Both President Nixon's and President Reagan's "new federalism" stressed that government programs should not come from a common mold: communities should set their own goals according to local conditions. While local governments are not mentioned in the United States Constitution, their political influence is ever present. Certainly local governments make their views known to the state legislature directly, or through their lobbying organizations, the Association of County Commissions of Alabama and the Alabama League of Municipalities.

Competition takes place between the states as each seeks to improve its economy and increase its tax base. Southern states have sought to attract industry to balance their agriculture, and global investment is sought from foreign companies. Alabama's community development program started with the Cater Act of 1949, which authorized the establishment of municipal industrial development corporations to finance, construct, and equip plants for lease to private firms, and the Wallace Act of 1951, which enabled local governing bodies to enter directly into contracts with prospective firms.

Both acts permit the financing of development projects within fifteen miles of the jurisdiction's limits. Bonds used to finance enterprises are repaid with lease revenues from the project, and the borrowing incurred is not charged against the city's debt limit. Unfortunately, some local projects have gone bankrupt, tarnishing Alabama's credit image. Since 1952, there have been more than 600 issues of industrial revenue bonds totaling over $2 billion and producing additional jobs for Alabama citizens. Some projects have been criticized by local businesses for subsidizing new outlets of nationwide chains or franchises. The quality of the development has come under scrutiny, for example as regards environmental effects and the demands for public services with an immediate governmental expenditure burden.

Relations with neighboring states also take several cooperative forms.

■ *Interstate compacts* may be approved by Congress. Article I, Section 10 of the United States Constitution reads: "No State shall, without the consent of Congress, . . . enter into any Agreement or Compact with another State." Originally designed to deter the states from ganging up against the new federal government, interstate compacts are used today to:

1. Provide consistent jurisdiction and services, such as the Driver License Compact. It allows Alabama and forty other states to ensure that each driver holds no more than one state's license and that offenses, no matter where committed, are reported on each driver's record.
2. Solve interstate problems, or provide facilities serving several states, such as the Southeastern Forest Fire Protection Compact. The Alabama Department of Youth Services administers the Interstate Compact on Juveniles, seeing to it that youngsters put on probation in another state who

move to Alabama are adequately supervised so that they do not revert to delinquent behavior.

3. Establish river basin administration, which oversees the dredging of navigable waterways, the enforcement of anti-pollution laws, and the allocation of water for drinking and irrigation. The Tennessee–Tombigbee Waterway Development Authority was established by an interstate compact involving Alabama, Mississippi, Tennessee, Kentucky, and Florida, approved by Congress in 1958.

4. Provide regulation, such as the Gulf Marine Fisheries Commission, to which Alabama appoints three representatives, as do Florida, Mississippi, Louisiana, and Texas.

■ *Uniform state laws* have been adopted in identical model form to facilitate transactions and move toward consistent legal practices. All fifty states have adopted the Uniform Commercial Code, which ensures that such business practices as a partnership or secured transactions (liens) mean the same thing everywhere. All states have agreed to secure the attendance of out-of-state witnesses, to the Controlled Substances Act, to child-custody jurisdiction, and to taxation legislation on gifts to minors. A uniform law is usually indicated by its title, such as Alabama's "Uniform Parentage Act" on DNA genetic testing.

■ *Informal executive understandings* may exist between the Alabama governor and those of neighboring states. These executive agreements are a widely used cooperative method, but are usually a commitment binding only upon the governors who made them.

In examining our governmental structure, then, we find that the United States Constitution, with the laws and international treaties made under it, is supreme law of the land. Providing they do not conflict with it, state constitutions and interstate compacts may be adopted. The powers of local gov-

ernments are defined by the state constitutions and state legislatures, yet the people under our democratic system retain
the ultimate political sovereignty.

Notes

1. The Supreme Court voided 8–0 the 30 constitutionally disenfranchising crimes: "Justices Strike Down a 1901 Law Designed
   to Bar Voting by Blacks; Poor Whites Also Disenfranchised," *New
   York Times*, April 17, 1985, p. 12.
2. *Davis v. Michigan*, 489 U.S. 803 (1989); *Sizemore v. Rinehart*, 611
   So.2d 1064 (1992).
3. *Chemical Waste Management, Inc. v. Hunt*, 112 S.Ct. 2009 (1992).
4. John F. Dillon, *Commentaries on the Law of Municipal Corporations*,
   5th ed. Boston: J. Cockroft, 1911. 1:448.

For Further Reading

Alabama Legislature. *Proposed Constitution* (Revised), 1979 Session;
1983 Session.
Code of Alabama, 1975. Charlottesville, Va.: Michie Co., annual sup-
plements. Volumes 1 and 2 contain the Alabama Constitution of
1901 and the latest amendments.
Code of Alabama, 1923. Vol. 1. *Political* (reprints the earlier Alabama
Constitutions).
Dodd, Donald B. "The Free State of Winston." *Alabama Heritage*,
Spring 1993, pp. 9–19.
Flynt, Wayne. *Poor But Proud: Alabama's Poor Whites*. Tuscaloosa: Uni-
versity of Alabama Press, 1989.
Going, Allen Johnston. *Bourbon Democracy in Alabama 1874–1890*.
University of Alabama Press, 1951. Reprint, 1992.
Hackney, Sheldon. *Populism to Progressivism in Alabama*. Princeton,
N.J.: Princeton University Press, 1969.
Knight v. Alabama, 787 Fed. Supp. 1030 (1991). (The Alabama college
desegregation lawsuit recounts its history in a 364-page opinion.)
McMillan, Malcolm C. *Constitutional Development in Alabama 1798–
1901: A Study in Politics, the Negro, and Sectionalism*. Chapel Hill,
N.C.: University of North Carolina Press, 1955.

Report of the Constitutional Commission. *Proposed Constitution of Alabama*, May 1, 1973.

Rodabaugh, Karl. *The Farmers' Revolt in Alabama, 1890–1896*. Greenville, N.C.: East Carolina University, 1977.

Stewart, William H. *The Alabama Constitutional Convention*. University: University of Alabama Press, 1975.

Stewart, William H. *The Alabama State Constitution*. Westport, Conn.: Greenwood Press, forthcoming.

Thornton, J. Mills III. *Politics and Power in a Slave Society: Alabama 1800–1860*. Baton Rouge: Louisiana State University Press, 1978.

Wiggins, Sarah Woolfolk. *The Scalawag in Alabama Politics, 1865–1881*. University: University of Alabama Press, 1977. Reprint, 1991.

Yarbrough, Tinsley E. *Judge Frank Johnson and Human Rights in Alabama*. University: University of Alabama Press, 1981.

THREE

Voters, Nominations, and Elections

Who May Vote?

In order to vote, a person must be registered as an eligible elector. In the past, Alabama, like many other states, had stringent statutory requirements for voting, such as lengthy periods of residence. Now that the United States Supreme Court has characterized voting as a fundamental right, there must be a compelling state interest (such as depriving convicted felons of the franchise) in order to impose any limitations.[1] Anyone can register to vote who is a United States citizen residing in Alabama, at least eighteen years old by the next election, and who has not been convicted of a disqualifying offense or legally declared mentally incompetent.

Alabama changed by a 1989 law from "permanent" voter registration to "periodic" removal for failing to vote in four years. Voters may reidentify themselves or names may be purged upon information of death, determination of insanity, or felony conviction. The state now maintains a computerized voter registration file, which has reduced duplicate listings as Alabamians move from one county to another, although a few counties have more people registered than were counted as eighteen or older by the census. Until Congress passed the "motor voter" act of 1993 to register when applying for a driver's license and requiring states to allow registration by mail, Alabama conducted registration in person at the county

NOTICE!   NOTICE!   NOTICE!

ALL REGISTERED VOTERS

The Montgomery County Board of Registrars is updating and correcting the Montgomery County Voting List. The law requires all voters to register in the precinct in which they reside. In order to do this, every registered voter is asked to fill out and return the form below or come in person to the Office of the Board of Registrars, Room 330, Montgomery County Court House and make sure that you are registered in the proper precinct.

Please fill in and return immediately to:

Board of Registrars
Montgomery County Court House
Montgomery, Alabama, 36104

NAME_____

RESIDENT   Last   First   Middle

ADDRESS_____
Street or Route

City   State   Zip

Date of Birth_____ Race _____ Sex _____

I hereby certify the above information is true and correct.

_____
Signature

Figure 3.1 Keeping voting lists up to date is a never-ending task.

board of registrars (or by deputies). Alabama allowed mail registration for citizens (plus their spouses and children) in the armed forces, working outside the country, or attending an institution of higher learning. In each Alabama county there is a three-member Board of Registrars[2] appointed by a state board composed of the governor, the state auditor, and the commissioner of agriculture and industries. In practice, each of these three officials chooses one registrar, sometimes upon the recommendation of state legislators from the county. Registration takes place during publicized periods (because some county registrars are paid to work a limited

Alabama Voter Registration Application

COUNTY: _____

COMPUTER REGISTRATION NO

Cnty   City
Prct ___ Prct ___ In ___ Out ___

NAME OF APPLICANT (PLEASE PRINT)

LAST   FIRST   MIDDLE OR MAIDEN

DATE OF APPLICATION
MONTH   DAY   YEAR

RESIDENCE ADDRESS

House or Apt. No. & Street (if Rural, Route & Box No.) CITY OR TOWN STATE ZIP

Mailing Address, if Different   DAYTIME PHONE

GIVE LOCATION

APPLICANT'S PLACE OF BIRTH

CITY OR TOWN   COUNTY   STATE   FOREIGN COUNTRY

DATE OF BIRTH
AGE MONTH DAY YEAR

SOCIAL SECURITY NO.   SEX (Circle One)   **RACE** (Circle One)

MALE FEMALE WHITE BLACK ASIAN AM INDIAN HISPANIC OTHER

PLACE OF LAST REGISTRATION

ADDRESS   CITY   COUNTY   STATE

If Naturalized Citizen,
Give Date and Number

Have You Ever Been Convicted of   YES   NO
any Felony? If Yes and If Pardoned,
Give Date and Number _____

Are You Currently Under a Judgment of
Mental Incompetence? (Circle One)   YES   NO

DATE APPROVED _____

_____
Board Member or Deputy Registering

_____
Board Member

_____
Board Member

I SOLEMNLY SWEAR OR AFFIRM TO SUPPORT
AND DEFEND THE CONSTITUTIONS OF THE
UNITED STATES AND THE STATE OF ALABAMA
AND FURTHER DISAVOW ANY BELIEF OR AFFILI-
ATION WITH ANY GROUP WHICH ADVOCATES
THE OVERTHROW OF THE GOVERNMENTS OF
THE UNITED STATES OR THE STATE OF ALA-
BAMA BY UNLAWFUL MEANS AND THAT THE
INFORMATION CONTAINED HEREIN IS TRUE, SO
HELP ME GOD

Form VR0001 1/16/90

_____
SIGNATURE OF APPLICANT

Figure 3.2   Alabama voter registration application.

number of days per month) up until ten days before an election, when the voter lists are compiled.

On election day, a voter appears at the polling place assigned by the county registrars (if confused, contact the county probate judge or city clerk for municipal elections) and is name-checked against the list (which is also publicly posted or printed in the newspaper). The voter signs the poll list for that precinct (sometimes called a "beat" in Alabama), and casts a ballot.

Voting procedures vary, depending on whether paper ballots or voting machines (either mechanical or electronic) are used. A person remaining in a voting booth over four minutes may be asked if assistance is needed by a poll worker, and if not, can remain for an additional minute, and then be asked to leave (if there is no line waiting, a voter can take all the time necessary to finish). Voters requesting assistance are entitled to another five minutes to finish with the help of a poll worker or anyone else they wish (except an agent of their employer or their union).[3] Voters may bring such aids as premarked sample ballots or lists for their personal help, as long as they do not distribute or leave them in the polling place. Campaigning is allowed on election day in Alabama, so long as it is done at least thirty feet from the door of the building where the polls are located.

A registered voter who will be absent on election day; is ill or has a physical disability that prevents travel to the polls; or is in the armed forces, is employed abroad, or is away at college, may vote absentee (as can that voter's spouse and registered children). The absentee ballot application can be obtained at city hall for a municipal election or the county courthouse for other elections and must be filled out or returned by U.S. Mail at least five days before the election. The absentee ballot can be personally handed to the voter or sent by U.S. Mail. The voter marks the ballot, seals it in the plain envelope supplied, and then seals both in an affidavit envelope (Figure 3.3), witnessed by a notary public or two witnesses eighteen or older. The voter can personally deliver the completed absentee ballot to the absentee election manager at the city hall or courthouse where the application was obtained, or send it by U.S. Mail so that it arrives by noon on election day. The high proportion (up to 25%) of absentee ballots to the total vote cast in some smaller Alabama counties has been a source of concern, but convictions for voting fraud have been rare. The polls in Alabama must be open for ten

ABSENTEE VOTING

"State of Alabama
"County of ....
"I, the undersigned, do swear (or affirm) that:
"(1) I am a resident of .... county in the state of Alabama.
"(2) My place of residence in Alabama is:
. . . .
(street)
. . . ., Alabama   . . . .
(city or town)   (zip code)
"(3) My voting precinct (or place where I vote) is: . . . .
. . . .
"(4) My date of birth is: . . . .
                              month   day   year
"(5) I am entitled to vote an absentee ballot because:
"Check only one:
_____ I have moved from Alabama less than thirty days prior to the election.
_____ I will be out of the county or the state on election day.
_____ I am physically incapacitated and will not be able to vote in person on election day.
"I further swear (or affirm) that I have not voted nor will I vote in person in the election to which this ballot pertains.
"I have marked the enclosed absentee ballot voluntarily and that I have read or had read to me and understand the instructions accompanying this ballot and that I have carefully complied with such instructions.
"Moreover, I further swear (or affirm) that all of the information given above is true and correct to the best of my knowledge and that I understand that by knowingly giving false information so as to vote illegally by absentee ballot that I shall be guilty of a misdemeanor which is punishable by a fine not to exceed $1,000.00 and/or confinement in the county jail for not more than six months.

. . . .
(Signature or mark of voter.)

"Note: Your signature must be witnessed by either: A notary public or other officer authorized to acknowledge oaths or two witnesses 18 years of age or older.
"Sworn to and subscribed before me this . . . . day of . . . . ,
19. . . . . . . I certify that the affiant is known (or made known) to me to be the identical party he claims to be.
. . . . (Signature of official)
(Title of official)
. . . .
(Address of official)
                              OR
"1st Witness   . . . .
                   Signature
               . . . .
                   Print name
               . . . .
                   Address
               . . . .
                   City   Zip Code
"2nd Witness   . . . .
                   Signature
               . . . .
                   Print name
               . . . .
                   Address
               . . . .
                   City   Zip Code"

Figure 3.3   Absentee voting affidavit.

CHALLENGE OATH—General or Municipal Elections

STATE OF ALABAMA, _____ COUNTY. _____ Precinct or Ward _____ Machine District or Box _____

I do solemnly swear (or affirm): 1. That I am a duly qualified elector under the Constitution and Laws of the State of Alabama.

2. That I have resided in the State of Alabama thirty days next preceding this day.

3. That I am eighteen years of age or upwards. 4. That I have not been convicted of any crime which disfranchises me.

5. That I have been duly registered. 6. I know of no reason why I am not entitled to vote.

7. I am generally known by the name under which I now desire to vote, which is _____

8. I have not voted and will not vote in any other precinct or ward (or if the precinct has been divided in districts, in any other voting district) in this election.

9. My occupation is _____ ,

the name of my employer is _____ .

10. My residence is _____ Alabama.

(If in a city or town, give street number).

11. That _____ and

have personal knowledge of my residence in the State of Alabama for thirty days.

This affidavit has been read to me. So help me God.

_____ Signature of Challenged Voter

Subscribed and sworn to before me this _____ day of _____ , 197 ___

_____ Inspector

PROOF OF IDENTITY

STATE OF ALABAMA, _____ COUNTY.

I, _____ , do solemnly swear (or affirm) that I have known

_____ (here insert the name of the person offering to vote) for the last thirty days next preceding this election, and that he has been a resident of this State for said time.

I do solemnly swear (or affirm) that I am a qualified elector of this precinct; that I have been a free holder and house holder in this State for thirty days next preceding this election; that my occupation is _____ ;

my residence is _____ ; my business address is _____

_____ Signature of Qualified Elector and a free holder and house holder

Subscribed and sworn to before me this _____ day of _____ , 197 ___

_____ Inspector

(Printed in accordance with Opinion of Alabama Attorney General, March 29, 1972 and Voting Rights Act of 1965.)

BROWN PRINTING CO., MONTGOMERY 1973

Figure 3.4
Citizens whose eligibility to vote is challenged take this oath.

consecutive hours, 8:00 A.M. to 6:00 P.M., but may open earlier or close later, depending on the type of election, with local hours set by the county commission or by the city for municipal elections.

Who May Run?

Alabama uses a party column form of ballot, which allows straight-ticket voting for all candidates of a party by marking a cross (x) in the circle under the name of the party. Deriving from the days when many voters were illiterate, each party in Alabama chooses an emblem. It may not be a representation of the national flag, money, state seal, likeness of a person, religious symbol, fraternal organization insignia, or industrial mark, and party emblems cannot be similar. Favorite identifications chosen are birds or beasts (see Figure 3.5). If more than one person is to be elected to an office, each vacancy to be filled is designated "Place No. 1," "Place No. 2," etc.

How does a candidate's name appear on the ballot? There are several nominating methods, the simplest one being self-announcement, which is used by write-in candidates. Caucus, or selection by a meeting of political leaders, was used by the Alabama Republicans prior to 1974, and by the state's Democrats to choose candidates for the legislature in 1983 and to certify the gubernatorial nominee in 1986. Andrew Jackson destroyed "King Caucus" to pick presidential candidates, but it is still used in smaller jurisdictions, and by new or minor parties. Nomination for statewide office by party convention can be used in several states, including Alabama. Alabama law authorizes political parties to hold a caucus, convention, or mass meeting to make nominations at least sixty days before the day of election. (This prevents primary election losers from being renominated or being nominated by two parties.) This assembly process can be used by small political parties

LEE COUNTY

Official Ballot, General Election, November 3, 1992

Names of Offices To Be Voted For	ALABAMA DEMOCRATIC	ALABAMA LIBERTARIAN	ALABAMA REPUBLICAN	INDEPENDENT	For Write-In
FOR PRESIDENT AND VICE-PRESIDENT OF THE UNITED STATES — (Vote for One)	( ) BILL CLINTON AL GORE	( ) ANDRE MARROU NANCY LORD	( ) GEORGE BUSH DAN QUAYLE	( ) LENORA B. FULANI MARIA ELIZABETH MUNOZ	
				( ) JOHN HAGELIN MIKE TOMPKINS	
				( ) LYNDON H. LaROUCHE, JR. JAMES BEVEL	
				( ) H. ROSS PEROT JAMES B. STOCKDALE	
				( ) JAMES WARREN ESTELLE DeBATES	
FOR UNITED STATES SENATOR (Vote for One)	( ) RICHARD C. SHELBY	( ) JEROME SHOCKLEY	( ) RICHARD SELLERS		
FOR UNITED STATES REPRESENTATIVE, 3RD CONGRESSIONAL DISTRICT — (Vote for One)	( ) GLEN BROWDER	( ) RODRIC D. TEMPLETON	( ) DON SLEDGE		
FOR ASSOCIATE JUSTICE OF THE SUPREME COURT, PLACE NO. 1 — (Vote for One)	( ) R. P. ALMON		( ) MARK ANDERSON		
FOR ASSOCIATE JUSTICE OF THE SUPREME COURT, PLACE NO. 2 — (Vote for One)	( ) JANIE SHORES		( ) REBECCA GREEN THOMASON		
FOR ASSOCIATE JUSTICE OF THE SUPREME COURT, PLACE NO. 3 — (Vote for One)	( ) J. GORMAN HOUSTON	( ) DAVID L. RAWLS			
FOR COURT OF CIVIL APPEALS JUDGE (Vote for One)	( ) SHARON G. YATES		( ) ROBERT J. "B.J." RUSSELL		
FOR PRESIDENT, PUBLIC SERVICE COMMISSION (Vote for One)	( ) JIM SULLIVAN	( ) BILL CREW			
FOR CIRCUIT COURT JUDGE, 37TH JUDICIAL CIRCUIT, PLACE NO. 2 — (Vote for One)	( ) ROBERT M. HARPER				
FOR DISTRICT COURT JUDGE, LEE COUNTY, PLACE NO. 1 — (Vote for One)	( ) MIKE NIX				
FOR DISTRICT ATTORNEY, 37TH JUDICIAL CIRCUIT (Vote for One)	( ) RONALD L. MYERS				
FOR MEMBER, LEE COUNTY BOARD OF EDUCATION, DISTRICT NO. 3 — (Vote for One)	( ) CARY L. SENN				

BALLOT STYLE 2

Figure 3.5 General election ballots are printed for each county listing local as well as statewide offices.

that received less than 20% of the vote in the last general election.

Persons seeking the Alabama Democratic or Republican party nominations must file a declaration of candidacy and pay a nonrefundable party assessment not to exceed 2% of one year's salary in office. Parties may set their own qualifying fees within the state limit, and this is a significant source for funding state party operations in Alabama. Candidates seeking nomination in a party primary election must file sixty days previously with the state party chair, or with the county party chair for county office.

If there is any competition for a party's nomination, a state primary election is held the first Tuesday in June. (Unopposed candidates for office are not listed on the ballot and are declared elected.) Primaries may be nonpartisan to narrow the field of candidates for the general election,[4] or they may be partisan to select the nominee of a political party or party officer. Depending on the state, partisan primaries can be "open" for participation by all voters, or "closed" to any but party members, so that the opposition cannot infiltrate into the nominating process to pick the weaker candidate for the general election. While Alabama law assumes a closed primary system, party affiliation is not listed when registering, and voters on election day are asked in which party primary they wish to vote, so Alabama operates an open system. (When constitutional amendments appear on a primary ballot, a voter not wishing to vote in a primary party election simply votes on the amendments.) Since several candidates may seek a party's nomination, none may receive a majority, necessitating a runoff (or second) primary election between the top two the last Tuesday in June. Alabama is one of ten states requiring a majority for nomination, which has been criticized for discriminating against African-American candidates who receive a plurality (more than other candidates), but are forced into a runoff against a white candidate, who presumably wins if voting is racially polarized. Alabama's effectively open primary system also allowed people who voted in the 1986 Republican primary for governor to "cross over" and vote in the Democratic runoff three weeks later (see next chapter). The present system defenses are that a nominee has the support of a majority (necessary for party coalition building) yet allows Alabamians to pick one party primary in which they wish to vote, depending on the candidates running.

To run as an independent candidate, a petition with the signatures of at least 1% of the registered voters in the jurisdiction of the office sought must be filed sixty days before the primary election. Independent candidates for county office file with the probate judge; all others file with the Alabama secretary of state. Write-in candidates are not allowed in Alabama primary elections, but voters may write in a person's name on the general election ballot.

In summary, Alabama candidates appear on the general election ballot after nomination by a political party holding a primary election, caucus, convention, or mass meeting for the purpose; as an independent candidate having filed a petition; or else as a write-in candidate in the blank column. Alabama's general elections are held the first Tuesday after the first Monday in November of even-numbered years.

Election Administration

Alabama adopted voting districts in conformity with the 1990 census blocks for reapportionment purposes, and in the future, county governing bodies will divide voting districts so that each precinct will not exceed 300 voters if paper ballots are used, or 600 electors if there are voting machines. Whether voting machines are used is up to the governing body willing to pay the cost. For each polling place there are three inspectors, two clerks, and a precinct returning officer appointed by a board consisting of the county probate judge, sheriff, and circuit clerk not running for election themselves. The political parties furnish lists of qualified electors from each voting place from which appointments are made. (Since the pay for a ten-hour-plus day is low, poll workers are sought and retirees often serve.) Each candidate in a primary election, and each party or political organization in a general election, may name a poll watcher to be present, but who cannot campaign or display buttons. Candidates convicted of election fraud are barred from office. Cities are responsible for the costs of municipal elections, and counties are responsible for all other elections, except that they are partially reimbursed by the state for noncounty contests. The county officials or the governor proclaim the election results, which may be challenged within twenty days, but if a recount is held and the contestant loses, he or she must pay the costs.

Voting Behavior: The People Decide

The candidate for public office knows every vote is important because relatively few citizens exercise their electoral privilege. The 1990 census counted nearly three million Alabamians eighteen and older, with 2.4 million registered voters (444,000 listed as black) in November 1992, yet less than 1.7 million voted. Voting turnout tends to decline from vigorously contested national elections, to state elections (where primaries in Alabama may draw more than general elections), to local elections, where only 10 or 15% of the citizens may go to the polls. While some issues may agitate the community (such as a controversial tax vote), many local offices are filled by default, since if only one candidate files for office in Alabama, no election is held. Financial referenda usually require two-thirds to pass in Alabama, so one "no" vote equals two "yes" votes, and bond issues can be defeated by a small minority of opponents.

Who votes in Alabama? In the absence of discrimination,

voting patterns follow those elsewhere: higher participation rates are found among the better educated, those with higher incomes, professionals and white-collar workers, and the middle-aged and elderly, rather than youth. The political effects of such tendencies in Alabama are examined in the following chapter.

Notes

1. See *U.S. v. Penton* 212 F. Supp. 193, and *Hadnott v. Amos* 401 U.S. 968 (1971), where lengthy Alabama residency requirements were rejected by the United States Supreme Court.
2. The United States Department of Justice, under federal voting rights laws, has authority to conduct registration in all Alabama counties when there have been instances of discrimination, but has not done so in recent years.
3. Alabama Secretary of State, *Alabama Poll Workers' Guide*, and *Election 1992*, "information provided in compliance with state election laws, federal laws, and the federal court order issued in *Harris v. Siegelman*."
4. Alabama municipal elections are nonpartisan and usually held on the fourth Tuesday in August, with any runoff election held the third Tuesday after the first vote.

For Further Reading

Alabama Secretary of State. *Alabama Election Laws, Jan. 1992 ed.* Charlottesville, Va.: Michie Co., 1992. (Reprints portions of the *Code of Alabama*, Title 17 "Elections," and the state's Fair Campaign Practices Act.)

Capstone Poll News. Public opinion telephone surveys on candidates and issues since 1980 conducted by the Department of Political Science and the School of Communication, University of Alabama, Tuscaloosa. A number of Alabama political scientists have also served as political consultants, whose findings have been reported in the news media before elections.

Chestnut, J. L., Jr. *Black in Selma.* New York: Farrar, Straus and Giroux, 1990. (Autobiography of a noted attorney for civil and voting rights.)

Journal of Politics. Published by the Southern Political Science Association, it contains articles on voting behavior and electoral studies.

FOUR

Politics in Alabama

Recent Elections

Alabama politics since Reconstruction has operated as a nominally one-party system, but with factional, sectional, and economic rivalry. In recent years there have been two new ingredients: the rise of Republicanism and African-American political participation. Several Republican congressmen were elected when Barry Goldwater carried the state in 1964, a United States senator in 1980, and the first Republican governor in 112 years was elected in 1986. Alabama has a potential black voting strength of 25% of the electorate, and by the early 1990s Alabamians had elected over 700 African-American public officials, the largest number of any state.

However, state politics is perhaps less visible to the average citizen for several reasons. Attention to this political arena, state politics, is distracted by other attractions in a three-ring circus of government. National and international affairs seem always to be in crisis, while local matters have the immediate interest of personal concern. State politics appears in third place, not as spectacular as national, nor as close as local affairs. The multiplicity of state functions examined in Chapter 7 fragments into technical spheres, making it difficult to keep abreast of the manifold activities. The communications media call things to our attention, but many state capitals, like Alabama's, are not in the main metropolitan area. Most newspapers other than those published in the capital city tend to ignore full coverage of state government, usually having only a weekly report that may emphasize the sensational, the illegal, or the trivial. Finally, issues may be obscured by the influence of special interests seeking to dominate certain areas of state policy.

Alabama municipal elections are *nonpartisan*, so that candidates are not identified on the ballot by party labels. But a nonpartisan system does not mean the absence of politics; rather it is a special kind of group politics with low visibility. Community power studies combining sociology and political science seek to answer the question, Who runs this town? by identifying the economic groups, civic clubs, and individuals who wield influence or "political clout."

What Is a Political Party?

Political influence is most often effective when it is organized into mass action. Alabama law defines a political party as any assemblage or organization that obtains more than 20% of the entire vote in a general election and is subject to regulation.[1] A new political party wishing to appear on the Alabama ballot must file a petition signed by registered voters equal to one percent of the total number of people voting in the last governor's race (currently some 15,000 signatures). The party must have a state executive committee, and there may be committees for each county and municipality to certify the names of candidates legally qualified to hold office and meeting any party qualifications. While party organization can be diagrammed as a hierarchy, each committee is largely autonomous, interested in winning the elections in its geographical jurisdiction. In 1978, a member of the Republican state executive committee declared himself to be "a born-again Democrat," and won the governorship. Rather than being a one-party state, Alabama might be described as a no-party system.

Campaigns

In such a system, personality, regional sectionalism, and factions within the party are important elements. A colorful personality helps distinguish the candidate from the mass of other Democrats seeking nomination. While sectionalism among different areas of the state is frequently commented upon, there are many local rivalries in which hometown or coming from the rural or urban areas of the county is important. One of the most damaging accusations made against Alabama politicians is the failure to carry their home area—"the folks who know you best."

Campaign strategy revolves around public opinion, the mass media, group appeals, and sometimes, unfortunately, smear tactics. How "the issues" are perceived is vital, and there are various propaganda devices that are commonly employed. *Name calling* goes beyond calling the opponent a crook, to more subtle ways of attaching negative symbols so that the desired reaction is based on the charge rather than facts. A false charge can take hold by constant repetition, resulting in *the big lie*. An *appeal to fear* or *attack ads* are often used in campaign advertising. *Glittering generalities* consist of associating positive symbols, slogans, and unsupported generalizations with an idea or person: "This act will benefit all Alabamians and help our state." *Transfer* conveys the attraction of strong positive symbols (e.g., the flag) or negative ones (inexperienced college kids) for the campaigner's purpose, but, again, citizens must determine if such uses are supported by the facts. *Testimonial* means the endorsement by prominent citizens, groups, athletes, and even coaches. *Plain folks*, or the common touch, is reassuring to many people who may not understand the "high-falutin'" issues. The picture of a candidate surrounded by spouse and children may indicate a fine family, but proves very little about qualifications for office. The *bandwagon* approach consists of giving the impression that everyone supports it, that victory at the polls is inevitable. *Card-stacking* presents the favorable side of a situation and is effective because it usually claims to cite some reliable facts—even if upon closer examination they turn out to be incomplete. Such one-sided argument can focus attention on a critical issue (a "winning" theme carefully chosen, after polling, to benefit the candidate), and if repeated by the news media, sets the political agenda, of which the candidate takes full advantage. Public awareness of such devices forces political oratory to address the issues.

Campaign Finance

Campaign finance is one of the most sensitive issues in politics. What it costs to run for office, how the money is spent, and where it is raised are favorite topics of political speculation.

Regulation of campaign finance in Alabama is a mixture of state law and party rules. The Alabama Fair Campaign Practices Act (FCPA) became effective in 1988 and covers candidates, elected officials, and political action committees (PACs). A person becomes a candidate upon having: received or spent certain threshold amounts ($10,000 for statewide, $3,000 for circuit or district, and $1,000 for county or municipal office); qualified for nomination with a political party; or submitted a petition to run as an independent candidate for election. Within five days of becoming a candidate in any of the defined ways, he or she must file a Principal Campaign Committee form (Figure 4.1) with the probate judge if seeking a county or municipal position, or with the Alabama secretary of state for all others. A PAC must file a statement of organization within ten days of reaching a $1,000 threshold of receiving contributions from or making expenditures to any candidate, elected official, principal campaign committee, proposition, party, or other political committee. Both candidates and PACs

THE FAIR CAMPAIGN PRACTICES ACT

APPOINTMENT OF PRINCIPAL CAMPAIGN COMMITTEE

FOR
OFFICIAL
USE
ONLY:

This form is due within five days of reaching the threshold amount, or within five days of qualifying with the party, or within five days of filing a petition as an independent candidate.

PLEASE PRINT OR TYPE

NAME OF CANDIDATE

OFFICE SOUGHT (INCLUDE DISTRICT OR CIRCUIT NUMBER)

ADDRESS (STREET OR POST OFFICE BOX)

CITY   STATE   ZIP CODE

IDENTIFICATION NUMBER

TELEPHONE NUMBER

TYPE OF COMMITTEE
(CHECK ONE OF THE FOLLOWING)

☐ I APPOINT MYSELF AS THE SOLE MEMBER OF MY PRINCIPAL CAMPAIGN COMMITTEE.

☐ I HEREBY APPOINT THE INDIVIDUALS LISTED BELOW TO ACT AS MY PRINCIPAL CAMPAIGN COMMITTEE.

IF YOU HAVE APPOINTED OTHERS TO SERVE AS YOUR COMMITTEE, YOU MUST SELECT AT LEAST TWO MEMBERS (ONE TO SERVE AS CHAIRMAN; ONE TO SERVE AS TREASURER) AND YOU MAY APPOINT UP TO FIVE MEMBERS. PLEASE TYPE OR PRINT THEIR NAMES AND ADDRESSES IN THIS SPACE. EACH APPOINTEE THEN MUST SIGN HIS/HER NAME.

NAME

ADDRESS

CITY   STATE   ZIP CODE

SIGNATURE OF APPOINTEE

NAME

ADDRESS

CITY   STATE   ZIP CODE

SIGNATURE OF APPOINTEE

NAME

ADDRESS

CITY   STATE   ZIP CODE

SIGNATURE OF APPOINTEE

NAME

ADDRESS

CITY   STATE   ZIP CODE

SIGNATURE OF APPOINTEE

NAME

ADDRESS

CITY   STATE   ZIP CODE

SIGNATURE OF APPOINTEE

"AS REQUIRED BY THE ALABAMA FAIR CAMPAIGN PRACTICES ACT, I HEREBY SWEAR, OR AFFIRM TO THE BEST OF MY KNOWLEDGE AND BELIEF, THAT THE INFORMATION CONTAINED HEREIN IS TRUE AND CORRECT, AND THAT THIS INFORMATION IS A FULL AND COMPLETE STATEMENT OF APPOINTMENT OF PRINCIPAL CAMPAIGN COMMITTEE AND OTHER REQUIRED INFORMATION."

SWORN TO AND SUBSCRIBED BEFORE ME THIS _____ DAY OF _____, 19_____.

SIGNATURE OF ELECTED OFFICIAL OR CANDIDATE   SIGNATURE OF CHAIRMAN OR TREASURER OF POLITICAL COMMITTEE

FORM REVISED 11/91

Figure 4.1   Appointment of principal campaign committee.

must file annual reports by January 31 for the previous year, and regular reports (Figures 4.2 to 4.6) before elections: forty-five days and again ten to five days before a primary; ten to five days before a primary runoff; and forty-five days plus ten to five days before the general election.

Failure to file can lead to denial of an election certificate to a winner, and criminal prosecutions (with penalties of up to a $2,000 fine and a year in jail) have been rare. All officials elected must file an annual report, and eventually the Statement of Dissolution must give a final report detailing contributions and expenditures not previously reported and the disposition of any residual funds. The FCPA requires that all political advertising (bumper stickers, signs, T-shirts, media ads, etc.) be clearly labeled and the sponsor identified by address. The Alabama Fair Campaign Practices Act also prohibits corrupt practices such as vote buying; making a contribution in someone else's name; misrepresentation as acting for a candidate, political committee, or party (no "dirty tricks"); or interfering (by jobs, financial reprisal, or other threats) with a person's right to cast a ballot freely.

Alabama also requires candidates for office and all state, county, and municipal elected officials to file a statement of economic interests with the State Ethics Commission, and their names can be removed from the ballot if they fail to file within ten days of announcing their candidacy. This statement is a public record of personal finances (Figure 4.7).

Campaigning has become increasingly expensive in recent Alabama elections. As a comparison, in the 1982 Democratic primary, the three gubernatorial candidates spent a total of $3 million and reported another $1 million spent in the runoff for the Democratic nomination. The Democratic and Republican candidates expended $3 million in the general election. By the 1990 governor's race, each of the five major Democratic candidates raised approximately $2 million for the primary, the two making it to the runoff reported spend-

THE FAIR CAMPAIGN PRACTICES ACT

SUMMARY OF CONTRIBUTIONS AND EXPENDITURES

FOR OFFICIAL USE ONLY:

FORM 1

PLEASE PRINT OR TYPE

NAME OF ELECTED OFFICIAL, CANDIDATE, OR POLITICAL COMMITTEE

OFFICE SOUGHT OR HELD (INCLUDE DISTRICT OR CIRCUIT NUMBER)

ADDRESS (STREET OR POST OFFICE BOX)

CITY STATE ZIP CODE

TELEPHONE NUMBER

☐ CHECK HERE IF ADDRESS IS DIFFERENT THAN PREVIOUSLY REPORTED.

IDENTIFICATION NUMBER ______

TYPE OF REPORT (CHECK ONE)

- ☐ 45-DAY PRE-ELECTION REPORT BEFORE PRIMARY ELECTION
- ☐ 10-5-DAY PRE-ELECTION REPORT BEFORE PRIMARY ELECTION
- ☐ 10-5-DAY PRE-ELECTION REPORT BEFORE PRIMARY RUN-OFF ELECTION
- ☐ 45-DAY PRE-ELECTION REPORT BEFORE GENERAL ELECTION
- ☐ 10-5-DAY PRE-ELECTION REPORT BEFORE GENERAL ELECTION
- ☐ ANNUAL REPORT
- ☐ TERMINATION REPORT

COMPLETE THIS BALANCE CHART

1. **BEGINNING BALANCE**
   FOR INITIAL ANNUAL REPORT THE BEGINNING BALANCE SHOULD BE ZERO; OTHERWISE SHOULD BE THE ENDING BALANCE ON THE LAST ANNUAL REPORT FILED.
   FOR PRE-ELECTION REPORTS, THE BEGINNING BALANCE SHOULD BE THE ENDING BALANCE ON THE LAST REPORT FILED, OR ZERO IF IT IS THE FIRST REPORT FILED. 1. ______
2. **TOTAL CASH CONTRIBUTIONS** (FOR THE REPORTING PERIOD)
   A. ITEMIZED CASH CONTRIBUTIONS (ATTACH FORM 2) 2A ______
   B. NON ITEMIZED CASH CONTRIBUTIONS 2B ______
   C. ADD ITEMS 2A AND 2B. THIS IS YOUR TOTAL CASH CONTRIBUTION. ______ 2. ______
3. **IN-KIND CONTRIBUTIONS** (FOR THE REPORTING PERIOD)
   A. ITEMIZED IN-KIND CONTRIBUTIONS (ATTACH FORM 3) 3A ______
   B. NON-ITEMIZED IN-KIND CONTRIBUTIONS 3B ______
   C. ADD ITEMS 3A AND 3B. THIS IS YOUR TOTAL IN-KIND CONTRIBUTION. ______ 3. ______
4. **TOTAL RECEIPTS FROM OTHER SOURCES** (FOR THE REPORTING PERIOD)
   INCLUDE INTEREST, LOANS, ETC. LOANS SHOULD INCLUDE THE IDENTIFICATION OF THE LENDER, THE IDENTIFICATION OF THE ENDORSERS, OR GUARANTORS (ATTACH FORM 4).
   THIS IS YOUR TOTAL IN RECEIPTS FROM OTHER SOURCES. ______ 4. ______
5. **TOTAL EXPENDITURES** (FOR THE REPORTING PERIOD)
   A. ITEMIZED EXPENDITURES (ATTACH FORM 5) 5A ______
   B. NON-ITEMIZED EXPENDITURES 5B ______
   C. ADD ITEMS 5A AND 5B. THIS IS YOUR TOTAL EXPENDITURE. ______ 5. ______
6. **ENDING BALANCE**
   A. ADD ITEMS 1, 2, AND 4.
   B. SUBTRACT ITEM 5. THIS IS YOUR ENDING BALANCE. ______ 6. ______

"AS REQUIRED BY THE ALABAMA FAIR CAMPAIGN PRACTICES ACT, I HEREBY SWEAR, OR AFFIRM TO THE BEST OF MY KNOWLEDGE AND BELIEF, THAT THE ATTACHED REPORT(S) AND THE INFORMATION CONTAINED HEREIN ARE TRUE AND CORRECT, AND THAT THIS INFORMATION IS A FULL AND COMPLETE STATEMENT OF ALL CONTRIBUTIONS, EXPENDITURES, AND OTHER REQUIRED INFORMATION DURING THE APPLICABLE PERIOD OF TIME."

SWORN TO AND SUBSCRIBED BEFORE ME THIS ______ DAY OF ______, 19______.

NOTARY PUBLIC

SIGNATURE OF ELECTED OFFICIAL OR CANDIDATE

PRINT NOTARY'S NAME

DATE COMMISSION EXPIRES

SIGNATURE OF CHAIRMAN OR TREASURER OF POLITICAL COMMITTEE

FORM REVISED 11/91

Figure 4.2 Summary of contributions and expenditures.

THE FAIR CAMPAIGN PRACTICES ACT

FORM 2: CASH CONTRIBUTIONS

PAGE ____ OF ____

NAME OF ELECTED OFFICIAL, CANDIDATE, OR POLITICAL COMMITTEE: ____

THE FCPA REQUIRES THAT THOSE CONTRIBUTIONS GREATER THAN $100 BE ITEMIZED. DO NOT LIST IN-KIND CONTRIBUTIONS OR LOANS ON THIS FORM. USE FORMS 3 AND 4 FOR THOSE LISTINGS.

CONTRIBUTOR (INCLUDE FULL NAME)	ADDRESS (ADDRESS SHOULD INCLUDE STREET OR P.O. BOX, CITY, STATE, AND ZIP)	SOURCE OF CONTRIBUTION (Check One)				DATE CONTRIBUTION RECEIVED (mo./day/yr.)	AMOUNT OF CONTRIBUTION
		BUSINESS/ CORPORATION	INDIVIDUAL	PAC	OTHER ( )		

TOTAL AMOUNT OF CASH CONTRIBUTIONS ON THIS PAGE

FORM REVISED 11/91

Figure 4.3 Fair Campaign Practices Act: Cash contributions.

THE FAIR CAMPAIGN PRACTICES ACT

FORM 3: IN-KIND CONTRIBUTIONS

PAGE _____ OF _____

NAME OF ELECTED OFFICIAL , CANDIDATE, OR POLITICAL COMMITTEE: _____

THE FCPA REQUIRES THAT THOSE CONTRIBUTIONS GREATER THAN $100 BE ITEMIZED. DO NOT LIST CASH OR LOANS ON THIS FORM. USE FORMS 2 AND 4 FOR THOSE LISTINGS.

CONTRIBUTOR (INCLUDE FULL NAME)	ADDRESS (ADDRESS SHOULD INCLUDE STREET OR P.O. BOX, CITY, STATE, AND ZIP)	NATURE OF CONTRIBUTION (CHECK ONE)										SOURCE (CHECK ONE)					DATE CONTRIBUTION RECEIVED	AMOUNT OF CONTRIBUTION
		ADMINISTRA-TIVE	ADVERTISING	CONSULTANT/ POLLING	EQUIPMENT	FOOD	RENT	TRANSPORTA-TION	OTHER ( )		BUSINESS/ CORPORATION	INDIVIDUAL	PAC	OTHER ( )			

TOTAL AMOUNT OF IN-KIND CONTRIBUTIONS ON THIS PAGE

FORM REVISED 11/91

Figure 4.4 In-kind contributions.

THE FAIR CAMPAIGN PRACTICES ACT

FORM 4: RECEIPTS FROM OTHER SOURCES
LOANS, INTEREST, OTHER

PAGE ____ OF ____

NAME OF ELECTED OFFICIAL, CANDIDATE, OR POLITICAL COMMITTEE:

THE FCPA REQUIRES THAT THOSE CONTRIBUTIONS GREATER THAN $100 BE ITEMIZED. DO NOT LIST CASH OR IN-KIND CONTRIBUTIONS ON THIS FORM. USE FORMS 2 AND 3 FOR THOSE LISTINGS.

SOURCE OF RECEIPT (INCLUDE FULL NAME)	ADDRESS (ADDRESS SHOULD INCLUDE STREET OR P.O. BOX, CITY, STATE, AND ZIP)	FORM OF RECEIPT			COMPLETE THIS BLOCK IF RECEIPT IS A LOAN — GUARANTORS [FCPA REQUIRES FULL NAME AND COMPLETE ADDRESS OF INDIVIDUAL(S) ENDORSING OR GUARANTEEING LOAN]	RECEIPT SOURCE (CHECK ONE)						DATE RECEIVED (mo./day/yr.)	AMOUNT OF RECEIPT
		INTEREST	LOAN	OTHER		LENDING INSTITUTION	PAC	INDIVIDUAL	BUSINESS	OTHER ( )			

TOTAL AMOUNT OF RECEIPTS ON THIS PAGE

FORM REVISED 11/91

Figure 4.5 Receipts from other sources.

66

THE FAIR CAMPAIGN PRACTICES ACT

FORM 5: EXPENDITURES

PAGE _____ OF _____

NAME OF ELECTED OFFICIAL, CANDIDATE, OR POLITICAL COMMITTEE: _____

THE FCPA REQUIRES THAT EXPENDITURES OVER $100 BE ITEMIZED.

VENDOR TO WHOM EXPENDITURE IS MADE (INCLUDE FULL NAME)	VENDOR ADDRESS (ADDRESS SHOULD INCLUDE STREET OR P.O. BOX, CITY, STATE, AND ZIP)	PURPOSE OF EXPENDITURE (PLEASE CHECK)											DATE OF EXPENDITURE (mo./day/yr.)	AMOUNT OF EXPENDITURE
		ADMINISTRA-TIVE	ADVERTISING	CONSULTANT/POLLING	FOOD	FUNDRAISING	LOAN	RETAYMENT	LODGING	TRANSPORTA-TION	OTHER ( )			

TOTAL AMOUNT OF EXPENDITURES ON THIS PAGE

FORM REVISED 11/91

Figure 4.6 Fair Campaign Practices Act: Expenditures.

STATE

Alabama Ethics Commission
770 Washington Street/Suite 330
Montgomery, Alabama 36130-2300

(see instructions on page 7)

STATEMENT OF ECONOMIC INTERESTS

01. FULL NAME, HOME ADDRESS and TELEPHONE OF FILING PERSON:

_____ _____ _____ _____ _____ _____
(Last)   (First)   (Middle)

_____ _____ _____ _____ _____ _____
(Street)   (Route)   (P.O. Box)   (City)   (Zip Code)   (County)   (Home Phone) (Business Phone)

If NAME changed within past year please indicate former NAME: _____ _____
                                                                  (Last)   (First)   (MI)

PLEASE FILL IN THE BLANKS OR CIRCLE THE CORRECT WORD(S) OR NUMBER(S) AS APPROPRIATE

02. Last year, I was a State   LEGISLATOR   in the   (SENATE)   (HOUSE OF REPRESENTATIVES).

02.1 Last year, I was a State (OFFICIAL) (EMPLOYED) of _____. Currently I am a State (OFFICIAL) (EMPLOYED) of _____.

02.2 As a State official or employee last year, my job title was _____

02.3 Last year, the name(s) of the (STATE) (COUNTY) (MUNICIPAL) Board(s), Commission(s), Authority(ies), Council(s), etc. of which I was a Member was _____

02.4 Last year in the aforenamed public position(s) in 02. thru 02.3 I earned: ($0-$1,000)   ($1,000-$10,000)   (MORE THAN $10,000).

03. I AM A CANDIDATE FOR THE (STATE) (COUNTY) OR (MUNICIPAL) OFFICE OF _____

04. Other than my public position(s) in 02. thru 02.3, my occupation or business last year was (including self-employment) _____

04.1 The name and address of my employer last year was _____

04.2 I was self-employed last year and the name and address of my business last year was _____

05. My spouse's name is _____ and his/her occupation last year was _____

05.1 The name and address of my spouse's employer last year was _____

06. Children or dependents for whom YOU and/or YOUR SPOUSE provided more than 50% of support last year are _____

07. Last year, from the occupations or businesses listed in 04 thru 05.1, I, my spouse and dependents earned an aggregate of: ($0-$1,000)   ($1,000-$10,000)   (MORE THAN $10,000).

07.1 Last year, (I) (MY SPOUSE) (DEPENDENTS) owned 10% or more of the stock in the firm(s) listed in   (04.1)   (04.2)   (05.1).

07.2 Last year, (I) (MY SPOUSE) was a consultant and earned more than $1,000 from each firm listed in   (04.1)   (04.2)   (05.1).

07.3 Last year, (I) (MY SPOUSE) served as an (OFFICER) (DIRECTOR) (TRUSTEE) of the firm(s) listed in   (04.1)   (04.2)   (05.1).

(1)

Figure 4.7 Statement of economic interests.

68

08. OTHER INCOME INFORMATION ON YOU, YOUR SPOUSE AND DEPENDENT CHILDREN

	Write in Type of Income Received	Check Appropriate Box			Last year, did YOU, YOUR SPOUSE, or YOUR DEPENDENT CHILDREN hold 10% or more of outstanding stock? (Check Appropriate Box)		Last year, did YOU or YOUR SPOUSE serve as: (Check Appropriate Boxes)			
	Salary, Fees, Commissions, Dividends, Profits, Rents, Treat., Interest, Other	Less than $1,000	$1,000 – $10,000	More than $10,000	YES	NO	Officer	Director	Trustee	Consultant earning more than $1,000
List names of ALL OTHER Occupations, Businesses, Firms, Partnerships, Professions, etc., not previously listed that do business in Alabama and all other State, Municipal or County Governmental Entities from which YOU, YOUR SPOUSE, or DEPENDENT CHILDREN received income last year.	Write in Type of Income Received									
08.1										
08.2										
08.3										
08.4										
08.5										
List names of Banks, Savings & Loan Companies, Credit Unions in Alabama from which YOU, YOUR SPOUSE, or DEPENDENT CHILDREN received income last year.	Write in Type of Income Received									
08.6										
08.7										
08.8										
08.9										
08.10										
List Company names of Stock and Bonds of Alabama Companies owned by YOU, YOUR SPOUSE, or DEPENDENT CHILDREN from which income was received last year.	Write in Type of Income Received				Last year, did YOU, YOUR SPOUSE, or DEPENDENTS hold 10% or more of outstanding stock of this company?					
08.11										
08.12										
08.13										
08.14										
List location of real or personal property sold by YOU, YOUR SPOUSE, or DEPENDENT CHILDREN from which money was received last year.	Write in Type of Income Received				Last year, did YOU, YOUR SPOUSE, or DEPENDENTS hold 10% or more of outstanding stock in a company selling the property?					
08.15										
08.16										
08.17										
08.18										

SPECIAL NOTE: ADD ADDITIONAL SHEETS AS NECESSARY.

(2)

Figure 4.7 (continued)

08. (CONTINUED) OTHER INCOME INFORMATION ON YOU, YOUR SPOUSE AND DEPENDENT CHILDREN

List title of any trusts from which YOU, YOUR SPOUSE, or DEPENDENTS received income from last year.	Write in Type of Income Received	Check Appropriate Box.			Last year, did YOU, YOUR SPOUSE, or YOUR DEPENDENT CHILDREN hold 10% or more of outstanding stock? (Check Appropriate Box)		Last year, did YOU or YOUR SPOUSE serve as: (Check Appropriate Boxes)			
		Less than $1,000	$1,000 – $10,000	More than $10,000	YES	NO	Officer	Director	Trustee	(Civilian) earning more than $1,000
	Salary, Fees, Commissions, Dividends, Profits, Rents Trust, Interest, Other									
08.19										
08.20										
List any other sources not previously shown from which YOU, YOUR SPOUSE, or DEPENDENTS received income last year.	Write in Type of Income Received									
08.21										
08.22										
08.23										

SPECIAL NOTE:
ADD ADDITIONAL SHEETS AS NECESSARY.

08.24 List any business not reported above in which YOU, YOUR SPOUSE or DEPENDENT CHILDREN received NO income but held 10% or more of the outstanding stock.

1. _____

2. _____

09. INFORMATION ON FAMILY MEMBERS

NAME OF ADULT CHILDREN	Address	Principal Occupation	Name of Employer/Business	Business Address
09.1				
09.2				
09.3				
NAME OF PARENTS				
09.4				
09.5				
NAME OF BROTHERS				
09.6				
09.7				
NAME OF SISTERS				
09.8				
09.9				

(3)

Figure 4.7 (continued)

70

10-10.2 (To be completed ONLY by ELECTED OFFICIALS, APPOINTED OFFICIALS or CANDIDATES for State, County or Municipal Offices.)

10. REAL ESTATE HOLDINGS

NOTE: EXCLUDE YOUR HOMESTEAD.

10.1 Did YOU or A BUSINESS WITH WHICH YOU ARE ASSOCIATED receive any rent or lease income from any governmental agency in Alabama last year?

_____ NO

_____ YES If yes, you must attach copies of the lease or rent agreement(s) and submit them with this report.

10.2 Did YOU, YOUR SPOUSE or DEPENDENTS own real estate for investment or revenue purposes last year?

_____ NO

_____ YES If yes, list each piece of real estate separately below and provide the requested information.

(CHECK APPROPRIATE BOXES)

Location of Alabama Real Estate (CITY and COUNTY)	What is the primary use of this property?			What is the fair market value?			What is the annual gross rent or lease income?		
	Residential	Commercial	Agricultural	Less than $50,000	$50,000 but less than $250,000	$250,000 or more	Less than $10,000	$10,000 but less than $50,000	$50,000 or more

SPECIAL NOTE:
ADD
ADDITIONAL
SHEETS AS
NECESSARY.

(4)

Figure 4.7 (continued)

11. PROFESSIONAL OR CONSULTING SERVICES

(To be completed if YOU or YOUR SPOUSE received income last year in return for professional activities. State the number of clients and check the appropriate boxes.)

☐ No income was received for Professional or Consulting Services for the categories of Clients shown below.

Categories of Clients	Number of Clients	Annual Gross Income During Reporting Year			Anticipated Annual Retainer Income	
		Less than $1,000	$1,000 but less than $10,000	$10,000 or more	Less than $1,250	$1,250 or more
11.1 Utilities						
Electric						
Gas						
Telephone						
Water						
Cable Television						
11.2 Transportation						
Intrastate Companies						
Interstate Companies						
Pipe Line Companies						
Oil or Gas Exploration						
Oil and Gas Retailers						
11.3 Finance and Insurance						
Banks						
Savings and Loan Institutions						
Finance Companies						
Life and Casualty Insurance			*			
11.4 Associations						
Trade						
Professional						
Governmental						
Employee						
Public Official		*				
Union						

Categories of Clients	Number of Clients	Annual Gross Income During Reporting Year			Anticipated Annual Retainer Income	
		Less than $1,000	$1,000 but less than $10,000	$10,000 or more	Less than $1,250	$1,250 or more
11.5 Government						
State						
County						
Municipal						
11.6 Miscellaneous						
Beverage Companies						
Beverage Distributors						
Construction						
Education, Private						
Funeral Homes						
Hospitals						
Machinery and Supply						
Manufacturing						
Mining						
Retail Companies						
Farming						
Medical or Health Related						
11.7 Other (Specify)						

(5)

Figure 4.7 (continued)

72

12. INDEBTEDNESS INFORMATION

(Report debts owed to all businesses operating in Alabama as of December 31 last year, EXCEPT indebtedness for the mortgage on the home in which you live. Include debts of YOUR SPOUSE and DEPENDENT CHILDREN.)

(CHECK APPROPRIATE BOXES)

TYPE	How many do you OWE?	How much do you OWE? (Check box that relates to the combined total in each category)		
		Less than $25,000	$25,000 but less than $50,000	$50,000 but less than $100,000	$100,000 or more
12.1 Banks					
12.2 Credit Unions and Savings and Loan Associations					
12.3 Insurance Companies					
12.4 Mortgage Firms					
12.5 Stock Brokers					
12.6 Other Businesses (Include Credit Card Indebtedness)					
12.7 Individuals					

13. DECLARATION OF REPORTING PERSON

I have read as completed, this Statement of Economic Interests, Form ASEC-1 (Revised), and do swear (or affirm) that the information contained in said Statement of Economic Interests is true and correct. I fully understand that anyone who violates the disclosure provision of this Act, shall be subject to a fine of $10.00 a day not to exceed $1,000 annually.

DATE: _____ SIGNED: _____

(Signature of Reporting Person)

Return completed form to:
Alabama Ethics Commission
770 Washington Street/Suite 330
Montgomery, AL 36130-2300

(6)

Figure 4.7 (continued)

ing another million, and the Democratic nominee spent $5.2 million losing to the incumbent Republican who spent $4.4 million to retain the Alabama governorship paying approximately $80,000 per year. Even candidates running unopposed for reelection have to raise hundreds of thousands of dollars, since advertising must be booked in advance before it is known whether there will be opponents. In fact, a large campaign fund accumulation may discourage rivals from filing.

Statewide campaigns needing mass media are very expensive; a sixty-second spot on a network television station ranges from $500 to $2,000 depending upon the time aired, and a quarter-page advertisement in a metropolitan daily costs $560 to $1,800 for the Sunday edition. This is the price of dissemination only; the campaign provides the promotional material. Alabama candidates have used public relations firms from both inside and outside the state for campaign management and to develop political advertising, which is the largest campaign expense. Other costs reported are for travel and meals, telephone, stationery and postage, copies of voters' lists for mailings in each county, polling, and rental of cars, office space, and equipment. Vendors often require prepayment since it is hard to collect from a losing campaign afterwards, and some candidates assume large personal debts.

Where does the money for campaigning come from? Individual donors, interest groups, those doing business in the state, state employees, teachers, and unions or professional organizations may feel access to the governmental machinery could be enhanced by helping a candidate. Incumbents (those who already hold office) usually find more assistance than do challengers. Such contributions are not necessarily made in cash, but may take such in-kind forms as sponsoring entertainment, providing transportation (loan of cars to a campaign is common), bringing legal business to a lawyer-legislator's firm, loaning the candidate secretarial help, and a multitude of other ways, which are supposed to be itemized if they exceed $100 in the reports required by the Alabama Fair Campaign Practices Act.

Alabama allowed businesses as well as nonprofit organizations to form political action committees (PACs) in 1981, and there are now more than 300 registered. "The 1982 legislative elections were the first in Alabama history to be mainly financed by PACs."[2] By the 1990 elections Alabama PACs reporting spending over $14 million, almost half of it by the top ten: AVOTE (Alabama Education Association), JOBPAC (whose largest contributor was dogtrack owner Milton Mc-Gregor), Alabama Trial Lawyers, Alabama State Employees, ALFA (Alabama Farmers Federation), Alabama Medical PAC, Alabama Builders Association, Alabama Power Company Employees PAC, Progress PAC (Business Council of Alabama), and the Alabama Democratic Conference (African Americans).[3] Since a number of Alabama state and local officials have been convicted of corrupt practices,[4] ethics regulation will continue to be of civic interest.

■ *Pressure Politics.* Interest groups can be distinguished from political parties primarily because they seek to influence policy rather than run candidates for office. They not only seek to persuade elective officials, but maintain close liaison with the bureaucracy carrying out government policy and cultivate a favorable attitude toward their cause. Thus such interests are sometimes called clientele groups, because they represent segments benefiting from certain policies, and seek to control the portions of government important to them.

The term *lobbyist* conjures up the image of a political wheeler-dealer, but actually legislative advocates come in all varieties and may represent more than one client.[5] Most will point out that the important thing in lobbying is access—the opportunity to state your case—rather than corruptly influencing officials. Effective lobbying is an exercise in communications.

Figure 4.8 Interest group representatives meet with legislators in the lobbies of the capitol, hence the term *lobbyists*. (Courtesy of the Alabama Film Commission. Used by permission)

Lobbyists concentrate on image (creating a favorable climate of opinion), contacts (personal acquaintances who can befriend the cause), sources of information, and convincing uncommitted decision makers (thus enforcing responsibility for an action).

When pressure politics has erupted into scandals, regulation of lobbying has been increased. Alabama lobbyists and their principal employers are required to register on the forms shown (Figure 4.9), but some do not, claiming the law's exemptions of "providing professional services" or only "isolated contact" in lobbying activities.

So many lobbyists are active in Montgomery that they have formed the Alabama Council of Association Executives. Many other groups have their own buildings surrounding the state

Lobbyist Registration Form
STATE OF ALABAMA
State Ethics Commission
770 Washington Street/Suite 330
Montgomery, Alabama 36130
(205) 242-2997

01 Name   Last   First   MI

02 Mailing Address   Street   City   State   Zip

03 Telephone No.   **04** *Name Of Person Or Association You Represent (Do not abbreviate)

05 Address of Principal   Street   City   State   Zip

* If your principal represents other clients in a lobbying capacity, attach a listing of the name and address of each client.

06 General Description Of Subjects On Which You Expect To Lobby
_____
_____

07 Name Of Person Signing As Your Principal _____

08 Title And Address Of Principal _____

09 What Is The Size Of Your Organization?   1-5   6-10   11-25   More than 25 Members

10 Is The Organization You Lobby For   (Incorporated)   (Unincorporated)?

11 Do You Serve As A Lobbyist For More Than One Organization?   (Yes)   (No)
(If yes, you must complete a separate registration form for each)

12 Are You Connected In Any Way With A Political Action Committee (PAC)?   (Yes)   (No)

13 Were You An Official/Employee Of The State During The Last 5 Years?   (Yes)   (No)
(If yes, show your position title)_____

Certification
I,_____ swear (or affirm) that the information contained in this Lobbyist Registration Report is complete, true and correct, and that no information is knowing withheld.

_____
Signature of Lobbyist   Date

Certification
STATE OF ALABAMA COUNTY OF _____
Sworn to and subscribed before me this
_____day of _____, 19____.

_____
Notary Public
My Commission Expires _____

Principal's Statement
I hereby certify I am the Principal named on this Lobbyist Registration Form. I further certify that I have read the Form and know it's contents; that acting for the Association or Organization, the named Lobbyist has been authorized to lobby on behalf of the Association or Organization and that no compensation will be paid to the named Lobbyist contingent upon the passage or defeat of any legislation.

_____
Signature of Principal

Figure 4.9   Lobbyist's registration statement.

Lobbyist Form

Monthly Statement of Lobbying Activities
State of Alabama
State Ethics Commission
770 Washington Street/Suite 330
Montgomery, Alabama 36130-2300
(205) 242-2997

General Information:
Reporting Person: _____
Address: _____
_____

Name of your Principal(s): _____

Month Covered by this Statement: ____(Month) ___(Year)
Latest Preceding Month for which this
Statement was filed: _____(Month) _____(Year)

Item 1

Did you do any lobbying activities during this reporting period?
☐ Yes (if yes, complete remainder of form)
☐ No (see paragraph below)

If Lobbyist (1) Performed no lobbying activities; (2) Made no expenditures for lobbying activities; (3) Loaned no money to any Legislator or anyone on behalf of a Legislator; (4) Had no direct business association with any Legislator or other public official or employee, then advance to Item 6.

Item 2

Categories of legislation subject to lobbying activities:
_____
_____
_____
_____

Item 3

Principal for whom expenditure made.
If no expenditure, check here ☐

First principal:
Name: _____
Address: _____

Amount of expenditures:
☐ Less than $1,000
☐ $1,000 to $3,000
☐ More than $3,000

Second principal (if any):
Name: _____
Address: _____

Amount of expenditures:
☐ Less than $1,000
☐ $1,000 to $3,000
☐ More than $3,000

Item 4

Loans made or promised to Legislators or to anyone on their behalf.
If none, check here ☐

Identification of recipient:
Name: _____
Legislative Branch: ☐ Senate ☐ House
District Represented: _____
Home Address: _____
_____

Name of recipient, if loan made or promised on behalf of Legislators:
Name: _____
Relationship, if any, of recipient to Legislator: _____

Home Address: _____
_____
Date of Loan: _____
Amount of Loan Made: _____
Amount of Loan Promised: _____

State in detail circumstances surrounding above loan :_____
_____
_____
_____
_____
_____

(Add Additional Sheets as Necessary)

Figure 4.9 (continued)

Item 5

Direct business association between reporting person (lobbyist) and member of Legislature or public official or employee.

    If none, check here   ☐

Identification of person having direct business association with reporting person:

Name: _____

Home Address: _____

_____

Branch of Government: _____

Position or Job Title: _____

_____

Name of Business in which directly associated: _____

_____

Business Address: _____

_____

Nature of business association: (Check one or more boxes):

  ☐ Serve as directors, officers, partners or employees in the same business.

  ☐ Have legal or beneficial ownership interest in same business.

  ☐ Identified person is employee, officer or director of reporting person.

  ☐ Identified person and reporting person are members of the same union.

  ☐ Identified person and reporting person are members of the same Trade or Professional Association.

State in detail the extent of any direct business association or partnership with any current member of the Legislature, public official/employee.

_____

_____

_____

_____

_____

_____

(Add Additional Sheets as Necessary)

Item 6

Verification of reporting person:

    I have read this Monthly Statement of Lobbying Activities and do swear (or affirm) that, according to my knowledge and belief, the information contained therein is true and correct.

Signed: _____

Date: _____

Sworn to and subscribed before me this

the _____ day of _____, 19____.

_____
                Notary Public

My Commission Expires: _____

Designated Filing Procedure

The Lobbyist's Form must be filed with the Commission by every person required to file between the first and fifteenth day of each month succeeding a month in which the Legislature was in session, covering the preceding month.

State of Alabama
State Ethics Commission
770 Washington Street/Suite 330
Montgomery, Alabama 36130-2300
(205) 242-2997

Figure 4.9   (continued)

Principal's Form

Monthly Statement of Lobbying Activities
State of Alabama
State Ethics Commission
770 Washington Street/Suite 330
Montgomery, Alabama 36130-2300
(205) 242-2997

Business/Association/Organization:
Name: _____
Address: _____
_____
Telephone Number: _____
Name and Title of Individual signing for Principal: _____

Month covered by this Statement:____(Month) ____(Year)

If principal is individual only, complete the following:
Name: _____
Address: _____
_____
Telephone Number: _____
Latest Preceding Month for which
Statement was filed: _____(Month) _____(Year)

Item 1
List all lobbyists employed/retained by principal:
Name of Lobbyist: _____
Address: _____

Expenditures Made: ☐ Yes ☐ No
Name of Lobbyist: _____
Address: _____

Expenditures Made: ☐ Yes ☐ No
(Add Additional Sheets as Necessary)

Item 2
Did you perform any lobbying activities during this reporting period?
☐ Yes (if yes, complete remainder of form)
☐ No (see paragraph below)

If Principal (1) Performed no lobbying activities; (2) Made no expenditures for lobbying activities; (3) Loaned no money to any Legislator or anyone on behalf of a Legislator; (4) Had no direct business association with any legislator or other public official or employee, then go to Item 7.

Were expenditures made in addition to any made by employed registered lobbyist?
☐ Yes
☐ No

Indicate amount of expenditures spent directly by principal (not by lobbyist):
☐ Less than $1,000
☐ $1,000 to $3,000
☐ More than $3,000

Item 4
Loans made or promised to Legislators or to anyone on their behalf.
If none, check here ☐

Identification of recipient:
Name: _____
Legislative Branch: ☐ Senate ☐ House
District Represented: _____
Home Address: _____

Name of recipient, if loan made or promised on behalf of Legislators:
Name: _____
Relationship, if any, of recipient to Legislator: _____
_____
Home Address: _____
_____
Date of Loan: _____
Amount of Loan Made: _____
Amount of Loan Promised: _____

State in detail circumstances surrounding above loan: _____
_____
_____
_____
(Add Additional Sheets as Necessary)

Figure 4.10 Principal's registration statement.

Item 5

Direct business association between reporting person (principal) and member of Legislature or public official or employee.

  If none, check here ☐

Identification of person having direct business association with reporting person:

Name: _____

Home Address: _____

_____

Branch of Government: _____

Position or Job Title: _____

_____

Name of Business in which directly associated: _____

_____

Business Address: _____

_____

Nature of business association: (Check one or more boxes):

  ☐ Serve as directors, officers, partners or employees in the same business.

  ☐ Have legal or beneficial ownership interest in same business

  ☐ Identified person is employee, officer or director of reporting person.

  ☐ Identified person and reporting person are members of the same union.

  ☐ Identified person and reporting person are members of the same Trade or Professional Association.

State in detail the extent of any direct business association or partnership with any current member of the Legislature, public official/employee.

_____

_____

_____

_____

_____

_____

_____

(Add Additional Sheets as Necessary)

Item 6

Categories of Legislation subject to lobbying activities:

_____

_____

_____

_____

_____

_____

_____

_____

Item 7

Verification of reporting person

  I have read this Monthly Statement of Lobbying Activities and do swear (or affirm) that, according to my knowledge and belief, the information contained therein is true and correct.

Signed: _____

Date: _____

Sworn to and subscribed before me this the _____ day of _____, 19____.

_____

Notary Public

My Commission Expires: _____

Designated Filing Procedure

The Principal's Form must be filed with the Commission by every person required to file between the first and fifteenth day of each month succeeding a month in which the Legislature was in session, covering the preceding month.

State of Alabama
State Ethics Commission
770 Washington Street/Suite 330
Montgomery, Alabama 36130-2300
(205) 242-2997

Figure 4.10   (continued)

State Ethics Commission **APPENDIX E**

State of Alabama
State Ethics Commission

RSA PLAZA
770 WASHINGTON STREET
SUITE 330
MONTGOMERY, ALABAMA 36130

COMPLAINT

I. **PERSON BRINGING COMPLAINT:**
Name: ____________________
Address: ____________________
City: __________ County: __________ Zip Code: __________
Telephone Number: __________ Area Code: __________
Complaint's Signature: ____________________

II. **PERSON AGAINST WHOM COMPLAINT IS BROUGHT:**
Name: ____________________
Address: ____________________
City: __________ County: __________ Zip Code: __________
Telephone Number: __________ Area Code: __________
Title of office or position held or sought: ____________________

III. **VIOLATION:**
List the statutory section(s) of the Code of Ethics which you believe has been violated by person named in paragraph II above:
____
____

IV. **STATEMENT OF FACTS:**
State in your own words the *detailed* facts and the actions of the person named in paragraph II which prompt you to make this complaint. The brief space provided below is not intended to limit your statement of facts. Please use the back of this form or additional sheets if necessary. Include relevant dates and times and the names and addresses of other persons whom you believe have knowledge of the facts:
____
____
____
____
____
____
____

Figure 4.11 State Ethics Commission complaint form.

Alabama Council of Association Executives Members

Alabama Alliance of Business and Industry
Alabama Asphalt Pavement Association
Alabama Association of Life Underwriters
Alabama Association of Home Health Agencies
Alabama Association of Realtors, Inc.
Alabama Association of School Boards
Alabama Bankers Association
Alabama Broadcasters Association
Alabama Cable Television Association
Alabama Cattlemen's Association
Alabama Chapter–American Academy of
  Pediatrics
Alabama Chemical Association
Alabama Coal Association
Alabama Concrete Industries Association
Alabama Consumer Finance Association
Alabama Council, American Institute of Architects
Alabama Council for School Administration and
  Supervision
Alabama Credit Union League, Inc.
Alabama Dental Association
Alabama Eagle Forum
Alabama Farm and Power Equipment Dealers
Alabama Farmers Federation
Alabama Forestry Association
Alabama Hospital Association
Alabama Independent Auto Dealers Association
Alabama Independent Insurance Agents, Inc.
Alabama League of Savings Institutions
Alabama Library Association
Alabama Manufactured Housing Institute, Inc.
Alabama Masonry Institute
Alabama-Mississippi Telephone Association
Alabama Mountain Lakes Association
Alabama Nursing Home Association, Inc.
Alabama Oilmen's Association and
  Alabama Association of Convenience Stores
Alabama Optometric Association
Alabama Parent-Teacher Association
Alabama Peanut Producers Association
Alabama Petroleum Council
Alabama Pharmaceutical Association
Alabama Poultry and Egg Association
Alabama Press Association
Alabama Primary Health Care Association
Alabama Propane Gas Association
Alabama Recreation and Parks Association
Alabama Retail Association
Alabama Retired State Employees Association
Alabama Retired Teachers Association
Alabama Road Builders Association
Alabama Rural Electric Association

Alabama Self-Insured Fund
Alabama Service Station Dealers Association
Alabama Society of CPAs
Alabama Society of Professional Engineers
Alabama Speakers Association
Alabama State Bar
Alabama State Chiropractic Association
Alabama State Employees Association
Alabama State Nurses Association
Alabama Textile Manufacturers Association
Alabama Travel Council
Alabama Trial Lawyers Association
Alabama Trucking Association
Alabama Water and Sewer Institutions
Alabama Wholesale Beer and Wine Association
American Subcontractors Association
Associated Builders and Contractors of Alabama
Associated General Contractors of Alabama
Association of County Commissions of Alabama
Association of State and Provincial Psychology
  Boards
Automobile Dealers Association of Alabama
Automotive Wholesalers Association of Alabama/
  Georgia
Better Business Bureau of Central Alabama, Inc.
BCA/EAA W/C Fund
Birmingham Association of Realtors
BTLS International, Inc.
Business Council of Alabama
Civitan International
Coalbed Methane Association of Alabama
Colquett & Associates
Consulting Engineers Council of Alabama
Crawford & Crawford
Diversified Consultants
Economic Development Association of Alabama
Envirosouth, Inc.
Greater Montgomery Home Builders Association
Home Builders Association of Alabama
Home Builders Association of Metro Mobile
Independent Community Bankers Association
Jefferson County Medical Society
Medical Association of the State of Alabama
Organization Management, Inc.
Professional Convention Management
  Association
Southern Building Code Congress International
Southern Gasoline Retailers and Automotive
  Services Association
T. R. McDougal & Associates
Yonce & Associates

Figure 4.12 Alabama Council of Association Executives.

capitol complex: the Alabama Education Association, utilities regulated by the state, agricultural interests, law enforcement fraternal organizations, bankers, county and municipal governments, and others representing the state's economic and social interests. Each of them watches developments of interest, and indeed serves as a primary source of technical expertise in formulating legislation. If one group demands too much, a coalition of opponents is likely to form a countervailing force to regain more balanced policies. Pressure politics can be a great force; public scrutiny is necessary for channeling it in constructive directions.

Notes

1. The party must maintain at least 20% of the vote in order to stay on the Alabama ballot during the next election year.
2. Mel Cooper, executive director, Alabama State Ethics Commission, interview, April 15, 1983.
3. Gita Smith, "Alabama PACs Spent $14 Million in 1990 Election," *Montgomery Advertiser*, July 21, 1991, 1D, 4D–7D.
4. An annual "Report to Congress on the Activities and Operations of the Public Integrity Section for [year]," by the Criminal Division of the United States Department of Justice gives a national tabulation of convicted public officials. From 1976 through 1990, 264 Alabama officials had been convicted, or 6.6 per 100,000 citizens of the state, compared to a United States average of 3.5.
5. The Alabama firm of Fine & Geddie is perhaps best known for forming several PACs.

For Further Reading

Bass, Jack. *Taming the Storm: The Life and Times of Judge Frank M. Johnson, Jr., and the South's Fight Over Civil Rights*. New York: Doubleday, 1993. (Alabama's political history and court orders on desegregation, prisons, and mental health institutional conditions.)

Black, Earl, and Merle Black. *Politics and Society in the South*. Cambridge, Mass.: Harvard University Press, 1987.

Grafton, Carl, and Anne Permaloff. *Big Mules and Branch-heads: James E. Folsom and Political Power in Alabama.* Athens, Ga.: University of Georgia Press, 1985.

Hrebenar, Ronald J., and Clive S. Thomas, eds. *Interest Group Politics in the Southern States.* Tuscaloosa and London: University of Alabama Press, 1992. (Chapter 11: "Alabama: Personalities and Factionalism" by David L. Martin.)

Raines, Howell. "Political Legacies Keep Alabama Down." *New York Times Magazine,* June 3, 1990, reprinted in the *Montgomery Advertiser,* June 22, 1990, p. 9A.

Sims, George E. *The Little Man's Big Friend: James E. Folsom in Alabama Politics, 1946–1958.* University: University of Alabama Press, 1985.

Smith, Dorothy. *In Our Own Interest: A Handbook for the Citizen Lobbyist in State Legislatures.* Seattle, Wash.: Madrona Publishers, 1979.

Taylor, Sandra Baxley. *Me 'n' George: A Story of George Corley Wallace and His Number One Crony Oscar Harper.* Mobile, Ala.: Greenberry Publishing, 1988.

Among the periodicals covering state politics are: *Inside Alabama Politics, Alabama Magazine, Montgomery Advertiser, Anniston Star, Birmingham News,* and *Birmingham Post-Herald.* Broadcasters are "Alanet News" (radio) and Alabama Public Television's program "For the Record."

The Legislature:
Your Representatives in Action

Structure and Composition

The Alabama legislature is divided into a 35-member state senate and 105-member house of representatives, all elected from single-member districts. The famous United States Supreme Court 1964 decision of "one person, one vote," requiring legislative districts of equal population size in both the Alabama senate and house caused the "reapportionment revolution" across the United States.[1] Although the 1901 constitution requires the legislature to reapportion itself after each decennial census, when it has failed to do so, the federal courts have ordered district boundaries in 1974 and 1983, and suits were pending at the time of writing in 1993. After the 1990 census, a perfectly divided house district would have about 38,500 Alabamians, and each state senator would represent 115,500 constituents. The courts have allowed up to 10% population deviation between the largest and smallest state legislative districts, and politically, the number of registered voters can vary. All of the 1990 census blocks are on computer, enabling legislative (as well as county commission and city council) districts to be constructed so that African-American or other minority votes are not diluted, as required by the federal Voting Rights Act. In Alabama, this has meant an increase in the number of majority black districts, but with convoluted boundaries cutting across existing counties or cities that were long used to being represented by one legislator.

■ *Legislative Sessions.* The Alabama legislature meets annually for thirty "legislative days" in regular session and up to twelve "legislative days" in any special session called by the governor. "Legislative days" are those on which either chamber meets during a 105-day calendar period for the regular session or a thirty-day calendar period for a special session. The normal practice is to hold floor sessions only two or three days per week (usually Tuesdays and Thursdays, with Wednesday committee meetings) so that legislators can go home to their districts on weekends.

The Alabama legislative schedule is that following their election in November (1990, etc.), the 140 legislators convene on the second Tuesday in January for up to ten calendar days in an organizational session. The new legislature canvasses (declares) the election results for state officials, decides any contested elections, elects its officers, appoints committees, and generally prepares itself for business. (Without legislative experience, some new members have later regretted passing the rules which they have to follow for the next four years!) In the first year, the regular session meets the third Tuesday in April (allowing the new governor time to formulate proposals), and extends until the thirty legislative days have been used up within the 105-day calendar period. During the second and third years, the legislature begins on the first Tuesday in February, a tradition in many states when the nonfarming time of year was used to conduct public business. In their fourth year, the Alabama legislators meet on the second Tuesday in January, allowing an earlier start on their reelection campaign when the regular session ends. At any time the governor may call legislators into special session to consider measures in his call; legislation on other subjects can only be passed in each house by a two-thirds vote of a *quorum* (a major-

Figure 5.1 The Alabama legislature meets in the Statehouse, 100 Union Street, Montgomery, across from the Capitol. (Photo by D. L. Martin)

ity of the members elected necessary for each house to conduct business). Timing is crucial politically, and Alabama governors have been prone to call five-day special sessions, the minimum period needed to pass their administration's package of bills. The Alabama legislature can only call itself into special session to consider impeachment of the governor,[2] unlike many other states' legislatures, which are "self-starting" or else meet year-round. Since the Alabama legislature began meeting annually in 1976, Governors Wallace, James, and Hunt all advocated return to biennial sessions, citing costs of sessions and that part-time legislators need to conduct their private businesses. The number of special sessions held (up to four some years) has not decreased with annual regular sessions.

■ *Terms of Office and Compensation.* Alabama state senators and representatives are concurrently elected for four years on the first Tuesday after the first Monday in November (in nonpresidential years: 1990, etc.), and their terms begin the day after the general election. They are paid the $10 per day salary fixed by the 1901 constitution, and two expense allowances (as of 1993): $2,280 per month and $50 for each day they claim legislative duties.[3] Thus individual members' pay varies, depending upon the days spent on committee business, but in the mid-1990s, Alabama legislators averaged some $30,000 per year.

■ *Qualifications.* State senators must be at least twenty-five years old, and representatives twenty-one at the time of their election. They must be citizens and residents of Alabama for three years prior to their election, and reside in their district during their term of office. State employees must obtain a leave of absence from their agency or else resign when they become candidates for any state office. No person convicted of embezzlement of public money, bribery, perjury, or other infamous (felony) crime is eligible to serve as a legislator, and members expelled for corruption can never be Alabama legislators again. An Alabama legislator is removed from office upon conviction of a felony or may be expelled by a two-thirds vote of the house in which he or she sits. The legislator can resume office if the conviction is reversed on appeal or a new trial is granted, but a pardon cannot restore one to office.

■ *Organization and Leadership in the Legislature.* From its membership, the state senate elects a president pro tempore to preside in the absence of the lieutenant governor, and the house of representatives chooses a speaker and a speaker pro tempore. In Alabama, the governor historically designated the persons favored, who were elected by the respective houses with little opposition. Contested elections for speaker occurred in January 1987 and 1991 with representatives not following the first Republican governor, who lacked the traditional "administration floor leaders." In contrast to Congress, where seniority ordinarily determines chairmanships, in many state legislatures, including Alabama's, committee assignments and those who chair committees are the choice of the presiding officers. In the absence of majority and minority leaders from the two parties in Alabama, a variety of influences (including the legislative black caucus) have produced diverse chairs and vice chairs, even newly elected members and an occasional Republican. Alabama governors have sought to ensure that the key rules and finance committees in each house have a majority of administration supporters, since these committees direct the flow of the governor's programs through the legislature. The speaker and lieutenant governor have tremendous influence on the legislative product, since they decide to which committee newly introduced bills will be assigned for consideration. Favored measures may be routed to a "safe" committee composed of supporters, but if the presiding officers oppose certain legis-

Figure 5.2 The lieutenant governor or the president pro tempore presides over the senate, with the senate secretary seated at one side, and reading clerks below. Note the legislative calendar on the projection screens. (Photo by D. L. Martin)

lation, the objectionable bill may be referred to a "burial" committee, whence it will never be heard of again.

Legislative business is conducted through approximately two dozen committees in each house, which are listed in Table 5.1 along with their abbreviations used in the computer system on status of bills. Local legislation committees consider bills that apply to parts of the state, their membership consisting of legislators from those areas.

While legislators might like to serve on all committees that may be of value to their constituents, the proliferation of committees is limited by the number on which an individual can effectively participate. Most senate committees have five or seven members, but rules has eleven, and finance and taxation grew to twenty-six. Alabama representatives serve on two to five committees.

The respective chambers choose a secretary of the senate and a clerk of the house who maintain the journals of each house, records, and facilities, with over one hundred legislative support staff, which doubles during sessions. The secretary and clerk are on annual salaries set by the legislature, which can range above $100,000, indicating their responsibilities and influence.

Who Are the Legislators?

In recent Alabama legislatures, nearly half the members are coming to Montgomery for their first term, although more incumbents sought and won reelection in 1986 and 1990. There are several reasons why turnover in state legislatures is greater than in Congress. Alabama legislative service is becoming less "part-time" and interferes with personal business and family life. While some use the legislature as a stepping-stone to run for higher office, others may become weary of the costs and attacks in political campaigning, or the lack

Table 5.1
Alabama Legislative Committees with Bill Status System abbreviations

Senate Committees		House Committees	
AC&F	Agriculture, Conservation & Forestry	A&FN	Agriculture, Forestry, Natural Resources
B&I	Banking & Insurance	BNKG	Banking
B&LR	Business & Labor Relations	B&L	Business & Labor
CT&U	Commerce, Transportation & Utilities	C&ID	Commerce & Industrial Development
EA	Economic Affairs	C&E	Constitution & Elections
ED	Education	ED	Education
F&T	Finance & Taxation	W&M	Ways and Means
GA	Governmental Affairs	HS	Highway Safety
HLTH	Health	HLTH	Health
		INS	Insurance
JUDY	Judiciary	JUDY	Judiciary
		LG	Local Government
LL#1	Local Legislation No. 1	LL#1	Local Legislation No. 1
LL#2	Local Legislation No. 2 (Jefferson Co.)	LL#2	Local Legislation No. 2
LL#3	Local Legislation No. 3 (Mobile Co.)	LL#3	Local Legislation No. 3
NR	Natural Resources	MA	Military Affairs
		O&G	Oil & Gas
		PU&T	Public Utilities & Transportation
PW	Public Welfare	PW	Public Welfare
RULE	Rules	RULE	Rules
RUL1	Rules, Day 1, etc.	SA	State Administration
SB	Small Business	SB	Small Business
SD&T	State Development & Tourism	TE&S	Tourism, Entertainment & Sports

of privacy and requirements for financial disclosure. Public criticism may lower the prestige of holding legislative office.

■ *Background of Legislators.* Alabama legislators, like those of most other states, tend to be men in their forties. Not until the 1970s did Alabamians elect more than a single female legislator, but in 1982 six women (four of them African-American) were elected, including the first to the state senate. An African-American woman first won a special election to the Alabama Senate in 1993, but two senators and a half-dozen representatives was a smaller percentage of women than in many state legislatures. The proportion of African-American legislators steadily increased after 1974 until by the 1990s minority representation reflected the state's population. Growing African-American representation in local legislative delegations and greater legislative influence through formation of the "black caucus" will result in appointments chairing committees. By the 1990s, Republicans held about one fifth of the seats in each house of the Alabama legislature.

Alabama legislators are likely to come from the usual state legislative occupations of attorneys, independent business (such as insurance, real estate, or others with flexible hours), and educators. They are likely to be Protestant (mainly Baptist or Methodist), married, with more years of education and higher incomes than their constituents. The principal changes in Alabama legislators' backgrounds over the past twenty years have been election of more African Americans, women, and Republicans, and fewer farmers.

The Legislative Process

■ *Powers and Limitations on Lawmaking.* The Alabama Constitution of 1901 contains numerous provisions limiting the exercise of legislative power. Article I lists a declaration of rights that "shall forever remain inviolate." Other articles regulate state finance, including the amounts the legislature can tax and borrow, and Article IV specifies legislative procedures on passing laws. A law in Alabama may be "general" (applying to the whole state or defined classes of municipalities), "special or private" (applying to an individual, association, or corporation), or else a "local" law (which requires newspaper legal notice before passage). Because there is no home rule granted to local governments in Alabama (see Chapter 2), a great amount of legislative business is local legislation pertaining only to certain sections of the state.

■ *Legislative Oversight and Investigation.* The Alabama legislature has several staff agencies to assist its operations.

The Legislative Reference Service conducts studies on matters coming before the legislature, maintains a reference library, and provides "spot" research for members. A major service is drafting bills upon request by legislators. The staff consists of a director, a dozen research lawyers, and additional workers during legislative sessions when business is heavy. It publishes the *Alabama Administrative Monthly*, which contains rules and regulations formulated by state agencies. The Legislative Reference Service is under control of the Legislative Council, which consists of the lieutenant governor, the speaker, both pro tempores, and chairs from a half-dozen powerful committees in each house (members are listed in the *Code* 29-6-2). Formed when Alabama legislators served part-time, the Legislative Council provides a continuing organization by meeting at least every three months, although development of legislative policy alternatives has been limited, compared to the proposals presented by the executive branch. The Alabama Law Institute, based at the University of Alabama Law School in Tuscaloosa, provides additional legal research and conducts an orientation for legislators shortly after their election.

The Legislative Fiscal Office compiles data on Alabama's

finances and the effects that legislative proposals would have if adopted (including comparisons with tax and spending policies in other states). Any bill that affects the revenue collection of cities, counties, or state government in Alabama or that appropriates money must have a "fiscal note" attached, showing an estimation of its costs by the Legislative Fiscal Office. This office maintains a budget tracking system to monitor the amounts available in the state's operating funds, giving the legislature its own independent analysis of changing financial conditions and estimated tax receipts, apart from the executive branch projections offered by the state budget officer. The Legislative Fiscal Office was created in 1975 to assist the house committee on ways and means and the senate committee on finance and taxation, operating under a joint fiscal committee.

A major legislative function is oversight into how money appropriated has been spent. The Department of Examiners of Public Accounts post-audits the books and records of all state and county agencies, and prescribes reporting systems in the expenditure of state funds. In the case of disputed expenditures, the chief examiner can issue subpoenas and conduct hearings, ordering repayment if necessary. Several cases of corruption in Alabama government given great publicity in recent years have been criminally prosecuted on evidence of financial irregularities discovered by the examiners in the course of their field audits. The chief examiner is appointed for a seven-year renewable term by the Legislative Committee on Public Accounts and confirmed by the state senate. The committee has a joint membership of five state senators and five representatives with the lieutenant governor as chair and the speaker as vice chair. Any expenditures and contracts not meeting legal requirements are reported by the department to the legislative committee and the governor, and audit reports are frequently the basis of "investigative reporting" by the news media.

There is continuing scrutiny by over thirty permanent legislative committees created by statute, with joint membership of equal numbers from both houses on such subjects as finances and budgets, highways, contract review, and municipal government. Additional topics of concern are studied by interim committees which meet between sessions of the whole legislature. Interim committees are used extensively in Alabama to gather facts on specific subjects, hold hearings, and report their findings to the next session of the legislature. Usually composed of members from both houses appointed by the lieutenant governor and the speaker, interim committees may sometimes also include nonlegislator experts appointed by them or the governor. Public concern over interim committee costs may limit their meeting days or budgets.

Legislative oversight is also exercised over state administrative actions. Under Alabama's administrative procedures act,

Figure 5.3 A joint legislative committee meeting with members from both chambers. (Photo by D. L. Martin)

the Legislative Council can suspend a rule or regulation proposed by a state agency until the next regular session of the legislature which can amend or repeal it—no objection constitutes approval. During the 1980s, Alabama and many other states passed "sunset legislation" which automatically abolishes agencies unless they are reauthorized (for four years) after legislative review.

Impeachment may be voted by a majority of the Alabama House of Representatives for willful neglect of duty, corruption in office, incompetence, intemperance that affects duties, or any offense involving moral turpitude. The state senate sits as a court of impeachment, presided over by the chief justice or else one of the associate justices if the governor or lieutenant governor is on trial. While a number of local officials have been impeached in circuit court and brought to trial in the senate, since 1901 no statewide elected official has been impeached. Most having charges brought against them have been induced to resign, since impeachment penalties do not extend beyond removal from office, and the accused is still liable to criminal indictment and punishment as prescribed by law.

How a Proposal Becomes Law

■ *A Bill Is Born.* In a democratic society, ideas for new laws come from many different sources. Interest groups frequently suggest legislation that calls forth counterproposals. State agencies and local units of government have ideas as to what needs to be done and may actually write the complex and technical legislation needed for programs. Legislators may write bills, or ask the legislative reference service to draft one in response to constituent desires. The Alabama governor is charged by law to prepare a general revenue bill for taxation and present a budget to the legislature. In addition to these, there may be many other administration bills which originate in the governor's office and embody his legislative programs.

■ *Introduction and Referral to Committee.* Whatever the source of the proposal, the Alabama constitution specifies that a member of the legislature must introduce the bill. Revenue bills must be introduced in the house of representatives, following the English tradition that taxation must originate in the lower chamber of the people. A legislator may introduce as many bills as desired, indeed, even indicating this is "by request" on behalf of others. Joint rules adopted by each house require that the bill be typed on $8\frac{1}{2}$ × 14-inch paper with double-spaced, numbered lines, and that above its title there be a brief synopsis of its contents. "Each law shall contain but one subject, which shall be clearly expressed in its title, except general appropriation bills, general revenue bills, and bills adopting a code, digest, or revision of statues."[4] Each begins: "Be it enacted by the legislature of Alabama . . ." and is divided into numbered sections according to subject, for convenience. Proposals changing existing laws must show the part to be deleted ~~stricken through~~ and new material <u>underscored</u>. Each bill usually concludes with a "severability" clause to the effect that only sections later found to be unconstitutional by the courts will be voided, a "repealer" that nullifies earlier laws which are inconsistent with the present law, and an "effective date" clause stating when the law goes into effect (upon date of approval, some other date, or if there are penalties, sixty days after approval in Alabama).[5]

All bills are entered in the ALERT (Alabama Legislative Evaluation and Research Terminal) computer system, which tracks them through the legislative processes listed in Table 5.2. Besides terminals located in the Statehouse, personal computer users can subscribe to ALERT, and some interest groups do. ALERT gives many types of information, such as bills' status in each house, their sponsors, committee meeting

Table 5.2

ALERT: the Alabama Legislative Computer

Step abbreviations used in the Bill Status System:

RD1	First Reading	RD2	Second Reading
RD3A	Third Reading: Adverse Calendar	RD3R	Regular Calendar
RD3C	Consent Calendar	RD3G	Third Reading Again
COMM	Committee	CONC	Concurrence
CONF	Conference	CNF2	2nd Conference
GOV	Governor	GOV2	Governor 2nd time
SEC	Secretary of State		

Action abbreviations used in the Bill Status System:

A/A	Adopted as amended
A/AS	Adopted as amended and substituted
A/S	Adopted as substituted
ADPT	Adopted
ADV	Adverse Calendar
AMD	With Amendment
AMDS	With Amendments
BASK	Died in the Basket (never taken up for action)
BIR	Budget Isolation Resolution
BL	Became Law
CHR	Call of the Chair
CHRU	Unfinished Business
COD	Carried over to Day _____
CODU	Unfinished Business
COT	Carried over to Time _____
COTU	Unfinished Business
EAMD	Executive Amendment
FAV	Favorable
IPP	Indefinitely Postponed
L/A	Lost as amended
L/AS	Lost as amended and substituted
L/S	Lost as substituted
LOST	Lost (defeated, not a missing bill)
P/A	Passed as amended
P/AS	Passed as amended and substituted
P/S	Passed as substituted
PEND	Pending
RECO	Reconsidered
RREC	Recommitted to Commmittee
RREF	Re-referred to Committee
S/A	With Substitute and Amendment
S/AS	With Substitute and Amendments
SIGN	Signed
SPEC	Special Order
SUB	With Substitute
UNF	Unfinished business
VETO	Veto
WD	Withdrawn

schedules, bills being considered by each committee, fiscal notes, subject matter by keywords, and related citations to the existing *Code of Alabama.*

Increasing legislative proposals have prompted many states, including Alabama, to allow "prefiling" before the session begins, permitting measures to be entered into ALERT and assigned to committees for informal study. On the first legislative day, prefiled bills are formally referred to committee, as are other new bills, which can be introduced until a legislative day (set by rule) late in the session with no time left for passage. Each bill given the senate secretary or house clerk will require three readings over separate days, so identical bills may be submitted simultaneously by cosponsors in each house to facilitate consideration. In the introductory "first reading" only the title is given (later reading at length, word for word, may be used as a delaying tactic), and consecutive numbers assigned: House Bill 1, H.B.2, Senate Bill 1, S.B.2; Senate Joint Resolution 1, S.J.R.2; House Joint Resolution 1, H.J.R.2, etc. The presiding officer refers the bill to a standing committee having jurisdiction, although political considerations or sponsor influence may result in exceptions. Studies of the Alabama legislature have shown that some committees (finance, judiciary, and Local Legislation No. 1) have a heavy workload, while others handle relatively few bills.

■ *Committee Consideration and Report.* The Alabama constitution provides that no bill may become law unless it has been referred to a standing committee in each house, acted upon by the committee in session, and reported to the floor. Measures appropriating money must also be referred to the house ways and means committee and the senate finance and taxation committee. Committee procedures vary according to the rules adopted by each Alabama chamber, with the senate using subcommittees like the Congress. A committee meets at the call of its chairperson (or by notice of a majority of its members) at times when the legislature is not in floor session. Committee meetings are held in designated rooms in the Alabama Statehouse, and public hearings are often held around the state by interim committees.

The committee may decide to report the original bill favorably, return it to be referred to another committee, make amendments, substitute a new bill, report it without recommendation, report it adversely, or not report it at all. The tendency in Alabama is to report a bill favorably (often amended), or not report it at all, and it is more likely that a bill will die in committee for lack of action than that it will be reported negatively. The usefulness (or even the political effectiveness) of public hearings and whether committees evade responsibility by not voting to report bills is a long-standing controversy in legislative literature. A favorite tactic is to delay reporting a bill until too late for passage in time-limited sessions like Alabama's, thus allowing legislators to tell supporters they voted for it in committee, while not wanting it to become law. Alabama Senate Rule 57 requires a recorded roll call final committee vote, but under House Rule 66 this is not required in the house unless two committee members request it.

■ *Debate on the Floor and Vote.* Bills reported by standing committees are placed on the regular calendar for floor consideration, which is the "second reading" required by the state constitution. Those with a negative committee report are listed on an "adverse calendar" and are not considered further unless a majority of the entire house votes to take up the measure. Noncontroversial legislation can be placed on the senate's "consent calendar," unless other members object, while late in the house session, each representative can call up a bill for unanimous consent (called "playing baseball" for rapid action).

Bills are supposed to be considered by the entire chamber

in the order in which they appear on the calendar. But since most bills are not reported out of committee until late in the legislative session, when time is short, most bills come to the floor under the special order calendar set by the powerful rules committee, which usually gives precedence to administration bills and those important to the operation of state agencies.

Debate and amendment on the floor by the entire chamber occur at this "third reading." Either house may resolve itself into a "committee of the whole" to discuss the bill informally clause by clause, and then reconvene into formal session. Members may refer to each other as "the senator (or representative) from (place)," creating some difficulty for the uninitiated observer. Ordinarily legislators are limited to speaking twice (for a maximum each time of ten minutes in the house and one hour in the senate), unless they are the bill's sponsor or chairing the committee reporting it. The bill's sponsor explains it, questions are answered, and a vote taken, first on each motion or amendment made, and then on the entire bill. Votes are *viva voce* (by voice) and if one-tenth of the members desire a roll call of the "yeas" and "nays," each senator is called alphabetically, while in the house an electronic voting system shows a green or red light beside the representative's name. (House members can see how the speaker votes, politically often indicating the administration's stand on the issue.) A majority of each chamber constitutes a quorum to do business (eighteen in the senate and fifty-three in the house), and the names of the members voting for and against final passage are recorded in the legislative journals as required by the Alabama constitution, although earlier procedural votes may determine the fate of legislation. A majority of the quorum present and voting passes the measure, with the exceptions noted below.

■ *Transmittal and Action by the Second House.* The amended bill as passed by one house is then engrossed[6] in final form

Figure 5.4 Alabama House of Representatives in floor session: the green and red lights beside each member's name indicate "yes" and "no" votes on the bill number shown on· the projection screens. (Photo by D. L. Martin)

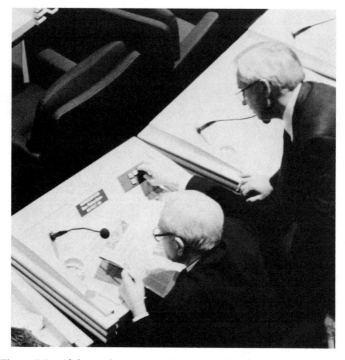

Figure 5.5 Alabama house member using the electronic voting system. (Photo by D. L. Martin)

and sent to the other chamber, where it goes through the same stages of committee consideration and floor action. It is quite possible that it will not survive this second test away from its house of origin. However, relatively few bills are defeated on the floor in Alabama; they are simply never reported out of committee. If the bill is passed without amendment, it is "messaged" back to its house of origin for enrollment to the governor.

■ *Conference Committee and Enrollment.* It is likely that the second chamber will pass the measure with some changes as a result of its consideration and debate. The house of origin may concur with these amendments readying the bill for enrollment, or possibly refuse to accept the changes made in the second chamber, in which case the bill is dead. Usually a motion will be made to appoint a conference committee between the two houses. Conference committees are ordinarily composed of three members from each chamber (appointed by the presiding officers), and must reach an agreement with a concurrent majority, that is, two senators and two representatives must approve each compromise. If the conferees cannot agree, or either house does not accept their report, even if another set of committee members is appointed, the bill is lost.

If both chambers approve the same measures, the bill is *enrolled*, or copied in identical form, and checked by the rules committees (actually by the computer, word for word). The presiding officers while sitting at the podium can be seen signing bills in pale blue covers in the presence of each house as required by the Alabama constitution, although reading "at length" is usually dispensed with by two-thirds vote of a quorum. The secretary or clerk then takes the bill and presents it to the governor's office, noting the time of delivery.

■ *Action by the Alabama Governor.* When legislation reaches the chief executive's desk, six things may happen. The governor may sign the measure, enacting it into law (cited as "Acts [year], No. ____" or "Act No. 93-__" if passed in 1993; the numbers are consecutively assigned by the secretary of state). If the governor disapproves—vetoes—the bill, it is returned with written objections to the house where it originated, although upon occasion, Alabama governors have personally addressed their discontent to the legislature. If a majority of those elected to each house vote to override the governor's veto, the bill becomes law without gubernatorial signature. Alabama is one of over forty states in which the chief executive can "item veto" a particular expenditure but approve the rest of an appropriation bill. The Alabama constitution gives the governor more flexibility than in other states in that the governor can propose "executive amendments," and if a majority of the members elected to each house agree, the amended bill is returned to the governor for signature. If the chief executive fails to act within six days (not counting Sunday) on a measure, it becomes law without the governor's signature if the legislature is in session.[7] Bills that reach the governor within five days before the end of the session may be signed by the governor within ten days after adjournment, otherwise they are "pocket vetoed," failing to become law. Since many bills are only presented to the governor at the end of the legislative rush created by constitutionally limited sessions, this gives the Alabama governor important final discretion.[8]

The power of the Alabama governor to secure acceptable legislation (especially through suggesting executive amendments) is illustrated by its final disposition. For example, in the 1990 regular session of the legislature, 1,677 bills were introduced, 772 were enacted by both houses, eleven were vetoed by the governor, and two were overriden by the legislature. The constitutional procedures and informal practices that have developed explain the governor's role as chief legislator for Alabama as much as a one-party political system or the personal popularity of the incumbent.

■ *Other Legislation.* There are three types of legislation that are handled somewhat differently than general bills: resolutions, local legislation, and constitutional amendments.

A resolution is a measure not having the force of law. A simple resolution is passed by one house, and a joint resolution, "Be it resolved by the Legislature of Alabama, both houses thereof concurring." Simple resolutions are mainly used for internal legislative purposes, such as adopting rules of procedure, setting up committees, appointing employees of the legislature, or requesting an advisory opinion from the state supreme court. Joint resolutions deal with matters affecting both houses, clarify legislative intent or policy, or more commonly, express the "will or sentiment" of the legislature in conveying sympathy or commending a constituent for an achievement. Such public-relations resolutions are read by title and passed on the following legislative day in a single vote unless some member objects to a particular one, which is then taken up separately. Resolutions dealing with procedures are referred to the rules committees and are reported like other bills. Joint (but not simple) resolutions require the Alabama governor's signature (except those dealing with adjournment, elections by each house, or constitutional amendments), but a veto may be overridden, as with bills.

Local legislation applies to a political subdivision (county or city) smaller than the whole state. A private or special bill applies to an individual, association, or corporation, meeting their special needs or exempting them from general laws. The Alabama constitution, sections 104 to 111, lists subjects upon which such laws cannot be passed, forbids passage of such legislation where relief can be provided by general law or the courts, and requires public advertisement of intent to introduce such proposals. Typical subjects of local legislation involve local finances or changing government structure, and private bills giving relief for injuries received from state action or correcting errors. Although local legislation has constituted up to one-third of all measures passed in Alabama, it is not considered by the entire legislature but rather by local legislation committees, usually composed of members from the areas affected. Other legislators automatically accept as "legislative courtesy" these bills proposed by colleagues who come from the area and presumably know about the situation. The local legislative delegation in effect acts for the whole legislature, giving it great power over community affairs. Local legislation thus affords members opportunities to build hometown political capital, but also creates risks of engaging in parochial feuds which distract from considering policy for the state as a whole.

Constitutional amendments or proposals for calling a constitutional convention (never called in Alabama since 1901)[9] are introduced in the same manner as other bills or joint resolutions and referred to the standing committees on constitutions and elections. The constitutional amendment is read at length, and if three-fifths (60%) of the members elected to each house approve, a popular referendum on the amendment is ordered set at least three months after final adjournment of that legislative session (ratification may be combined with the next general election). These constitutional measures do not have to be submitted to the governor for approval: the Alabama executive merely issues a proclamation declaring the amendment part of the constitution if it receives a majority of votes cast at the election.

Legislative Problems

After the Alabama legislature in 1970 was ranked[10] fiftieth in the nation according to its being functional, accountable, informed, independent, and representative, reforms were instituted. Alabama opinion surveys have consistently shown the legislature to rank low in public esteem, and indeed, among the strongest critics have been Alabama legislators themselves. What are some major areas of concern?

Legislative failure to pass education and general fund budgets on time led voters to pass Amendment 448 giving them priority, but since 1984, three-fifths of a quorum present have routinely attached a "B.I.R." (budget isolation resolution) to all other bills enabling passage before the budgets. A more fundamental political problem, it is charged, is the legislative habit of holding the budgets hostage until certain expenditures are included and of appropriating whatever funds are

Figure 5.6 Citizens exercising their constitutional right to petition the government for the redress of grievances are a frequent sight at the Statehouse. (Photo by D. L. Martin)

forecast, so that if revenues fall with changing economic conditions, state budgets are "prorated" in percentage cutbacks.

The weakness of a competitive party system has meant the absence of majority and minority leaders actively promoting their careers through committee work. Without partisan checks and balances, committee procedures are very important. By the 1980s each body had adopted some minimum procedures, but only the senate (not the house) rules had defined each standing committee's jurisdiction. While a majority of committee members can convene a meeting if the chairperson refuses to act, this rarely happens. A favorite tactic for sidetracking a particular bill is to call a committee hearing so late in the session that it has no chance of passage, even though the committee reports it favorably and one house passes it, thus allowing legislators to tell constituents they voted for a measure even though they did not actually support it. Because special interest lobbyists know that a majority of eighteen Alabama senators can block any measure, that body has (rightly or wrongly) gained such a reputation.

The legislative workload is likely to increase in Alabama. More bills are being introduced—and more are lost because they are still in the legislative process when the constitutionally limited sessions have to adjourn. This means that necessary bills, including local legislation, have to be reintroduced in the next session, or special sessions called. Alabamians can watch on public television the last legislative day as the clock ticks toward midnight, and the politics played with "stopping the clock" to continue the session past the calendar deadline into the small hours of the following morning (the courts have upheld the validity of such a continuous meeting). As frustrated legislators complain on live television about their lack of knowledge of the contents of bills being rushed to passage, this can hardly increase the public's confidence.

What responsibilities should individual legislators have beyond winning at the ballot box? The Alabama constitution provides that a legislator who has a personal or private interest in any proposal before the legislature shall disclose it and not vote on such measures. Officials, including legislators, cannot begin office until they have filed a financial disclosure statement with the five-member State Ethics Commission. Joint rules of the legislature provide that all persons (including government officials) who seek to influence legislation must register as lobbyists. Citizens wishing to express an opinion "on an isolated basis and without intent to continue beyond a single day during a session" are exempted.[11]

In the mid-1990s over 350 lobbyists and their principal employers registered, but many had multiple clients, making it difficult to know for whom exactly they were working. The advisory opinions issued by the State Ethics Commission interpreting the 1973 law have been criticized as too restrictive by some legislators, who have sought to abolish the commission.

STATE SENATE

――――――― **Session 19____**

LOBBYIST REGISTRATION FORM

Pursuant to Joint Rules of the two houses of the Alabama Legislature, Rules 15 thru 23

NAME _____

BUSINESS ADDRESS _____

BUSINESS PHONE _____

NAME OF PRINCIPAL _____

BUSINESS ADDRESS OF PRINCIPAL _____

GENERAL & SPECIFIC AREAS OF LEGISLATIVE INTEREST _____

DURATION OF AGENCY _____

Extent of any direct business association or partnership with any current member of the Legislature _____

Sworn to and subscribed before me this _____   I certify under oath the above information

day of _____, 19___   signed: _____

――――――――――――――――――――
Notary Public

Figure 5.7 Anyone wishing to lobby Alabama legislators must fill out these cards in the senate and the house.

A final concern of Alabamians is: How does a citizen find out what is going on in the legislature? Since the legislature moved into the Statehouse in 1987, there can no longer be an excuse of inadequate facilities. Each legislator, for the first time, has a small private office with a direct phone line and can listen to floor debate in either chamber or a half-dozen committee rooms via an audio link. Shared secretaries have computer terminals to the ALERT system. The fifth floor of the Statehouse contains the house of representatives chamber, and the offices of the speaker, most members, and the clerk, where the public can get copies of bills. The sixth floor has the house visitors' gallery, the remaining representatives' offices, the legislative reference service and library, the legislative fiscal office, plus committee rooms and auditoriums for hearings used by both the house and senate. The Statehouse seventh floor is occupied by the senate chamber, offices of the senators, the president pro tempore, the senate secretary, and hearing rooms. The top (eighth) floor contains the senate visitors' gallery and the joint briefing room 807, commonly called the "star wars" room for its advanced audiovisual equipment. Although there are press and camera facilities located in the corners of each chamber, the visitor galleries are separated from the chambers by glass. There are no public access terminals to the ALERT computer system (an annual subscription is expensive), so citizens can only scan the lobby notice boards for committee meetings or try to call a bill status telephone number. An Alabamian interested in pending legislation must still rely on an assessment of its political fate from a legislator or lobbyist who is concerned with the measure. Unlike members of Congress, few Alabama legislators can afford to send periodic newsletters to their constituents since they do not have a free mailing privilege. While political candidates exhort us to "look at the record," its availability to most of the public depends upon what is reported in the news media. Citizens need to know what their representatives are doing in order to make an informed choice at election time.

Notes

1. *Reynolds v. Sims* 377 U.S. 533 (1964).
2. The Alabama Constitution of 1901, Sec. 173.
3. Following pay controversies, in 1991 a Legislative Compensation Commission was set up (see *Code* 29-1-40) and amounts recommended by the commission would have to be adopted by a majority of both houses in order to go into effect for the next four-year term. The mileage allowance for legislators is the same as for state employees, but "actual expenses" for out-of-state travel have been subjected to media scrutiny.
4. Alabama Constitution, Sect. 45.
5. There may be a "saving clause" if the bill deals with judicial procedures or crimes to prevent interference with legal processes under way.
6. Engrossment means checking the accuracy of the amended bill; in Alabama practice, the senate secretary simply "endorses" and the house clerk "certifies" the bill as passed to the other body.
7. Should the legislature be in recess, an objectionable bill must be returned within two days after the legislature reassembles; otherwise it becomes law.
8. The Alabama Supreme Court ruled in 1991 that the governor cannot line-item veto a budget after adjournment, but must accept or reject the entire budget. *Hunt v. Hubbert* 588 So.2d 848 (1991).
9. Only a majority of the legislators elected to each house have to approve the calling of a constitutional convention. If the voters agree to a convention, it would have virtually complete freedom to amend, revise, or alter the state constitution.
10. Citizens Conference on State Legislatures, *The Sometime Governments.* New York: Bantam Books, 1971. Paperback condensation of the complete report *State Legislatures: An Evaluation of Their Effectiveness.*
11. Joint Rule No. 20 of the two houses of the legislature of Alabama, 1991.

For Further Reading

Couch, Jim F., Keith E. Atkinson, and William F. Shughart II. "Ethics Laws and the Outside Earnings of Politicians: The Case of Alabama's 'Legislator-Educators.'" *Public Choice*, 73 (March 1992), 135–45.

Legislature of the State of Alabama (Year). *House Roster, Alphabetical, by Districts; Standing Committees. Senate Roster, Standing Committees, Committee Assignments.*

McCurley, Robert L., Jr., ed. *The Legislative Process: A Handbook for Alabama Legislators*, 5th ed. Tuscaloosa: Alabama Law Institute, 1991.

Rules of the House of Representatives of Alabama. Legislative Document No. 1, annual.

Rules of the Senate of the State of Alabama. Senate Document No. 1, annual.

Senate Manual State of Alabama. Senate Document No. 2, annual.

Elected State Officials:
Leadership Has Many Faces

In contrast to New Jersey and Maine, where the people elect only the governor, most American states have a wide range of elective administrative officials. In Alabama the people elect the governor, lieutenant governor, secretary of state, attorney general, treasurer, auditor, commissioner of agriculture and industries, eight members of the state board of education, and three public service commissioners—a total of eighteen officials in nine agencies. So many separately elected officials (each of whom can claim a mandate from the voters) with a constitutional limitation upon their succeeding themselves in office is often viewed as part of a checks and balances system. Alabama's elected executives are allowed two successive terms under a 1968 amendment, reducing the "musical chairs" shuffle from one office to another. In this fragmented governmental structure, the governor provides the primary leadership.

Who Can Be Governor of Alabama?

The qualifications given in the 1901 constitution are that the governor must be thirty years of age, a United States citizen for ten years, and a resident of Alabama for seven years before election. The governor and the other Alabama executive officers are elected for four-year terms and take office on the first Monday after the second Tuesday in January (1991, etc.).

The Alabama governor is paid approximately $81,000 per year (this 1993 amount varies as constitutional officers have been made eligible for cost of living increases by the legislature), slightly less than most American governors. The governor receives an office expense allowance and a governor's "contingency fund" appropriated at the discretion of the legislature. Among the other perquisites of office are a governor's mansion built in 1907 and later purchased by the state, and a vacation home at Gulf Shores. The beautifully furnished staterooms of the Greek revival–style mansion, located at 1142 South Perry Street in Montgomery, are open by appointment to the public. A car driven by an Alabama state

Figure 6.1 The Governor's Mansion, 1142 South Perry Street, Montgomery. (Courtesy of the Alabama Bureau of Publicity and Information. Used by permission)

trooper and state-owned aircraft and a helicopter are at the governor's disposal for official travel. Although the constitution forbids a pension for elected state executives, two-term governors are appointed "governor's councillors" at the age of sixty, at $18,000 per year. Finally, there is the courtesy of being called "governor" after holding office.

The Governor as Civic and Political Leader

As the central figure in state politics, the governor plays many roles. From cutting ribbons to crowning beauty queens, the governor presides as ceremonial head of state and speaks for Alabama to other governments. With press, radio, and television coverage, the governor becomes a leader of public opinion whose statements are better known than those of any other state politician. Media coverage is important, for the state capital is not the state's largest metropolitan area.

As chief legislator, the governor can call the state legislature into special session, and under Alabama custom, designate choices for the speaker of the house and president pro tempore of the senate. The houses usually elect these presiding officers and their assistants, who are known as "the governor's floor leaders." Both presiding officers often cooperate with the governor in making appointments to the standing committees of the legislature, which gives the governor willing to exercise it a degree of control. All bills and joint resolutions (except proposed constitutional amendments) passed by the legislature must be signed by the governor to become law unless a majority of the members elected to both chambers vote to pass the measure over the governor's objection or veto. As described in Chapter 5, under the Alabama constitution the governor may suggest executive amendments to the legislation presented, and these are then reconsidered by both houses. In appropriation bills the governor can item veto individual expenditures but accept the rest. The president of the United States does not have these powers.

As chief administrator, the Alabama governor presides over some 150 separate departments, boards, commissions, and other state agencies. Service on many of these is *ex officio* (by virtue of office), or by appointing the heads or members of them, sometimes with the consent of the state senate. If the legislature is not in session, the governor may make interim appointments, or if the senate refuses confirmation, incumbent appointees may serve until their successors have qualified. If the position is not under the state merit (career personnel) system, the governor is able to fill the job under political patronage with supporters. The governor may remove any state official whom he or she has appointed, provided the position is not covered by the merit system, and can fill vacancies in most state and local elective offices until the next election. The Alabama chief executive has full responsibility for preparing the state's budget and submitting it to the legislature for approval.

As party leader, the governor's endorsement is influential in campaigns, raising money for candidates, and trying to control, not always with success, the state executive committee of the governor's party. Alabama governors have usually headed the state's delegation to their party's presidential nominating convention, but have not been as active as other governors in national party activities.

As formal head of state, the governor is commander in chief of the 20,000-member Alabama Army and Air National Guard. On the office wall of most high state officials is a certificate appointing each an "Aide de Camp to the Governor of Alabama and Honorary Lieutenant Colonel in the State Militia," plus an automobile tag saying "Governor's Staff." Under the National Guard Act of 1916, however, state forces were integrated into the United States armed forces reserve units, and the governor appoints an adjutant general to serve as the active head of the State Military Department. The officers appointed by the governor must be qualified to receive a reserve commission in the United States Army or Air Force. Choices influenced by politics have been questioned in the Alabama news media, although the Pentagon does have standards for promotions. The guard plays an important role in times of natural disaster or civil disorder, but any governor who adopts an untenable position[1] may become a general without troops, as the guard is "federalized" or put under control of the United States government.

Policy Leadership: Persuasion and the Governor's Staff

To enable the governor to carry out the responsibilities for faithful execution of the laws, there are a number of staff assistants.

The executive secretary is the chief of the governor's staff, an important figure around the capitol, seeing that the governor's orders are carried out. The appointments secretary keeps track of all the vacancies coming open on the myriad state boards and commissions, maintains a résumé file of job seekers, and evaluates their qualifications to ensure that if appointed, they do not embarrass the governor. The confidential secretary answers the governor's personal mail and screens requests and visitors to ensure that the chief executive's busy schedule is put to best use. There may be several political aides (sometimes carried on the payroll of other state departments) who dispense patronage, manage the next campaign, and serve as the extended eyes and ears of the governor.

The press secretary issues statements to the media, organizes the governor's appearances, and answers requests for information. Because the governor is expected to make "appropriate remarks" on numerous occasions, the press secretary arranges for speechwriting and answering routine letters.

The legislative aide is the governor's liaison to the legislature, not only pushing enactment of the governor's programs, but reviewing bills passed. During each session a huge stack of bills arrives from the legislature awaiting action (see Chapter 5), so some Alabama governors have appointed two liaisons, one for each chamber. The legislative aide(s) must read through the fine print of each measure to judge if it is acceptable to the governor's administration.

The budgetary function is institutionalized in Alabama in the Department of Finance, with a director appointed by the governor. The director of finance and the state budget officer act as the governor's chief financial advisers in matters of state taxation and spending.

As chief of the state, the governor is vested with executive clemency powers. A reprieve can be granted to those sentenced to death or their sentences can be commuted to life imprisonment. The Alabama legislature, under Amendment 38, removed from the governor and vested in the three-member Board of Pardons and Paroles the clemency functions of a *pardon* for those convicted (an exoneration sparingly used, when a miscarriage of justice has occurred) and *parole*, or conditional release from incarceration prior to the expiration of a sentence (see Chapter 7).

Besides receiving legal advice from the elected state attorney general, the governor also has a legal adviser. This attorney may handle extradition requests, hold clemency hearings with the condemned and their victims or families, advise the governor on litigation or appeals, and review state contracts. There may be other attorneys or administrative assistants on the staff to oversee the state bureaucracy.

Finally, included in the governor's entourage may be bodyguards, for which events have shown the tragic necessity. In Alabama, these are state troopers (sometimes in plain clothes) who also drive the governor's official car.

Some Recent Alabama Governors

With these varied duties and a complex state government, it is obvious that the Alabama governor has to provide a great deal of personal persuasion and leadership. In examining some recent occupants of the Governor's Mansion, it appears that whatever their political differences, all of them share one thing in common: vigorous personalities.

James E. Folsom, governor from 1947 to 1951, 1955 to 1959, and an unsuccessful candidate several times afterwards, was universally known as "Big Jim" because of his six-foot, eight-inch stature. Also known as "Kissin' Jim" because of his affection for the ladies, he perfected an entertaining campaign style, which personalized Alabama politics. Warming up the crowds with country music by the Strawberry Pickers, Big Jim would appear, waving a "corn shuck mop," promising to "clean out" the state capitol and passing the "suds bucket" for campaign contributions. Behind the hillbilly façade, Folsom represented the populist coalition of the Wiregrass and north Alabama. Colorful and outspoken, "the Little Man's Big Friend" advocated minimum salaries for teachers and the establishment of the Department of Pensions and Security (now Human Resources), for an old-age pension system based on need. One of Governor Folsom's most popular measures was the "Farm to Market Road Program," which paved highways in rural areas. No segregationist, his "grass-roots" movement won support from labor and liberal groups and hatred from the Black Belt, Birmingham industrialists, and vested interest groups. Not all the Folsom program was enacted; there was opposition in the legislature, the representation of which favored conservatives in sparsely populated areas. Earlier Alabama governors had found that they might win a popular majority but that the 1901 apportionment of the legislature was stacked against them. During his two terms, Governor Folsom repeatedly called the legislature into special session to reap-

Figure 6.2 James E. "Big Jim" Folsom on the campaign trail. Governor 1947–1951; 1955–1959. (Courtesy of the Alabama Department of Archives and History. Used by permission)

portion itself, without success, and indeed reapportionment on the basis of "one person, one vote" was not achieved until 1974 by federal court order.

John M. Patterson, governor from 1959 to 1963, was the youngest—at thirty-six—ever to reach the office, and his ascent came as a result of dramatic events. While he was practicing law with his father in Phenix City, the elder Patterson was nominated in 1954 as attorney general, pledging to clean up the vice-ridden city. He was assassinated by a hired gunman, and John Patterson was selected by the Democratic executive committee to take his father's place as candidate for attorney general. The murder shocked Alabama, and the national guard was sent in under qualified martial law to replace the corrupt officials and police. As attorney general, John Patterson was noted for vigorous enforcement of state laws regulating insurance, the competitive bidding for government purchases enacted under the Folsom administration, and segregation laws. By the late 1950s, integration had become the prime Alabama political issue, and in 1958 John Patterson defeated George Wallace for governor in a campaign noted for the candidates' trying to "out-seg" each other. Under the Patterson administration, bonds were passed to build roads, educational facilities, and state docks in inland rivers. After his governorship, John Patterson served into the 1990s as presiding judge of the Alabama Court of Criminal Appeals.

George Corley Wallace, governor from 1963 to 1967, 1971 to 1979, and 1983 to 1987, held the office longer than anyone else in the state's history. He was Alabama's best-known politician due to his presidential campaigns, and he dominated state politics for twenty-five years. Born in 1919, he attended Barbour County High School and took an early interest in politics, serving as a page in the state senate when he was fifteen. During the Depression, the Wallaces lost their farm and home when a mortgage was foreclosed, but George worked his way through the University of Alabama, graduating from its law school in 1942. In 1943 he married Lurleen Burns, a sixteen-year-old Tuscaloosa store clerk whom he had met while a student. After World War II service as a flight sergeant, he returned home to campaign for Big Jim Folsom and became an assistant state attorney general.

From 1947 to 1952 he served Barbour County in the legislature, becoming known as the sponsor of the Wallace Industrial Act (discussed in Chapter 2) and bills establishing five new trade schools to increase the state's skilled labor, as well as serving on the Tuskegee Institute Board of Trustees for two years. Elected circuit judge for the Black Belt counties of Barbour and Bullock in 1953, George Wallace defied the United States Civil Rights Commission seeking Negro voting records, maintaining that registration was a prerogative of the states. Defeated for governor in 1958 (the only statewide race he would ever lose), Wallace practiced law in Clio until his successful 1962 campaign. His younger brother, Jack, was elected to his old circuit judgeship, and his other brother, Gerald, an attorney, was an aide.

In his famous 1963 inaugural address, Governor Wallace pledged, "Today I have stood where Jefferson Davis stood and took an oath to my people . . . and I say . . . segregation now . . . segregation tomorrow . . . segregation forever."[2] Six months later, Governor Wallace "stood in the schoolhouse door" at the University of Alabama in an unsuccessful attempt to bar enrollment of African-American students. Constitutionally barred from succeeding himself as governor in 1966, George Wallace ran his wife, openly avowing, "Both of us will be the Governor of this state, I will make the policy decisions during her term of office."[3] Lurleen Wallace easily won the Democratic primary nomination over nine male opponents (including former governors Folsom and Patterson) to become the third American woman governor and the first in Alabama's history. Occupying the office with dignity and charm, she exercised her own interest in mental health to em-

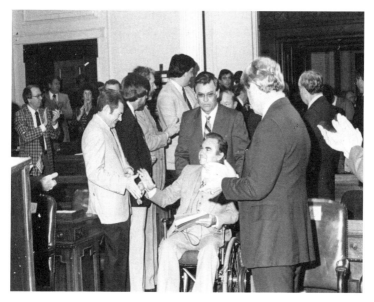

Figure 6.3 Governor Wallace addresses the legislature carrying the state budget. (Courtesy of the governor's office. Used by permission)

phasize these state programs, and her social concerns won great popularity.

When Lurleen Wallace succumbed to cancer during May 1968, she was succeeded by Albert Brewer, the first lieutenant governor to be elevated to office under the 1901 constitution. A practicing lawyer, Albert Brewer had been elected to the legislature at the age of twenty-six, and at thirty-four, in 1963, became the youngest Alabama speaker of the house. His legislative experience gained passage of the Wallace administration's program, including a 1968 amendment allowing two consecutive terms for elected state executives.

George Wallace faced tough races to regain the governorship in 1970. In the May Democratic primary he ran second (416,443 votes) to incumbent Albert Brewer (428,146). African Americans were registering rapidly and voting, so that for the first time more than a million Alabamians went to the polls in the primary elections. In the June Democratic runoff with the "liberal" Brewer, Wallace was failing to carry the Black Belt, his initial segregationist base, and losing Jefferson County, the state's most populous, by 40,000 votes, mostly African Americans in Birmingham. Due to a 15,000-vote lead in Mobile, where fewer blacks were then registered, Wallace beat Brewer by 34,000 votes. But it was a lesson in electoral calculus that was repeated in November 1970, as an African-American dentist from Huntsville, Dr. John Cashin, running on a third ticket, the National Democratic Party of Alabama, received 15% of the vote. (The Republicans did not run a candidate.)

Back in office, Governor Wallace campaigned for the presidency in 1972 until an assassination attempt in Laurel, Maryland, left him paralyzed from the waist down. Lieutenant Governor Jere Beasley became acting governor until Governor Wallace returned to the state, although many months of therapy ensued. In the 1974 Alabama elections, Republicans held their first statewide primary, but Governor Wallace won two-thirds of the vote in the Democratic primary and easily won in November, as it was widely commented that race was not the prevailing issue for the first time in fifteen years. During his third term, Governor Wallace appointed the first African-American member to his cabinet (as director of the Office of Highway Safety) and forged ties with the increasing number of black elected county and municipal officials by state funding of local projects. Governor Wallace in 1971 had married Mrs. Cornelia Ellis Snively, a niece of former Governor Folsom. They were divorced in 1978 after the existence of a telephone tape-recording system was revealed at the governor's mansion.

Since Governor Wallace was constitutionally barred from seeking another consecutive term in 1978, the political arena was opened to a political newcomer, Forest H. James, Jr. "Fob"

James, after playing football at Auburn University, graduated as a civil engineer and founded a successful sporting-goods manufacturing firm in Opelika. Declaring himself a "born-again Democrat," he defeated the "three Bs" (former Governor Brewer, Attorney General Baxley, and Lieutenant Governor Beasley) in a professionally managed campaign with extensive media advertising. Promising "a new beginning" for Alabama at his 1979 inauguration, Governor James found his proposals often frustrated in the legislature, which he did not seek to manage. Defeated in his attempts for a new constitution and "unearmarking" of designated state revenues, Governor James did cut the employees on the state payroll, and he created the Alabama Heritage Trust Fund for future public construction projects from Mobile Bay petroleum royalties.

Three experienced Democrats entered the 1982 elections for governor: House Speaker Joe McCorquodale, Lieutenant Governor D. H. McMillan, Jr., and George C. Wallace, with the latter two in the primary runoff. With just over one million votes cast, McMillan, endorsed by the black Alabama Democratic Conference, lost to Wallace by less than 24,000 votes, the closest margin of the sixteen Alabama elections Wallace won. With a worsening state economy, Governor Wallace's ads, "Alabama needs jobs, Jobs, JOBS!" gained 60% of the November gubernatorial vote, defeating Republican Montgomery Mayor Emory Folmar and five minor party candidates. When the legislature was organized after the 1982 elections, newspapers headlined, "Wallace keeps his 'promise': Four Blacks Appointed Chairmen of Committees,"[4] and other African Americans were named to important legislative positions.

After his fourth term, increasingly afflicted by his injuries, Governor Wallace announced that he was retiring from politics in 1986. Lieutenant Governor Bill Baxley, who had been elected the nation's youngest attorney general in 1970 at age twenty-nine, entered the 1986 Democratic primary along with former Governor James, former Lieutenant Governor McMil-

lan, and Attorney General Charles Graddick. Graddick, a former Republican district attorney in Mobile, had switched parties and been elected attorney general in 1978. Consequently,
the Alabama Democrats in 1979 had adopted a party rule for-
bidding anyone who had voted in another party's primary or
promoting an independent candidate from "crossing over" to
vote in Democratic primaries. The Democratic state chairman
recommended that all voters be asked, at the second or runoff
election between Baxley and Graddick, if they had voted earlier in the GOP primary; Republicans responded that this in-
vaded the privacy of the ballot. On the June 24, 1986, runoff
election night, Attorney General Graddick thanked the
470,051 Alabamians, including Republicans, who had voted
for him compared to 461,295 for Lieutenant Governor Baxley, and then ordered the impoundment of ballots in thirty-
six of Alabama's sixty-seven counties to prevent fraud. After
a variety of federal and state suits, joined by Baxley saying the
election was "stolen," the Alabama Supreme Court ruled that
the Alabama Democratic Party had authority to settle the contest, and five officials certified Baxley as the nominee, stating
that Graddick's 8,756 lead came from illegal crossover votes
by Republicans. Graddick then waged a write-in campaign until dropping out shortly before the general election. After
these bitter battles, in November 1986, 696,203 Alabamians
turned to elect Guy Hunt as the first Republican governor of
Alabama in 112 years, compared to 537,163 votes for Baxley.
Guy Hunt had accumulated debts as the Republican nominee
for governor, losing in 1978, and only 30,000 Alabamians had
voted in the 1986 Republican primary. A farmer, Amway
products distributor, part-time Primitive Baptist preacher,
and former Cullman County probate judge, Governor Hunt
proclaimed "Alabama open for business."[5] He formed a number of commissions to study educational reform and sought
to limit the importation of hazardous waste into the state. In
1990, a record number of Republicans ran for statewide of-

fices, but only Governor Hunt was reelected—by 633,520 votes over 582,106 for Democratic nominee Paul Hubbert, the long-time leader of the Alabama Educational Association. In December 1992, Governor Hunt was indicted for converting campaign funds to personal use, and after a jury trial, was found guilty of violating the state ethics law by using his office for personal gain. Upon his felony conviction on April 22, 1993, Governor Hunt, a Republican, was removed from office and succeeded by Lieutenant Governor James Folsom, Jr., a Democrat, and the son of Big Jim Folsom.[6] The younger Governor Folsom had cosponsored, with State Treasurer George

Figure 6.4   Electronic media enables "live" coverage of Alabama politics. Governor Hunt was removed upon conviction. (Photo by D. L. Martin)

Wallace, Jr., the Wallace-Folsom prepaid college tuition plan, allowing Alabama parents to invest for their children's education. Thus recent Alabama history has been personalized in generational politics.

Other State Elective Offices

The following state executive officers are elected concurrently with the governor for four-year terms in even-numbered, nonleap years (1990, 1994, etc.). The state constitution requires that candidates for attorney general, secretary of state, state treasurer, state auditor, and commissioner of agriculture and industries have the following qualifications: be at least twenty-five years of age, a citizen of the United States for at least seven years, and a resident of Alabama for five years preceding the election. There are no other requirements except winning the election. All may be removed upon impeachment by the Alabama house of representatives and conviction by the state senate. No statewide executive officers have been impeached this century, although a state treasurer in 1978 and the governor in 1993 were removed from office following criminal convictions.

■ *Lieutenant Governor*: in succession without success. Historically, Alabama's lieutenant governors have been politically unable to be elected governor on their own, perhaps being blamed for the fate of legislation in the senate. The lieutenant governor must have the same qualifications as the Alabama governor and assumes the office if there is a vacancy (due to death, resignation, or upon criminal conviction when the trial judge notifies Alabama's chief justice). The lieutenant governor becomes acting governor if the governor is impeached, is absent from the state more than twenty days, is judged unsound of mind by the Alabama Supreme Court, or is otherwise disabled, until the governor is acquitted, returns to the state, or is cured of the disability. The ordinary function of the lieutenant governor is to preside over the state senate, although without a vote except in case of a tie (which occasionally happens). For the dual role as a legislative officer, the 1901 constitution specifies the same $12-a-day salary as that for the speaker of the house (while performing the duties of governor, the lieutenant governor is paid accordingly). The lieutenant governor and speaker receive a $3,780 monthly expense allowance and the same per diem as other legislators, but are likely to work more days thus averaging over $50,000 per year. A recent campaign question has been whether the Alabama lieutenant governorship should be full-time (some incumbents have kept their private law practice or business), and paid accordingly. The lieutenant governor chairs the legislative committee on examiners of public accounts, is a member of the legislative council, and serves on, or appoints members to, a number of other state commissions.

■ *Attorney General*: enforcer for the people. This official, whom the Alabama Supreme Court ruled must be "learned in the law" (a licensed attorney), serves as the state's chief legal officer. Alabama's attorney general may initiate criminal prosecutions and intervene in or even take over cases from local prosecutors, and also represents the state in all criminal appeals. On the order of the governor, Alabama Supreme Court, or a grand jury, the attorney general can institute impeachment proceedings against state or local officials.

The attorney general represents the state and its agencies in all court proceedings in which Alabama is a party or has an interest, including extradition matters in conjunction with the governor's office. Assistant attorneys general (often recent law school graduates) are assigned to state agencies to prepare legal documents such as contracts, to review rules, and to conduct litigation. The attorney general reviews legislation for constitutionality, interprets statutes, and issues advisory opinions at the request of state officials, legislators, and local prosecutors. The attorney general is often asked for a legal opinion on proposed actions by local governments and upon request by a city may represent the municipality before state appellate courts when the constitutionality of an ordinance is challenged. These advisory opinions are published quarterly, and while not as authoritative as those of the Alabama Supreme Court, serve as guidance for government agencies. The attorney general is an *ex officio* member of many state boards needing legal advice and is responsible for the enforcement of Alabama's Fair Campaign Practices Act and ethics laws. Citizens with a consumer complaint can take it to the attorney general's office, which investigates antitrust violations and fraud.

The Alabama attorney general's office thus includes criminal and civil sections, provides legal opinions for state and local governments, and has a consumer protection division. The total staff of 150 consists of an appointive deputy attorney general, assistant attorneys general, legal research aides, investigators, and supporting clerical personnel. A continuing issue has been which outside legal counsel has been hired for specialized work, since the Alabama attorney general is paid approximately $90,000 per year, but receives election campaign donations from law firms. In other states, the office has been a frequent stepping-stone to the governorship (especially if the attorney general made a crusading reputation exposing crime and corruption in the administration of the incumbent of the opposite party), but historically this has not been the trend in Alabama (see listing of governors in Appendix B and their backgrounds).

■ *Secretary of State* and *State Treasurer*: record keepers. Women were elected as Alabama's secretary of state from 1944 until 1978 and as state treasurer from 1958 until 1986.

The secretary of state is custodian of the Great Seal of Alabama which, affixed to all laws and many other official documents signed by the governor, attests that these bear a genuine signature. All original statutes and other records are kept in Montgomery, and the secretary of state distributes copies to officials and the public. A major duty is managing statewide and special elections, listing candidates to appear on the ballot, and certifying the final voting results (or a recount, if necessary) as the "official returns." Being secretary of the Board of Adjustment means handling all claims filed against the state. As in most states, the secretary has commercial responsibilities: keeping the records of incorporation and trademarks of firms doing business in Alabama and administering "secured transactions" (financing liens) under the Uniform Commercial Code. DIALUP (Direct Information Access Link Using PCs) allows personal computer users to check UCC filings, business incorporations, campaign finance records of candidates and political committees (PACs), legislative acts, and a listing of all notary publics in Alabama. The pay of the secretary of state is currently $57,200.

The state treasurer is responsible for state funds and payment of the state debt. The treasurer receives and accounts for money paid to the state and deposits these millions of dollars in financial institutions throughout Alabama. The treasurer negotiates how much is put in each bank and the amount of interest received; candidates for this office have found it easy to raise campaign funds. After an Alabama state treasurer was convicted of ethics laws violations (favorable loans to her husband's business) and removed in 1978, pressure grew for banks to bid competitively to pay the most interest, as in other states. George Wallace, Jr., was elected to his first office in 1986, pledging to improve cash management by electronic fund transfer to maximize interest received.

Rather than keep funds in the treasurer's vault seen in many older state capitols, the modern official issues a state warrant (two signatures are required on the check) on a particular account when payment needs to be made. The treasurer keeps a file of all receipts, warrants, and disbursement of funds at each of the depositories and issues an annual report on the state's financial condition. As trustee of the state's sinking funds, or amounts put aside to repay debts coming due, and as custodian of the investments of the employees' and teachers' retirement systems and the state self-insurance fund, the treasurer is involved in securities management. The treasurer keeps records of the state's own bonds, and destroys those turned in at repayment. The office employs about fifty accountants, computer operators, and secretaries, and the Alabama treasurer is paid $57,200.

■ *State Auditor*: the checker. This official post-audits (after the transaction) the accounts and securities held by the state treasurer, the records of the Department of Finance, and the payrolls of all state departments and maintains an inventory of all state property. Property management and the inventory of state vehicles are continuing tasks. The auditor makes an annual report to the governor showing all taxes and revenues collected by source and all disbursements paid out by item. Since reorganizations (especially in 1939) have transferred major accounting functions to the state Department of Finance and the Department of Examiners of Public Accounts, the auditor's office has fewer powers than as created in 1819. In 1993, the incumbent auditor recommended abolishing the office. The state auditor is paid approximately $57,200 per year, and between the mid-1950s and 1990 women were elected to the office in Alabama.

■ *The Commissioner of Agriculture and Industries* must have the same qualifications as the other constitutional officers, as well as being "of good moral character, of recognized executive ability and trained in the practice and science of agriculture" (*Code* 2-2-2).

This official serves as executive head of the Department of Agriculture and Industries directed by a board of eleven, consisting of the governor, the commissioner, the directors of the Alabama Cooperative Extension Service and agricultural experiment station at Auburn University, four outstanding farmers, and three industrial leaders appointed by the incumbent governor with senate confirmation. The department enforces regulations (against livestock theft), is responsible for weights and measures (its seal is found on gasoline pumps and scales), and conducts inspection of many agricultural products and pesticides for consumer protection. The commissioner serves on a number of bodies promoting industry, agriculture, and marketing (such as establishing farmers' markets), and recent elections have witnessed contests between agribusiness interests and small farmers. The commissioner is paid approximately $56,800, and board members receive per diem expenses up to twenty days per year.

■ *The State Board of Education* consists of eight members elected by district and is chaired by the governor. Districts were redrawn by federal court order to equalize population and assure minority representation, and members must be registered voters within the area they represent for four-year staggered terms. There are no other qualifications, except that a member cannot have been employed by the board or been a professional educator within the five years preceding election. The board has been divided in ideology over curriculum issues and textbook selection in recent years. An increasing number of Alabama's children are enrolling in private or home schools.

The state superintendent of education acts as the executive officer in carrying out the board's instructions and serves at its pleasure (backing the superintendent over the governor in the early 1990s). The superintendent is an *ex officio* member of several public educational institutions' governing boards and is paid approximately $115,000 per year, while board members receive $500 per month plus daily expenses and a travel allowance. As a professional educational administrator, the superintendent approves the budgets of all county and city school systems and manages the State Department of Education (discussed in Chapter 7).

■ *Public Service Commissioners*: regulating for the people. The Alabama Public Service Commission supervises and regulates public utilities, common carriers (transportation), and contract carriers (shipping). It investigates complaints of unreasonable rates and holds hearings on the establishment and abandonment of service by issuing permits to operate. It furnishes information to the state Department of Revenue to assist in the assessment of taxes upon utilities. The Alabama commission was established by statute in 1881, and the legislature sometimes debates whether to alter it. Legislation passed in 1977 gives the state attorney general responsibility to represent consumers in hearings before the commission. The commissioners must decide what is a "fair rate of return" (profit, once depreciation has been calculated), although rates can go into effect pending appeal to the Alabama Supreme Court, but if the utility loses, the commission decides refunds to customers.

The three commissioners are elected for four-year staggered terms by the entire state, but no two members can come from the same congressional district. They must be registered voters, but cannot own stock or have a financial interest in any public utility. Commissioners are required to reside in Montgomery and devote full time to their duties, for which they are paid approximately $51,000 (the president earns $600 more), plus a $670 monthly expense allowance.

As federal deregulation has occurred, there has been increasing public concern over rates within the state for electricity, gas, water, telephone, and radio communications services, and there are twenty-eight railroads, four airlines, and hundreds of motor carriers (trucks, buses, limousines, and taxis) operating in Alabama. The consumer services section investigates complaints regarding utility operations and services and enforces weight limits, safety standards in shipping hazardous wastes, and financial responsibility (insurance). The Public Service Commission's staff numbers a hundred auditors, utility analysts, attorneys, safety inspectors, engineering specialists, and enforcement officers to deal with the experts hired by the private utilities.

In summary, all these elected officials are responsible for their own departments, but they are only a portion of the state administrative structure, which is described in the following chapter.

Notes

1. Such as "standing in the schoolhouse door" to try to bar integration at the University of Alabama in 1963.
2. Inaugural Address, January 14, 1963.
3. *Time* Magazine, March 4, 1966, p. 28.
4. *Montgomery Advertiser*, January 13, 1983, p. D-1.
5. Guy Hunt, *Alabama Development Office 1989 Annual Report*, p. 1.
6. See articles in "Convicted: Hunt vows to appeal; Folsom in," *Birmingham Post-Herald*, April 23, 1993.

For Further Reading

Carter, Dan. *The Politics of Rage: George Wallace and His America*. New York: Simon and Schuster, forthcoming.

Grafton, Carl, and Anne Permaloff. *Big Mules and Branch-heads: James E. Folsom and Political Power in Alabama*. Athens, Ga.: University of Georgia Press, 1985.

Lesher, Stephan. *George Wallace: American Populist*. New York: Addison-Wesley Publishing, 1994.

Sims, George E. *The Little Man's Big Friend: James E. Folsom in Alabama Politics, 1946–1958*. University: University of Alabama Press, 1985.

Taylor, Sandra Baxley. *Me 'n' George: A Story of George Corley Wallace and His Number One Crony Oscar Harper.* Mobile, Ala.: Greenberry Publishing, 1988.

Wallace, George C. *Stand Up for America.* New York: Doubleday, 1976. (Autobiography.)

Videotape: "George Wallace," Alabama Public Television, 1988.

SEVEN

State Administration: Services and Selected Agencies

An organizational chart of Alabama state government shows a bewildering maze of bureaucracies. A greatly simplified diagram appears in Figure 7.1. This chapter will examine the major services provided by the state, and the agencies that administer them.

Some Major State Functions

■ *Agriculture* was historically the base of Alabama's economy, but the percentage of the state's labor force engaged in agriculture has dropped from nearly 20 in 1950 to less than 3% today. As workers have left the land, farming operations have increased in size, becoming agribusinesses that require large capital investment. The Department of Agriculture and Industries, headed by the elected commissioner, seeks to promote agricultural productivity and adopts standards for grading products. Its regulatory activities are indicated by some of its divisions: agricultural statistics; seed and plant inspection; uniformity of weights and measures (including petroleum products); meat and poultry inspection; pesticide management and licensing of commercial applicators; shipping-point inspection of grain and produce; enforcing pure food and

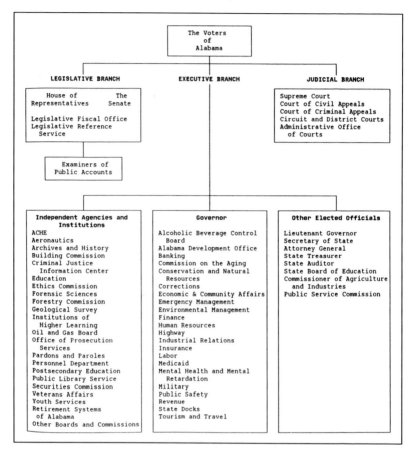

Figure 7.1 A representative sample of state agencies. A full Alabama state government chart would be considerably more complex. (Courtesy of the Department of Finance, *State of Alabama Annual Financial Report, 1989*, p. 15)

Table 7.1
Alabama's Largest State Agencies

Agency	No. of employees
Mental Health and Retardation	6,141
Public Health	4,491
Human Resources	4,444
Highways	4,225
Corrections	3,492
Industrial Relations	1,734
Conservation and Natural Resources	1,588
Economic and Community Affairs	1,431
Revenue	1,344
Public Safety	1,335
Other state agencies ranged from 1 to hundreds	
state total	38,129

Source: State Personnel Department, *The Alabama Merit System, 1991*, p. 25.

drug laws and use of agricultural chemicals; and publication of informational materials. The state veterinarian heads the animal industry division, which tests for diseases and supervises stockyards, brands, and transportation of animals. The poultry division collects an inspection fee for grading eggs and levies assessments on producers to promote eggs and poultry products. Marketing promotion is an example of government effort on behalf of private enterprise to increase product consumption in state farmers' markets and exports abroad. Thus the department issues market news on prices and trends in livestock and commodities.

■ *Business Promotion and Regulation.* The regulatory activities of the Alabama Public Service Commission were discussed in the previous chapter, but there are other units concerned with certain activities of commerce. The Department of Aero-

Table 7.2
Leading Alabama Crops and Livestock

	Ala. rank in 50 states	Percentage of total U.S. production
Peanuts for nuts	3	13%
Sweet potatoes	5	6
Cotton lint	10	3
All chickens	9	4
Broilers	2	14
Eggs	12	3
Catfish	2	13

Source: *Alabama Agricultural Statistics*, Bulletin 34 (1991), p. 7.

nautics approves airfield sites within the state, licenses their operation, investigates aircraft accidents, and aids local governments in developing airports. The department is financed by the state tax on aviation fuel. The Alabama Liquefied Petroleum Gas Board issues permits to ensure safety in its storage, transport, and sale to consumers. The Department of Insurance licenses all companies and their agents doing business in Alabama, monitoring the financial condition of over 600 property and casualty and 700 life insurance companies, and seeks to reduce losses by working with the state fire marshal, who inspects public buildings and mobile homes sold, supervises the storage of fireworks, and investigates cases of suspected arson. In Alabama, there is no price regulation over life, accident, and health insurance (except certain Blue Cross–Blue Shield and Medicare supplement policies), but most property and liability rates are subject to state approval.

The State Banking Department decides whether to issue state charters to financial institutions in Alabama and examines their operations to ensure that they are in sound financial condition. If a bank or credit union does not include the word *national* or *federal* in its name, then it was established under state authority. In Alabama, there are over 160 banks with 600 branches, 800 consumer finance (small loan) licensees, and (starting in 1992) 200 pawn shops under state supervision. The Alabama Securities Commission (consisting of the attorney general, state superintendent of banks, commissioner of insurance, a lawyer, and a certified public accountant) registers securities dealers and salespersons and regulates the mutual funds, stocks, and bonds qualified to be sold in Alabama.

The Alabama Development Office (ADO) and the Alabama Department of Economic and Community Affairs (ADECA) seek to promote economic growth (such as minority and small business programs and enterprise zones) and to attract new industry. Located in the Alabama Center for Commerce (financed by the state retirement systems), a briefing room with computer graphics can show plant locations meeting an employer's needs, and workers are trained at state expense through vocational education programs. Through a variety of loans and grants, the state offers financing to stimulate business investment and grants money to local governments for industrial development. The state Industrial Development Authority, which issues bonds, is an example of public corporations formed to circumvent the limitations placed upon state debt discussed in Chapter 2.

■ *Occupational Licensing Boards.* Alabama has some forty entities regulating entry into and practice of a trade or profession within the state. These bodies must certify a practitioner's competence from head (psychologists) to foot (podiatrists). The boards, created by statute, typically consist of three to nine members appointed by the governor for staggered terms from within the ranks of the trade they regulate. Sometimes the state professional organizations make nominations directly. (The ultimate identity is attained by the state

Board of Medical Examiners, composed of the Board of Censors of the Medical Association of Alabama.) The boards ordinarily administer an entrance examination (thus regulating entry into practice), enforce laws relating to the occupation, making the necessary rules, and revoking (after a hearing) the licenses of violators. They are financed by the examination, inspection, and license renewal fees they collect (which the state examiners have found, on occasion, they were unable to account for). Persons not properly certified can be prosecuted for practicing without a license. Such regulation is for protection of the public, and a citizen with a complaint can present it to the appropriate board for disciplinary action. More practitioners are now being required to take mandatory continuing education to keep them up to date in their fields. Table 7.3 shows the occupations now covered in Alabama; the first to be licensed were harbor pilots in 1852. In many states, consumer groups have called for public members (not from the profession) and an end to anticompetitive regulations such as barring professionals from advertising or listing prices.

■ *Conservation and Waterways.* The State of Alabama owns more than 250,000 acres of land and 900,000 acres of inland waters. The Department of Conservation and Natural Resources operates twenty-four state parks, twenty-three public fishing lakes, two waterfowl refuges, and two wildlife sanctuaries; manages twenty-nine wildlife areas (in which hunting may be allowed); administers public trust lands for other agencies; and enforces fish and game and water safety laws. Nearly one million Alabamians buy hunting or fishing licenses annually, and there are 300,000 boats registered in the state. Fifty marine police patrol recreational waterways making several thousand arrests each year enforcing water safety and offshore fishing laws, and there are 150 conservation enforcement officers. The department conducts research on the best utilization of natural and marine resources, runs fish hatcher-

Table 7.3
Occupational Licensing in Alabama

Occupations regulated in all states, including Alabama:

1. Accountant
2. Architect
3. Attorney
4. Barber
5. Chiropractor
6. Cosmetologist
7. Dental hygienist
8. Dentist
9. Emergency medical technologist
10. Engineer, professional
11. Funeral director, embalmer
12. Insurance broker, agent
13. Nurse
14. Optometrist
15. Osteopath
16. Pharmacist
17. Physical therapist
18. Physician/surgeon
19. Podiatrist
20. Psychologist
21. Real estate broker, agent
22. Social worker
23. Teacher, public school
24. Veterinarian

Occupations licensed, certified, permitted in Alabama:

25. Abstractor
26. Adoption/Child placement
27. Athletic trainer
28. Auctioneer
29. Audiologist/Speech pathologist
30. Automobile dealer
31. Beekeeper
32. Cleaner, dyer
33. Collection agency operator
34. Contractor, general, building, home improvement
35. Contractor, heating and air conditioning

36. Cotton buyer
37. Counselor, professional
38. Dietitian/nutritionist
39. Driver training instructor
40. Electrical contractor
41. Employment agency operator
42. Forester
43. Foster care
44. Hearing aid dealer
45. Interior designer
46. Junk dealer
47. Landscape architect
48. Medical technician
49. Merchant, transient
50. Midwife
51. Mine operator
52. Motion picture operator
53. Nurseries operator
54. Nursing home administrator
55. Optician/occulist
56. Pawnbroker
57. Pest control/pesticide applicator
58. Physician's assistant
59. Plumber/gas fitter
60. Polygraph examiner
61. Private detective
62. Real estate appraiser
63. Ship pilot
64. Sanitarian
65. School bus driver
66. Securities broker
67. Soil classifier
68. Surveyor, land
69. Tree surgeon
70. Veterinary technician
71. Wastewater treatment operator
72. Weighmaster
73. Welldriller

ies, and propagates oysters and shrimp. The department is largely self-supporting through user fees: park entrance and rentals; fishing and hunting permits; saltwater licenses; excise taxes on sporting arms and gear and marine fuels; and oil, gas, and timber revenues.

The Forestry Commission (separated from the conservation department in 1969), through a professional state forester and staff, manages state forests and three nurseries for improved seedlings, fights forest fires, loans fire trucks to rural communities, and provides technical assistance, including nursery stock, to private landowners. About one-third of Alabama's forests are owned by the wood products industry, 62% by individuals, and 5% by government, with the forested acreage increasing.

The Surface Mining Commission and the sixty-seven county soil and water conservation districts engage in land reclamation measures, as well as programs for flood prevention and water supply for municipal and industrial use. The state Oil and Gas Board, through the state geologist, regulates the drilling for petroleum and natural gas, setting limits to maximize subsequent production. All of the foregoing agencies are financed by charges for their services, license fees, and appropriations from the general fund voted by the legislature.

Development authorities have been established for the state's rivers (such as the Coosa, Tennessee–Tombigbee, Elk River, and Bear Creek) to dredge navigable waterways and for water conservation and irrigation purposes. The various authorities are composed of public officials from affected cities or counties, state officials, or appointed citizens and are financed through the sale of bonds that are repaid from the developed projects or state appropriations.

■ *Education.* The state has founded many institutions of higher education: the University of Alabama with campuses at Tuscaloosa, Birmingham, and Huntsville; Auburn University at Auburn and Montgomery; Alabama Agricultural and Mechanical University at Huntsville and Alabama State University at Montgomery, still with predominantly African-American enrollments; the University of Montevallo; the University of South Alabama at Mobile; the University of North Alabama at Florence; Livingston University; Jacksonville State University; Athens State College; and Troy State University in Troy, Dothan, and Montgomery. Although some institutions were founded in times of segregation by race or gender, the state's eagerness to bring affordable education within thirty miles of every Alabamian has meant investment in sixteen campuses of four-year colleges or universities, plus forty two-year institutions: junior, community, and technical colleges. The state also gives annual financial support to four private institutions: Tuskegee University; Talladega College; Marion Military Institute; and Lyman Ward Military Academy.

Of the $3 billion that Alabama spent annually on education in the early 1990s, one-third typically went to higher education and two-thirds for elementary and secondary schools. The "minimum program" set a level of state support for teacher salaries and instruction, based upon pupil attendance (thus parents upset with local schools would keep their children home to force negotiations with the board by financial pressure). Alabama public school education is 14% federally financed, 65% from the state, and 21% from local sources, compared to a 1992 national average 6-48-46 federal-state-local ratio. However, in late 1991, a federal judge ordered reallocation of resources to overcome previous effects of segregation in higher education,[1] and in 1993, a state court ruled that Alabama's public schools, because the richest districts spent twice as much per pupil as the poorest, violate the Alabama constitution (Art. XIV, Sec. 256) by failing to provide equitable and adequate educational opportunities, thus neces-

ALABAMA INSTITUTIONS OF HIGHER EDUCATION

PUBLIC SENIOR INSTITUTIONS
1. Alabama A&M University (A&M)
2. Alabama State University (ASU)
3. Athens State College (ASC)
4. Auburn University (AU)
5. Auburn University at Montgomery (AUM)
6. Jacksonville State University (JSU)
7. Livingston University (LU)
8. Troy State University (TSU)
9. Troy State University at Dothan (TSUD)
10. Troy State University in Montgomery (TSUM)
11. University of Alabama (UA)
12. University of Alabama at Birmingham (UAB)
13. University of Alabama in Huntsville (UAH)
14. University of Montevallo (UM)
15. University of North Alabama (UNA)
16. University of South Alabama (USA)

PUBLIC JUNIOR COLLEGES
17. Alexander City Junior College
18. Bishop State Junior College
19. Brewer State Junior College
20. Chattahochee Valley Community College
21. Jefferson Davis State Junior College
22. Enterprise State Junior College
23. Faulkner State Junior College
24. Patrick Henry State Junior College
25. Jefferson State Junior College
26. Northeast Alabama State Jr. College
27. Northwest Alabama State Jr. College
28. Snead State Junior College
29. Southern Union State Junior College
30. L.B. Wallace State Junior College

PUBLIC COMMUNITY COLLEGES
31. Calhoun State Community College
32. Gadsden State Community College
33. Lawson State Community College
34. Shelton State Community College
35. G.C. Wallace State Community College–Dothan
36. G.C. Wallace State Community College–Hanceville
37. G.C. Wallace State Community College–Selma

PUBLIC TECHNICAL COLLEGES
38. Alabama Aviation and Technical College
39. Atmore State Technical College
40. Ayers State Technical College
41. Bessemer State Technical College
42. Carver State Technical College
43. Drake State Technical College
44. Fredd State Technical College
45. Hobson State Technical College
46. Ingram State Technical College
47. MacArthur State Technical College
48. Muscle Shoals State Technical College
49. Northwest Alabama State Technical College
50. Nunnelley State Technical College
51. Opelika State Technical College
52. Patterson State Technical College
53. Reid State Technical College
54. Southwest State Technical College
55. Sparks State Technical College
56. Trenholm State Technical College
57. Walker State Technical College

PRIVATE SENIOR INSTITUTIONS
58. Birmingham-Southern College
59. Faulkner University
60. Huntingdon College
61. Judson College
62. Miles College
63. Mobile College
64. Oakwood College
65. Samford University
66. Southeastern Bible College
67. Spring Hill College
68. Stillman College
69. Talladega College
70. Tuskegee University

PRIVATE JUNIOR COLLEGES
71. Concordia College
72. Marion Military Institute
73. Selma University
74. Walker College

Figure 7.2   Institutions of higher education in Alabama.

sitating reform of educational finance.[2] The Alabama Special Education Trust Fund presently receives a dozen designated state (primarily income and sales) taxes.

Public control over education is exercised in a variety of ways. All of the four-year institutions have their own boards of trustees, often with members from the legislature, a few of whom are also presidents of or work for state institutions, and a position of chancellor of postsecondary education was created in the 1980s to coordinate the two-year institutions. The

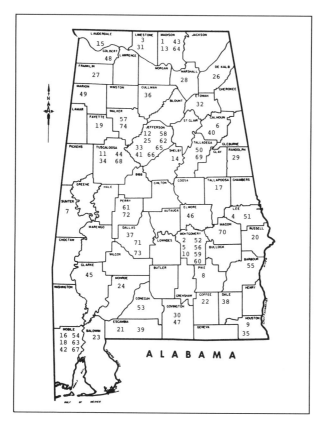

Figure 7.2 (continued)

chancellor is appointed (under contract like the state superintendent of education) by the elective state Board of Education. The Alabama Educational Television Commission, composed of seven members appointed by the governor, operates the Alabama Public Television Network, which broadcasts programs for instructional use and public information and entertainment.

Primary and secondary schools are under locally elective boards of two types in Alabama: sixty-one city and sixty-seven county school districts. (The state Department of Youth Services operates its own schools). A municipality with a population greater than 5,000 may establish separate city schools; otherwise they are under the county system. City school boards ordinarily consist of five members appointed by the city council for five-year staggered terms, although a few municipalities have elective boards, and bills are being introduced in the legislature to make all city boards elective. Members of county school boards are ordinarily elected for staggered six-year terms from districts, fostering a proprietorial attitude toward "their" schools. Compensation of school board members varies under local acts passed by the legislature. The boards set educational regulations within state policies and hire personnel through an executive officer, the superintendent of education. Most county superintendents are elected for four-year terms, but city superintendents and some county superintendents are appointed under contract by the boards at their pleasure. The Alabama Code, Title 16 on education, sets the superintendent's professional qualifications.

Finally, the state sets the requirements for teacher certification, with tenure being granted upon three years' satisfactory service, and administers a teachers' retirement system. A textbook committee recommends books to the State Board of Education for adoption (meaning the state will pay most of the cost of the texts adopted by local boards from the list), and the tenure commission hears appeals when teachers are fired by local boards.

■ *Health and Welfare.* Originally started to quarantine the spread of infectious disease, public health services now comprise a variety of functions. All counties have public health departments that conduct sanitary inspections of public eating places, food processing operations, schools, and jails. Public health officials sample dairy products and water supplies for purity, operating clinical laboratories for testing (including premarital blood examinations required by Alabama law). Communicable diseases are contained through immunization programs, vector (pest) control, and inspection of animal and solid waste disposal sites (dumps). Maternal and child health services include issuing permits to midwives, screening of children in clinics, and offering family planning programs. Air and water pollution control, hazardous waste disposal, and inspection of radiation (X-ray) equipment used in the state reduce public exposure to unnoticed harm. Personal services include preventive dental education, setting standards for nursing care, and providing home health aides for convalescent patients. The Alabama Department of Public Health conducts surveys of medical need and licenses hospitals and nursing homes, approving facilities as meeting standards for the federal Medicare and Medicaid programs. Certification responsibilities include licensing all ambulance services, attendants, and hearing aid dealers. The state collects and analyzes vital statistics, thereby gauging the health of the community (Figures 7.3 and 7.4).

Alabama is unusual in that the Medical Association of Alabama (all practicing doctors) constitutes the state Board of Health. This body elects, determines the salary ($135,000 in 1993), qualifications, and term of the state health officer, who heads the department.

The first patient committed in 1861 to Alabama's then newly established insane asylum was a middle-aged, would-be Confederate warrior from Fort Morgan, who was diagnosed as suffering from "Mania A . . . the alleged exciting cause—political excitement." Custodial confinement was the traditional practice, but the high costs of institutionalization meant Alabama was under federal court order during most of the 1970s and 1980s to improve its mental health facilities and hire trained professional personnel.

The Alabama Department of Mental Health and Mental Retardation runs institutions for those adjudged criminally in-

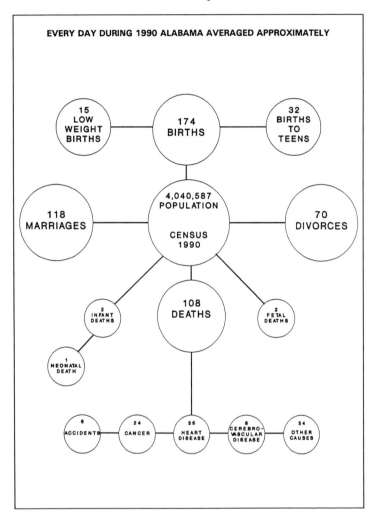

Figure 7.3 Collection of vital statistics is an important public health function. (Chart courtesy of the Alabama Department of Public Health)

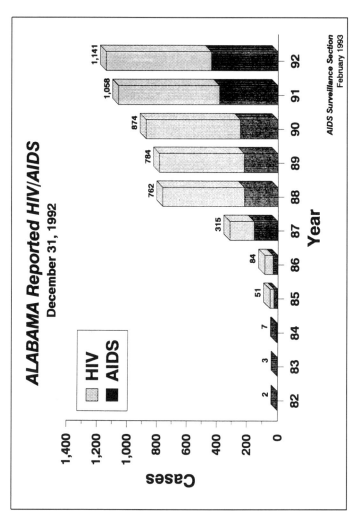

Figure 7.4 The growth of AIDS in Alabama, 1982–1992. (Chart courtesy of the Alabama Department of Public Health)

sane (Taylor Hardin Secure Medical Facility), those committed for psychological disturbances (Bryce and Searcy Hospitals, Eufaula Adolescent Center, and three geriatric nursing homes), and the mentally retarded (residential centers in Decatur, Tarrant City, Tuscaloosa, Wetumpka, and Mobile). While the state maintains a mental illness residential capacity of some 2,400, and some 1,200 spaces for the mentally retarded, approximately 100,000 Alabamians are served by community-based programs for mental health, substance abuse, and services for the retarded. Such preventive measures are reducing the number institutionalized to those incompetent to care for themselves.

The concept of public welfare, rather than just private or religious charity, is traced to the Elizabethan Poor Law of 1601, which levied a tax for relief and gave responsibility to secular authorities. Until the twentieth century, the city workhouse and the rural poor farm symbolized the work-ethic approach to poverty. During the Great Depression of the 1930s, local and private relief agencies, unable to care for the millions of Americans out of work (pictured by the Farm Security Administration photographs taken in Alabama), prompted federal intervention in financing programs largely administered through state agencies.

Table 7.4
Primary Reason for Substance Abuse Treatment

Alcohol	51%
Alcohol with other drugs	11%
Crack	21%
Cocaine	5%
Other drugs	12%
21,452 clients served	100%

Source: Alabama Department of Mental Health and Mental Retardation, *Statistical Review, 1991–92*, p. 63.

The Alabama Department of Human Resources (originally Pensions and Security) is the primary welfare agency at both state and county levels. In each county there is a welfare board chosen by the county and city governments, which appoint a county welfare director, who is an employee of and administratively responsible to DHR. The state Board of Human Resources is chaired by the governor, with six other members (at least two of whom must be women) appointed with state senate confirmation for six-year staggered terms, and chooses the commissioner to administer a departmental budget of over $350 million. The state pays a supplement to federal programs as shown in Table 7.5 and administers the JOBS programs required of recipients of Aid to Families with Dependent Children. Caseworkers verify the eligibility of recipients for each program and attempt to detect fraud.

The Department of Human Resources received over 43,000 reports of child abuse or neglect (placing 4,500 children in foster care) and 8,000 reports concerning elderly or disabled Alabamians in a recent year. It enforces child support collections from absent parents to reduce welfare payments. The department approves adoptions and licenses child-placing agencies in the state, as well as licensing nearly 4,000 day-care facilities and group homes for children. Homemaker services are designed to help the elderly and disabled stay out of nursing homes and institutions where care is much more costly.

In recent years, nearly 400,000 poor Alabamians received over $1.5 billion in Medicaid benefits (Table 7.6), with the state's share exceeding $400 million per year, indicating why health-care reform is on the nation's agenda. Alabama's infant mortality rate is among the country's highest; more than 30% of the babies are born in the state to unwed mothers; and nearly one Alabama child in three lives with a single parent, the highest proportion in America.[3]

■ *Labor and Industrial Relations.* All states have enacted workers' compensation insurance covering employee injury or

Table 7.5
Public Welfare in Alabama

	1990–91 monthly cases	average payment
Financial assistance[a]		
Old age pensions	5,380	$ 54
Aid to the blind	99	$ 57
Aid to permanently disabled	4,127	$ 58
Aid to families with dependent children	47,389	$119
Refugees	58	$116
Disasters (declared by pres.)	32	$135
Social services[b]		
Child day care	10,259	$133
Adult day care	911	$157
Child foster care	2,617	$237
Adult foster care	148	$104
Food stamps (households)	186,281	$175

[a]State supplement to federal payment
[b]Average payment per case
Sources: Alabama Department of Human Resources, *1991 Annual Report* and *Statistical Report Fiscal Year 1991*.

death on the job (Table 7.7). The Department of Industrial Relations operates the state Employment Service with local offices and administers unemployment compensation, which is financed by a tax on both employers and employees. This tax has traditionally been kept low in Alabama, resulting in a maximum weekly benefit of $165 in 1993. The industrial relations department enforces the child-labor, mine, and industrial-safety statutes. The Alabama Department of Labor investigates wage and labor disputes, attempting to mediate equitable settlements in order to avoid costly work stoppages.

Table 7.6
Medicaid in Alabama

Benefit Payments		Recipients	
Hospitals	44%	Female	70%
Nursing Homes	20%	Male	30%
Mental Health	8%	White	60%
Community Services	7%	Nonwhite	40%
Medicine	6%	5 years & younger	14%
Physicians	6%	6 to 20 years	13%
Insurance	5%	21 to 64 years	34%
Health Services	2%	65 years & older	39%
Finances			
Benefit payments	97.5%	Federal funds	72.5%
Administrative costs	2.5%	Alabama funds	27.5%

Source: Alabama Medicaid Agency, *Statistical Summary, Fiscal Year 1992.*

It records strike vote ballots, reviews reports by labor unions, and arbitrates labor disputes. For all building projects with state money, the department determines prevailing wages in the area before construction begins at the rates determined.

■ *Highways.* Alabama has over 11,000 miles of state highways (including the interstate system) constructed and maintained by the Department of Transportation, which has over 4,200 employees. Since 1939 the state highway director has been appointed by and serves at the pleasure of the governor, with no qualifications prescribed by law. The department is responsible for the construction, maintenance, and repair of state highways, bridges, and roads on state-owned land. The department may contract out work to private construction firms or enter into agreements with other states and the federal government when necessary. The director prescribes the placement of utility lines along public highways, issues regula-

Table 7.7
Workers' Compensation in Alabama

Injuries reported		Claims settled	
eyes	2%	temporary disability	37,778
fingers/thumbs	8%	permanent partial disability	7,081
hand	8%	permanent total disability	23
arm	7%	deaths	56
foot/toes	10%	state total	44,938
leg	12%		
body/head	53%	compensation paid	$197 million

Source: Alabama Department of Industrial Relations, *1992 Annual Report*, pp. 22–23.

tions on vehicle weight loads, makes rules concerning advertising along state highways, and tries to see that junkyards within 1,000 feet of a road are screened from view. The state is geographically divided into nine divisions, each supervised by a professional engineer.

Various bureaus of the department conduct planning of existing highways, their usage, and future transportation needs; acquire rights of way; prepare maps; conduct research in road engineering and test materials; and design roads and bridges. The Bureau of Construction examines bids received for work to be done by private firms and makes recommendations to the director (about half of the expenditures made are contracts). The Bureau of Secondary Roads coordinates the work of the Transportation Department with the counties and administers various aid programs. The department closely coordinates with the federal government on programs, funding, and urban planning for transportation.

Highway construction and maintenance in Alabama are financed through fuel taxes (16 cents per gallon on diesel and gasoline and 6 cents on lubricating oil), motor vehicle license and carrier fees ($13 on private cars and up to $845 on com-

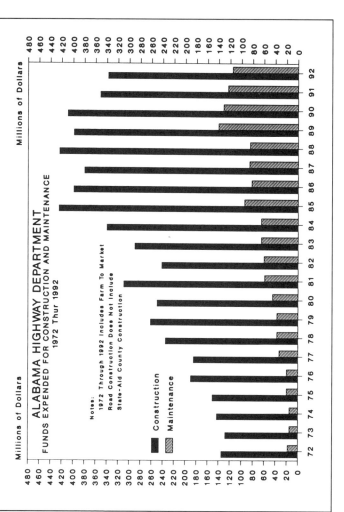

Figure 7.5 State highway construction and maintenance expenditures. (Chart courtesy of the Alabama Highway Department, *Annual Report, 1991–92*, p. 79)

mercial trucks depending upon weight), and petroleum products inspection fees. Several highway finance corporations have been formed to issue bonds for construction, so that debt service means less departmental budget for maintenance or new construction. Counties and cities receive a proportion of the motor vehicle registrations and fuel taxes, plus reimbursement for any work upon state highways within their boundaries. Such assistance (as for example, the state's installing a traffic light if the city will keep it up) prompts local officials to want main routes through towns designated as part of the state highway system.

■ *State Enterprises: Docks and Liquor.* Various states own proprietary enterprises, operating them for the benefit of the public. In Alabama, the state owns shipping docks at Mobile and inland ports (some sold to local governments) and controls the sale of liquor.

The Alabama State Docks were opened at Mobile in 1927, and in 1991 earned $20 million from shipping coal, with the rest of the $46 million in revenues coming from its "roll-on/roll-off" facility, terminal railway, bulk handling, grain elevators, and warehouse (including cold storage) operations. Alabama has more than 2,000 miles of navigable inland waterways, connected by the Tennessee–Tombigbee Waterway with twenty-three other states.

Since 1937 the sale of alcoholic beverages has been through state stores, although the legislature is considering getting out of the retail business. To choose "wet" or "dry" status, 25% of the number voting at the last general election must petition for a referendum, which can be called only at two-year intervals (to allow negotiation of state store leases, which traditionally have been awarded to the politically influential). Over the years, several counties have changed their status back and forth, but by the 1990s, forty-one were wet, with seven cities in the twenty-six dry counties allowing liquor to attract tourist

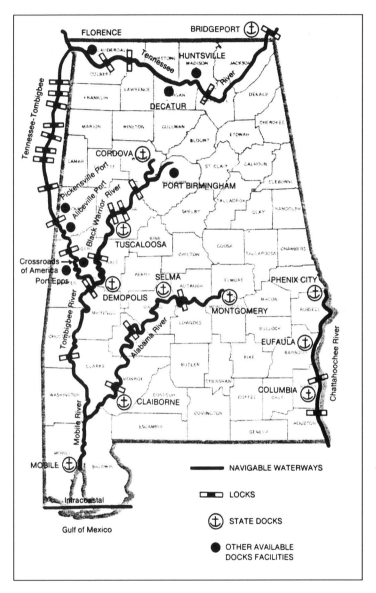

Figure 7.6 Alabama state docks and inland ports. (Map courtesy of the Alabama Department of Economic and Community Affairs, *Alabama County Data Book, 1990–91*, p. 20)

trade (Figure 7.7). Private licensees selling beer and wine compete with state stores by staying open longer hours.

The Alcoholic Beverage Control (ABC) Board consists of three members appointed for staggered six-year terms, but since they serve at the pleasure of the governor, the practice has been a new board with each new administration. The board selects the brands and sizes of alcoholic beverages sold in state stores (such discretion has caused scandals in the past) and sets price lists. If a customer desires to purchase any brand not regularly stocked, a special order may be placed at any ABC store. Another responsibility of the board is to hear cases of licensees cited for failure to observe laws or regulations. The board may reprimand licensees or temporarily suspend or revoke a license as a result of violations. There are over 850 ABC board employees, almost all under the state merit system.

Taxes collected and profits from sale of alcoholic beverages are an important revenue source for Alabama, totalling more than $130 million in fiscal year 1991. Such government levies on sumptuary consumption are often designated for beneficial purposes. For example, the state beer tax of five cents per twelve fluid ounces yielded $43 million in 1991, with two cents of every nickel going to the Special Education Trust Fund, one cent to the Department of Human Resources, half a cent divided equally among the wet counties, and a penny and a half to the state general fund. A continuing battle in Alabama liquor politics has been whether dry jurisdictions should receive ABC revenues, since stores in wet counties have thirsty neighbors. Taxes and profits on liquor and wine sold in state stores, as well as income derived from license and permit fees, are distributed according to complicated formulas as the legislature enacts new revenue measures.

■ *Public Safety and Correctional Agencies.* Under its "general police power" the state is responsible for public order. There

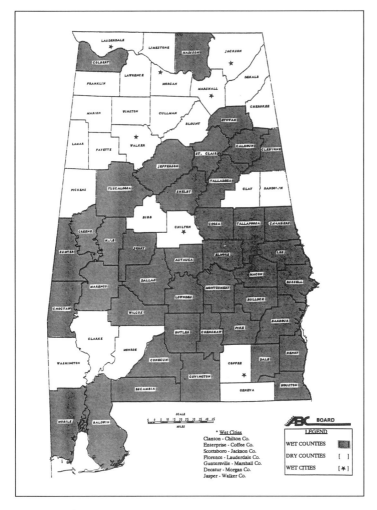

Figure 7.7 "Wet" and "dry" counties and cities. (Map courtesy of the Alabama Alcoholic Beverage Control Board)

are some 360 state and local law enforcement agencies in Alabama. The Department of Public Safety enforces motor vehicle laws for state highways and county roads, issues drivers' licenses to three million Alabamians, and provides technical assistance to local law enforcement agencies. The Alabama Bureau of Investigation investigates major crimes, auto theft, missing children, and it conducts fingerprinting and polygraph examinations. The Department of Public Safety has over 900 officers, most of whom are state troopers assigned to highway patrol, and a narcotics division. Personnel are hired under the state merit system, and there is a trooper cadet program for nineteen- to twenty-one-year-olds.

Other state enforcement agencies include campus police, the Alcoholic Beverage Control Board, which employs 150 agents to regulate liquor laws, and the Department of Conservation and Natural Resources, which has fish and game wardens as well as marine police on patrol. The Alabama Criminal Justice Information Center is part of a nationwide computer network with terminals in each major law enforcement agency, which allows patrolling officers to receive instant information on vehicles, persons, or property wanted by other jurisdictions. It also compiles the annual report *Crime in Alabama*.

There is an elected sheriff in each of Alabama's sixty-seven counties who has general law enforcement duties and serves judicial writs (except when done by a few elected constables), but usually does not have responsibility for automobile accident investigations, which are handled by the state troopers or city traffic officers. There are approximately 1,800 regular sheriff's deputies, but the size of sheriffs' offices varies greatly, with rural ones being quite small. In offices with a staff of less than ten, the sheriff after each election is likely to hire assistants personally, whereas in large counties having over fifty officers there is apt to be a career system.

There are nearly 300 municipal police departments in Ala-

Table 7.8
Crime in Alabama

Offenses	Clearance rate[a]	Stolen property	recovered
Homicide	71%	Locally stolen vehicle	38%
Rape	54%	Consumable goods	10%
Aggravated Assault	46%	Firearms	9%
Robbery	35%	Clothing, furs	8%
Theft	20%	Household goods	6%
Vehicle theft	17%	Currency, jewelry	5%
Burglary	13%	Office equipment	5%
		Electronics	4%
Violent offenses	45%	Livestock	4%
Total offenses	22%	Total property value	19%

[a]One arrest may clear more than one offense.
Source: Alabama Criminal Justice Information Center, *1992 Crime in Alabama: A Preliminary Report.*

bama, employing 5,500 police officers. The police chief is appointed by the city government and has general law enforcement authority within the city, extending to an area of "police jurisdiction" outside the city limits (see Chapter 9). Municipal police forces vary in size from one or two officers to large city departments.

All Alabama law enforcement officers must complete an initial training course at the Alabama Police Academy based at Selma or regional centers. Besides these regular officers, Alabama state and local law enforcement agencies employ some 2,900 full-time civilian personnel. There is a statewide average of one law enforcement officer for every 555 Alabamians, and about 8% of the sworn officers are women.

Public fear of crime led Alabama in 1980 to pass mandatory sentencing laws with the number of inmates serving longer sentences rising to an all-time high of 17,000. Several new

Table 7.9
Alabama's State Prison Population

Race	Male	Female	Age	
White	32%	2%	20 or younger	5%
Black	61%	4%	21 to 30	40%
Other less than 1%			31 to 40	35%
			41 and older	19%

Length of sentence		*Level of custody*	
up to 2 years	9%	Maximum/Close	3%
2 to 4 years	11%	Medium	51%
5 to 9 years	9%	Minimum	23%
10 to 14 years	16%	Trusty	1%
15 to 19 years	17%	Community	12%
20 to 24 years	10%	Quarantined	3%
25 to 35 years	8%	All Others	7%
over 35 years	4%		
Life	11%	17,800 inmates	
Life w/o parole	4%	as of February 1993	
Death:	less than 1%		

Source: Alabama Department of Corrections, *Inmate Sentences and Demographics*, February 1993.

state prisons have been built (including one for those infected with AIDS) to comply with a federal court order that had found overcrowding and other unconstitutional conditions. Limiting intake into the state prison system has meant, on occasion, a backup of state prisoners in county and city jails. Keeping a prisoner locked up is very expensive: more than $30,000 to build a single cell, more than $12,000 annually for each inmate kept in prison, and state reimbursement does not cover local costs. A Supervised Intensive Restitution program in community-based facilities is less expensive, but the public becomes concerned about inmates serving much less time than their original sentences.

The state Board of Pardons and Paroles investigates adult prisoners to determine their fitness for parole, and through a staff of probation and parole supervisors, oversees offenders outside the institutional system (including those from out of state, under an interstate compact). The three members of the Board of Pardons and Paroles are appointed for six-year staggered terms by the governor from a list of three qualified persons for each vacancy, nominated by a panel consisting of the chief justice of Alabama, the presiding judge of the court of criminal appeals, and the lieutenant governor.

During the 1980s, the Alabama legislature restricted the board's power to parole serious "Class A" felony prisoners. In order to be released on probation (by the judge) from a sentence of less than ten years, or be paroled (by the board) from the state prison system, inmates must have a satisfactory home and employment situation, which is often difficult to secure. Over 200 probation and parole supervisors (qualified college graduates who are sworn law enforcement officers hired under the merit system) located in field offices throughout the state seek to integrate offenders back into the community. Electronic surveillance (wearing a transmitter) is beginning to be used in Birmingham, Mobile, and Montgomery. The board holds weekly public hearings (victims of violent crime are notified under Alabama law) and can grant pardons, remit fines or forfeitures, and restore civil and political rights (such as those of carrying firearms and voting) to those who show evidence of being rehabilitated by living as good citizens.[4] The Crime Victims Compensation Commission awards limited amounts from the restitution paid by offenders.

The Alabama Department of Youth Services was established in 1973 to prevent juvenile delinquency and rehabilitate those eighteen and younger. The department provides half the salary of juvenile-court probation officers in each Alabama county, subsidizes community-operated youth detention centers, licenses foster care and operates group homes for children in

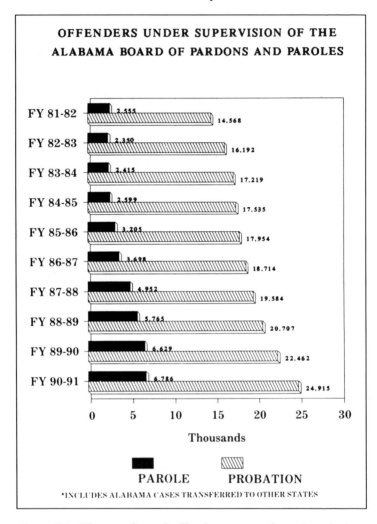

Figure 7.8 The number of offenders on parole and probation. (Chart courtesy of the Alabama Board of Pardons and Paroles, *Annual Report 1990–91*, p. 31)

need of supervision (CHINS: ungovernable behavior, truancy, runaways), and has room for 600 youths at three state training schools, two located near Birmingham and the third at Mount Meigs (which is now surrounded by a security fence). Of 22,000 juvenile court appearances in a recent year, 30% were dismissed, 53% placed on probation or consent decree not to repeat the offense, 2% were transferred to adult court, and 10% were committed to DYS, with the state providing medical care, remedial education, and vocational training.

Trained personnel are needed by virtually all Alabama correctional agencies, which seek college graduates interested in helping others. Conditions have been improved as a shift toward community-based corrections reduces the number of prisoners placed in isolated facilities. The high costs of recidivism serve as a further incentive to prison reform, showing the need to pursue rehabilitative efforts.

■ *Military and Emergency Powers.* Members of the Alabama National Guard are perhaps most conspicuous by their distinctive vehicle license tags, one of which is issued free to each member. The state Military Department, headed by the adjutant general who serves at the pleasure of the governor, is responsible for maintaining 140 armories around the state and conducting training. The Alabama Army National Guard numbers approximately 19,000 and the Air Guard 3,000, giving the state one of the largest forces in the nation (units were sent to the Persian Gulf in 1991) and the largest per capita force based on population.

Guard personnel enlist for a six-year term, having a duty obligation of certain weekends for training. Unless the guard is federalized (called into national service) operational costs are paid by the state, with equipment (weapons, vehicles, aircraft) supplied by the United States government. Spending by the guard is important to the economic and political life of many Alabama communities. During natural disasters or civil

Figure 7.9 Alabama National Guard engineers install a temporary bridge for residents after a flood. (Courtesy photo provided by Headquarters, Alabama National Guard)

disorders such as riots, the civil authority may be unable to respond adequately. Local officials may request assistance, or the governor may order in the guard to conduct rescue operations or maintain order. Thus in a typical year, the guard may be activated after tornadoes and floods, maintain order during a strike, haul water during local supply shortages, search for missing persons, or assist law enforcement agencies.

In times of emergency, local officials may impose a curfew and close liquor outlets or stores selling deadly weapons. If necessary, the governor may declare martial law, superseding local authority. Or, after natural disasters, the governor may ask the president to proclaim a certain region to be a disaster area, making it eligible for federal assistance and low-cost loans to rebuild.

Administrative Organization and Control

The problems of coordinating government operations become apparent when we consider that the State of Alabama employs over 38,000 persons, not only in Montgomery, but spread across the state. By custom, the governor may designate "cabinet" members as advisers, who usually carry the title of director of key state agencies.

Alabama's Government Human Resource Management System provides computerized personnel and payroll records for all state agencies. Government jobs can be filled either through patronage (appointment by elected officials) or through some type of merit selection process resulting in a career force that remains despite political changes. Currently, over 32,000 employees are "classified" under the state merit system, meaning they are appointed, promoted, and have job security under its rules. There are 2,000 government positions that are specifically exempt, 3,600 are unskilled and often temporary jobs, and another 180 are "unclassified," meaning they are under civil service pay scales and leave policies, but serve at the pleasure of their appointers. The motto of earlier party politics was "To the victor belong the spoils," but the requirement that programs with any federal funds must hire employees under an objective merit process obliged state and local governments to create civil service systems. Jobs are classified according to the skills required and prevailing wages ("equal pay for equal work"); vacancies are publicly announced, followed by written or oral examinations to demonstrate educational qualifications or practical tests to measure skills and experience; the result is ranking of applicants by scores into an "eligible" hiring register from which, under Alabama law, the appointment must be made from the top three. Examinations may be open to all who wish to compete or closed in order to promote subordinates from within. After serving a probationary period (six months in Alabama), a new employee with a satisfactory rating can only be dismissed for grave cause through a hearing process conducted by retired state judges. State employees can appeal disciplinary actions to the state Personnel Board, consisting of two members appointed by the governor, one each appointed by the lieuten-

Announcement Date __4/28/93__

State of Alabama
Personnel Department
64 North Union Street
Montgomery, AL 36130-2301

(BIOLOGIST I - ECOLOGY OPTION - 70721-048)
($21,666 - $32,786)

<u>Training and Experience Exam and Who May Apply</u>
An <u>open-competitive</u> and a <u>promotional</u> register will be established by an evaluation of the extent and quality of the applicants' training and experience as shown on their application. A <u>promotional</u> register will be established for present State employees who have permanent status as a <u>Biologist Aide I, II, or III</u>, and who meet the minimum qualifications. For the <u>promotional</u> register, the evaluation of applications will constitute 90% of the final grade and an average of service ratings for the last three years will constitute the remaining 10%. On the <u>open-competitive</u> register, the evaluation of training and experience will comprise 100% of the final grade.

<u>Purpose of Exam</u>
To establish an eligible register from which to fill __1__ vacancy in <u>Montgomery with the Highway Department</u> and any future vacancy in State service.

<u>Required Minimum Qualifications</u>
B. S. Degree in Biology, Biological Resources, or Ecology/Environmental Science/Management. (Horticulture degrees will not be accepted).

<u>Kind of Work</u>
This is scientific research work in the study, development, and improvement of State fish, wildlife, and plant resources. Employees may identify potential wetland or hazardous waste sites; recommend wetland relocation; recommend handling of hazardous waste; perform taxonomic research and population studies; analyze water samples; identify plant/animal species; compose reports and journal articles; maintain research equipment; schedule auxiliary research teams; and other related duties.
NOTE
Extensive travel with some overnight travel. Ability to work outdoors in all weather conditions.

<u>How to Apply for Current Exams</u>
Use an official Application for Examination form which may be obtained from this office or from any local Alabama Employment Service Office. Applications must be returned to the State Personnel Department at the above address by the close of business on __May 17, 1993__. Applications received after this date will be REJECTED and applicants' names will be placed on the mailing list to be notified when this class is again open for application. The State Personnel Department cannot be responsible for delays in the receipt of applications caused by the mail service. Photocopied and facsimile (fax# 205-240-3171) applications will be accepted.

Note:
Individuals currently on the register <u>and</u> who meet the criteria listed under the sections "Required Minimum Qualifications" and "Who May Apply", must reapply to remain eligible for employment from the new register.

Note:
Veteran's credits are NOT allowed on promotional examinations.

The State of Alabama is an equal opportunity employer.

Figure 7.10 Position announcements describe the job, responsibilities, and qualifications.

ant governor and the speaker of the house, and the fifth elected by merit system employees, all for six-year staggered terms.

Bureaucracy: People Administering Programs

Public administration as implementation of policy consists of organization (structure) and management (action). It seeks

GENERAL INFORMATION
ALABAMA MERIT SYSTEM EXAMINATIONS

WHO MAY APPLY FOR MERIT SYSTEM POSITIONS?
(Anyone may apply for any number of examinations, but a separate application form must be submitted for each one.)

Residence--Residence in Alabama is not generally required, but preference may be shown to legal residents of this State.

Age--Unless specific minimum or maximum age limits are stated in the announcement, any qualified person under the statutory retirement age of 70 may apply.

Training and Experience--An applicant must fulfill requirements that are established by the employing departments and the Personnel Board before he can be admitted to an examination.

Education--Most state jobs require high school graduation or the equivalent. Satisfactory "GED" test results from the Armed Forces or from schools authorized by the State Superintendent of Education are acceptable. Some jobs require college graduation. Others require elementary or junior high school education.

HOW DOES A PERSON QUALIFY?
Each person must meet the requirements listed in the QUALIFICATIONS part of the examination announcement. This should be described as completely as possible on the application and submitted to the State Personnel Department; Montgomery, Alabama. Be sure to fill in all information called for. Incomplete or unsigned applications or applications filled out in pencil will be returned. All statements on the application are subject to verification.

Everyone who applies will be notified of his acceptance or rejection. Applicants who meet the entrance requirements will be individually notified where and when to report for written examinations.

WHAT DOES THE EXAMINATION CONSIST OF?
The examination may consist of a written test, a performance test, an evaluation of training and experience, an oral examination, or a combination of these.

WHO IS PUT ON THE ELIGIBLE LIST?
The minimum grade required for a place on the eligible list is 70. (The final grade is made up of grades on all parts of the examination combined on the basis of the announced weights.) A register of these eligibles is made starting with the person with the highest grade. Failure in any part of the examination may disqualify the candidate from further consideration.

Candidates are notified of their grades as soon as possible after all parts of the examination have been graded. Each candidate who qualifies is notified of his grade and standing on the eligible list.

HOW ARE APPOINTMENTS MADE?
Appointments are made by the various State department heads and not by the Personnel Department. When a vacancy occurs in any department, the Personnel Department submits the three highest ranking names on the eligible list for the department head to choose from. The two remaining names go back on the eligible list which stays in effect until a new examination is given and a new list established.

Appointments are ordinarily made at the minimum salary of the salary range for the class. Increases in salary are given on the basis of merit. There are no automatic salary increases or promotions because of length of service.

WHAT IS THE PROBATIONARY PERIOD?
All appointments to permanent positions are made for a probationary period of not less than six months. During this period the work and conduct of the employee are systematically checked and reported on by his supervisor to determine whether he merits permanent appointment to the position.

Figure 7.10 (continued)

to answer such questions as: When operations expand, how are coordination and control maintained? How can decisions be made in the public interest? How can administrative sprawl with a proliferation of governmental segments be avoided?

Some basic administrative concepts are: *span of control,* or the number of persons or operations which can be supervised

Form 3 — Revised 1991

APPLICATION FOR EXAMINATION
RETURN TO
STATE PERSONNEL DEPARTMENT
MONTGOMERY, ALABAMA 36130

AN EQUAL OPPORTUNITY EMPLOYER

ENTER SOCIAL SECURITY NUMBER HERE

GENERAL INSTRUCTIONS:

A separate application is required for each job. Do not write in shaded areas. Type or print clearly in dark ink and sign. Complete all parts of the application form. Applications not properly completed will be returned.

Full Name _____
First   Middle   Last

Title of Examination for Which you are Applying:

Address _____
House or Apartment No.   Street

Option (if Applicable)

City   State   County   Zip Code

Telephone Number: Home _____ Work _____

Date of Birth: Mo Day Year

The following information is required for Governmental reporting or recordkeeping purposes only:

Sex (Check One)
1 | | Male
2 | | Female

Race (Check One)
1 | | White   2 | | Black   3 | | Hispanic   4 | | Asian or Pacific Islander
5 | | American Indian or Alaskan Native   6 | | Other

EDUCATION High School Graduate or GED? | | Yes | | No   If No, circle highest grade completed
1 2 3 4 5 6
7 8 9 10 11 12

Name and location of high school attended	FROM (Mo) (Yr)	TO (Mo) (Yr)	Did you Graduate?	Date of Graduation	Area of Study

Name and location of Colleges and Universities Attended	FROM (Mo) (Yr)	TO (Mo) (Yr)	Did you Graduate?	Fields of Study Major(s) Minor(s)	Degree and Date

Name and location of business, correspondence or vocational school attended

If you attended college, but did not graduate, show credit received
Sem. hrs _____ Qtr hrs _____

List professional certificate or license if applicable _____

COMPLETE THIS SECTION IF YOU ARE CLAIMING VETERAN'S PREFERENCE

If you claim Veteran's Preference, check the type below. Attach copies **(which will not be returned)** of the required documents to your application to support your claim

1 | | Veteran (5 points) — Requires DD214 or document showing dates of service and type of discharge. **If this has been submitted previously & is on file with this office, you may disregard this requirement.**

2 | | Disabled Veteran (10 points) — Requires DD214 or other document as above & letter of disability from V.A. dated within last 6 months. **V.A. letter must be kept updated until register is established or you lose the extra 5 points.**

3 | | Veteran's widow (10 points) — Requires DD214 or other document as above & marriage & death certificates. Cannot be claimed if widow remarries

4 | | Disabled Veteran's wife (10 points) — Requires DD214 or other document as above & V.A. letter of disability dated within last 6 months. Cannot be claimed unless still married to disabled veteran

5 | | Permanently Disabled Veteran (10 points) — Requires DD214 or other document as above indicating veteran is permanently disabled, or DD214 or other document & V.A. letter indicating permanent disability

COMPLETE THIS SECTION IN ORDER TO BE SCHEDULED FOR WRITTEN EXAMS

Written exams will be given periodically in any of the places listed below for which a sufficient number of applicants express preference. Indicate by number your 1st, 2nd and 3rd choices

01 | | Alexander City   07 | | Linden
02 | | Andalusia   08 | | Mobile
03 | | Birmingham   09 | | Montgomery
04 | | Decatur   10 | | Selma
05 | | Dothan   11 | | Sheffield
06 | | Anniston   12 | | Tuscaloosa

If you qualify, you will receive a notice showing the place and time you are to report for the exam

NOTICE: The processing of an application or admission to a test does not preclude the subsequent removal of an applicant's name from an eligible register for any disqualifying reason.

CERTIFICATE (Must be signed in ink by applicant):

I certify that all statements on or attached to this application are true and correct to the best of my knowledge. I understand that any false statements may cause me to be refused the opportunity of examination, to be removed from an eligible register, or terminated from employment. I further authorize the release of all relevant prior employment, military service and criminal records. If employed I agree, consistent with applicable laws, to receive compensatory time off in lieu of overtime compensation for any overtime hours worked.

Signed _____ Date _____

Figure 7.11 Application for Alabama civil service examination.

REFERENCES

List three reliable persons, not relatives or present employer, who know you well enough to give information about you

Name	Address and Phone Number	Employer

I. If you need special testing aids and/or services in order to accommodate a disability or health problem, (e.g., interpreters or reading devices), please indicate these requirements in the space below

II. Have you ever been involuntarily terminated, discharged, forced or asked to resign, from any job or employment? (   ) Yes (   ) No
If you answered **Yes** to the above question, attach an explanation on a separate sheet noting any mitigating or extenuating circumstances.

NOTE: A CRIMINAL CONVICTION WILL NOT NECESSARILY BE A BAR TO CONSIDERATION FOR EMPLOYMENT, EXCEPT THAT A FELONY CONVICTION WILL BAR EMPLOYMENT IN A LAW ENFORCEMENT JOB. THE DISCLOSURE OF A MISDEMEANOR CONVICTION WILL NOT AUTOMATICALLY RESULT IN DISQUALIFICATION. CRIMINAL HISTORIES WILL BE SUBMITTED TO THE NATIONAL CRIME INFORMATION CENTER (NCIC) FOR VERIFICATION. FAILURE TO DISCLOSE A CONVICTION MAY BE CONSIDERED AS GROUNDS FOR DISQUALIFICATION. FOR THESE REASONS, APPLICANTS SHOULD BE CAREFUL TO DISCLOSE **ALL** CRIMINAL CONVICTIONS IN THE SPACE BELOW.

III. Have you ever been convicted of a misdemeanor or felony crime? (   ) Yes (   ) No
If you answered **Yes** to the above question, list in the space below, all prior misdemeanor and felony convictions and any extenuating or mitigating circumstances regarding such convictions. If necessary, you may use a separate sheet or sheets and attach to application.

WORK HISTORY
THIS SECTION MUST BE COMPLETED REGARDLESS OF WHETHER OR NOT A RESUME' IS ATTACHED

Begin with your PRESENT or most recent employment, list in REVERSE ORDER periods of employment. **Each time you changed jobs or your title changed should be listed as a separate period.** Describe in detail your specific duties. (Attach additional sheets if needed.)

Current or Last Employer	Your Official Job Title
Address	Type of Business

Number/Title of Employees You Supervised — Equipment You Operated — Reason for Leaving

Name, Title, and Phone Number of Supervisor

Describe Your Duties in Detail

Figure 7.11 (continued)

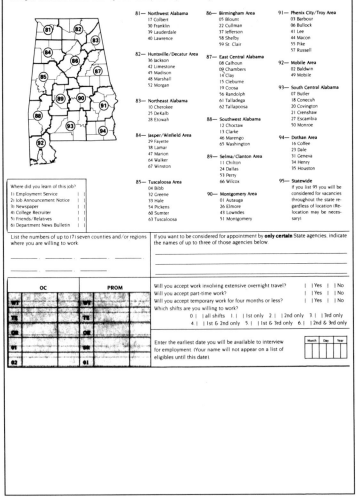

Figure 7.11 (continued)

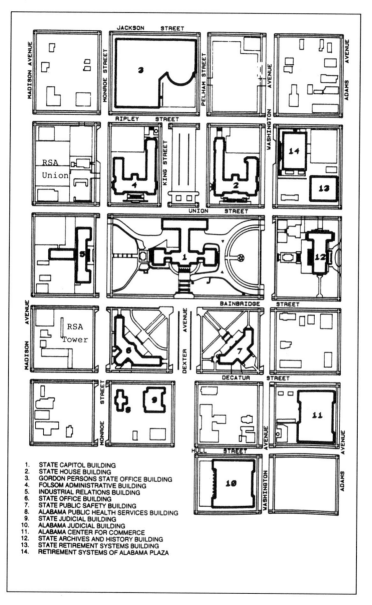

Figure 7.12 Alabama's state capitol complex. (Map courtesy of the Alabama State Telecommunications Division)

adequately in a functional area. This results in *delegation of authority* downward, decentralizing operations so that decisions can be made quickly at an appropriate level. This entails *accountability* for those decisions upward, including *feedback* to the top so that necessary corrective action can be taken. One organizational response to these goals is dividing functions into "line" (primary operations) and "staff" (supporting activities). Another approach is *total quality management* in which workers meet in cooperative groups to make decisions. *Performance budgeting* is a type of financial management that allocates resources not by line item (one fire engine, hose, etc.), but by program area (fire suppression, training, etc.), enabling comparison of results for amounts expended.

Such concepts result in "bureaucracy," a certain way of organizing institutions (hierarchy, rational division of labor, etc.), which is sometimes looked down upon. Yet how can productivity in government (citizens may politically demand ser-

Figure 7.13 The Gordon Persons State Office Building. (Photo by D. L. Martin)

vices considered necessary, but unprofitable) be achieved? Government is often forced to rely on the institutionalization of standards so that all are treated equally under the law.

Notes

1. *John Knight et al. v. State of Alabama*, 787 Fed. Supp. 1030 (1991).
2. *Alabama Coalition for Equity v. Hunt, Governor of Alabama*, Cir. Ct. for Montgomery, AL, CV-90-883-R (April 1, 1993).
3. U.S. Census Bureau, summarized in Chris Roberts and Jerry Roberts, "Not Married with Children," *Birmingham News*, March 28, 1993, p. 1, 10A.
4. The Alabama Supreme Court has held that a pardon cannot restore the eligibility to hold public office. See *Randolph County v. Thompson* 502 So. 2d 357 (Ala. 1987), and *Sumbry v. State* 562 So. 2d 224 (Ala. 1990).

For Further Reading

Each Alabama state agency is required by law to compile an annual report, which contains detailed information about its operations. The *Code of Alabama* contains the legislative mandate for each state agency.

March, Ray A. *Alabama Bound: Forty-Five Years Inside a Prison System.* University: University of Alabama Press, 1978.
Thigpen, Richard A., ed. *Alabama Government Manual.* 8th ed. Tuscaloosa: Alabama Law Institute, 1990.

EIGHT

Alabama's Judicial System

Every year Congress and our state legislatures pass thousands of new acts. It is the duty of the judiciary, federal and state, to apply these laws fairly and in accordance with the United States Constitution, the supreme law of the land. Periodically, legislative acts are codified, or arranged according to subject, together with the relevant court cases interpreting the meaning of the law. In our state, this was done in 1923, 1940, 1958, and currently in the *Code of Alabama, 1975.* Found in most law offices and many public libraries, the Code resembles an encyclopedia set, divided into forty-four titles, each dealing with a certain subject, such as motor vehicles and traffic. Alabama laws are cited by three numbers: title-chapter-section. After the Alabama legislature has adjourned, a slip-in cumulative supplement to each printed volume is issued, listing the new laws passed during that session. The Code is also available "on-line" to law offices that subscribe to the ALERT computer system and on compact disk (CD-ROM), enabling a complete electronic search rather than using the paper index. Other laws passed by local jurisdictions, such as city ordinances, may not be codified, but can be found in the minutes of the local governing bodies.

These written laws largely incorporate the English common law derived from centuries of usage, and equity, or legal procedures and doctrines. As in most states, the practice of these two legal branches is now fused. Our system is often called a "government of laws and not of men."

Alabama's Courts

Alabama has had a unified judicial system since voters passed a new judicial article (Amendment 328) to the state constitution in December 1973. Besides these constitutional revisions, the Alabama State Bar Association, which is composed of the more than 7,300 lawyers licensed to practice in the state, has sought to improve the machinery for justice. Since the state has had two law schools approved by the American Bar Association (the University of Alabama School of Law and the Cumberland School of Law at Samford University), all persons wishing to practice law must pass an examination administered by the state bar. About 75% of the candidates pass the first time they take it (five attempts are allowed). The state bar also requires practicing attorneys to attend continuing legal education programs. In cases of criminal or unethical behavior, the state bar can recommend to the Alabama Supreme Court that an attorney be disbarred or suspended from practice.

Alabama, like most states, has a hierarchy of courts, consisting of a supreme court, two intermediate appellate courts, trial courts of general jurisdiction, and courts of limited jurisdiction. Judicial power can also be exercised by the state senate, sitting as a court of impeachment, to try state executive officials for their conduct in office. These state courts are concerned with enforcing the Code of Alabama and hearing cases between citizens. The jurisdiction of each of these courts is described below.

■ *The Alabama Supreme Court* is the state's "court of last resort." Only if it can be shown that there is a "substantial federal question," usually involving a constitutional issue, can its decisions be appealed to the United States Supreme Court (which hears less than 200 cases annually from across the country).

The Alabama Supreme Court sits in Montgomery[1] and has statewide jurisdiction. It has original jurisdiction in answering "certified questions" of state law requested by a court of the United States, issues remedial writs (or orders) necessary to give it general supervision and control of other Alabama courts, and has duties in certain matters assigned to it by the state constitution. These include giving legal opinions on important constitutional questions upon written request of the governor or by resolution of either house of the legislature, which is a rather unusual practice, since most courts decide only specific cases or controversies rather than issuing advisory opinions.

The work of the Alabama Supreme Court is chiefly appellate: the law may provide a "direct appeal" of a decision by a trial court, and the supreme court has discretion to issue a "writ of certiorari" to review any case (usually at the appeal of the losing party). It has exclusive jurisdiction in civil suits (between private parties) where the amount involved exceeds $50,000, and it reviews regulatory decisions appealed from the Alabama Public Service Commission.

The Alabama Supreme Court sits together (*en banc*) to consider petitions for certiorari in death penalty cases, utility-rate cases, decisions declaring a legislative act to be unconstitutional or overruling a prior decision of the courts, and advisory opinions requested by the governor or the legislature. To expedite the rest of the more than 2,000 new filings each year, the court divides itself into two divisions of four associate justices, with the chief justice sitting on both panels. If all five members in a division agree, then this is a majority opinion, but if not, the case is considered by all nine members of the court.

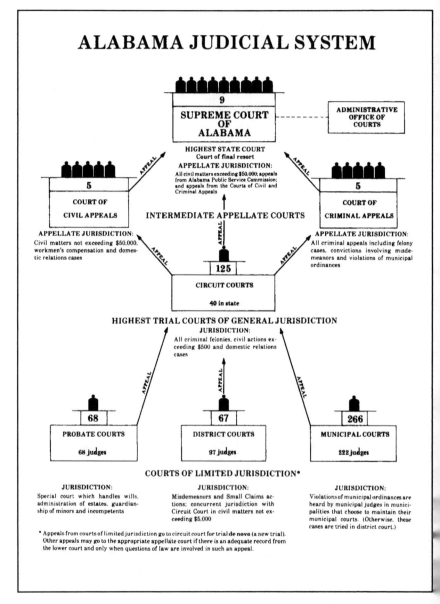

Figure 8.1 Alabama judicial system. (Courtesy of the Administrative Office of Courts, State of Alabama)

Table 8.1
The Alabama Supreme Court

Workload		From	
Direct Appeals	43%	Ala. Circuit Courts	54%
Criminal Petitions for		Ala. Court of Criminal	
Certiorari	33%	Appeals	37%
Civil Petitions for		Ala. Court of Civil Appeals	8%
Certiorari	7%	Other (Fed. court, lawyer	
Certified Questions,		disciplinary actions, etc.)	1%
writs, misc.	17%		
	100%		100%

How cases were decided

Affirmed	27%
Affirmed in part/Reversed in part	4%
Reversed and remanded	11%
Reversed and rendered	less than 1%
Remanded	less than 1%
Petition/Writ denied	47%
Petition/Writ quashed	6%
Petition/Writ granted	2%
Other	1%
	100%

Reasons for reversal given in cases

Case law construction	28%
Sufficiency of evidence	23%
Admission or exclusion of evidence	5%
Interpretation of statute or rule	13%
Constitutional interpretation	3%
Statute of limitations (time expired for a case)	2%
Jurisdiction (lacking)	2%
Jury instruction (by judge)	2%
Inconsistent judgments	2%
Other reasons or not available	20%
	100%

Source: *Alabama Judicial System 1992 Annual Report.* Workload: FY 1992 dispositions, p. 15; Court of origin, p. 17; Cases decided, p. 16; Reason for reversal, p. 17.

The Alabama Supreme Court consists of a chief justice (currently paid $108,125) and eight associate justices (paid $107,125), with the number set by the legislature and the salaries set by a judicial compensation commission subject to legislative approval. All state judges in Alabama are elected for six-year terms (with no limit) on a partisan ticket. The chief justice and three associate justices were chosen in 1994, three in 1992, and two in 1990. In 1974 the first woman and in 1980 the first African American became Alabama Supreme Court justices.

The supreme court has general supervisory authority and responsibility over the other state courts and the attorneys who practice in them. It establishes the rules of practice and uniform procedures. Alabama judges (except county probate judges) must be licensed attorneys, but no judge can engage in law practice while holding full-time office. The chief justice has the authority to assign state judges as necessary to improve the efficiency and effectiveness of the courts. (Those called—even from retirement—are termed "supernumerary" [extra] judges.) The Administrative Office of Courts, operating under the chief justice, assists in case management, budgeting, records and "one-step" juror summoning, education, and statistical evaluation. With ever-increasing litigation, the state's three appellate courts have adopted the goal of releasing an opinion within 280 days after filing of a direct appeal. A new $33 million State Judicial Building on Dexter Avenue near the Capitol was completed in late 1993, centralizing the three appellate courts and the Administrative Office of Courts (level 2). Near the entrance to the lobby's massive rotunda are the clerks' offices for the courts of civil and criminal appeals and the state law library (levels 3 and 4). The civil and criminal appeals court judges' offices, their staffs, a courtroom, and a conference room are on level 5. The Alabama Supreme Courtroom is on level 6, with a visitors' balcony on level 7 and the offices of the clerk and the reporter of decisions.

There are two intermediate appellate courts in Alabama that hear civil and criminal appeals from the trial circuit court. There are five judges on each court, who must have the same qualifications as supreme court justices. Their salaries, set by the judicial compensation commission, are currently $106,125 per year, except that the two presiding judges receive $500 more.

■ *The Alabama Court of Civil Appeals* has statewide jurisdiction over all civil appeals where the case does not involve more than $50,000 and makes final determinations in appeals from state administrative agencies (except the Public Service Commission), for workers' compensation, and for juvenile and domestic relations cases (Table 8.2). The five judges of the court of civil appeals are partisanly elected by the people of the state for six-year terms (one judge every even year, until the 1993 legislature added two judges to the court), and the judge who has served longest on the court presides.

Table 8.2
Alabama Court of Civil Appeals

Types of Litigation with Opinions		Decisions	
Administrative agencies	6%	Affirmed	64%
Divorce	19%	Reversed	22%
Child Custody, Adoption	18%	Affirmed in part	
Juvenile	13%	Reversed in part	7%
Damages, contracts, etc.	14%	Dismissed/other	7%
Workers' compensation	15%		100%
Teacher tenure	3%	Less than 1% argued orally	
Other cases	12%	before the court: 99% submitted	
	100%	in written briefs by attorneys.	

Source: *Alabama Judicial System 1992 Annual Report*, pp. 22–23.

■ *The Court of Criminal Appeals* has statewide jurisdiction, handling some 2,000 cases per year. It has exclusive jurisdiction of criminal appeals: final judgment of all misdemeanors (including violations of municipal ordinances), but decisions on felonies may be reviewed by the supreme court on writ of certiorari. Death penalty cases are automatically appealed to the state's highest court. It receives many petitions (Table 8.3), since it can grant "extraordinary writs" such as *habeas corpus*, which is used by a person to obtain release from unlawful imprisonment, or *mandamus*, where the court orders something to be done.

There are five judges on the court of criminal appeals, and they may sit in panels of three to hear the caseload, but if so, all three judges (a majority of the court) must concur in the verdict. The judges are partisanly elected by the voters of the state for six-year terms, two being chosen in 1990 and three in 1994.

Alabama's three appellate courts review the actions or decisions of the trial courts on questions of law or allegations of procedural error. Alabama's trial courts are of four types: probate courts, municipal courts, district courts, and circuit courts. A jury trial is available only in circuit court; cases in the others are heard by the judge alone.

Table 8.3
Alabama Court of Criminal Appeals

Disposition of cases:		Petitions:	
Affirmed the trial court	69%	Denied	93%
Reversed and remanded	7%	Granted	7%
Reversed and rendered	1%	Two thirds of the appellants	
Dismissed	23%	were indigent.	
	100%		

Source: *Alabama Judicial System 1992 Annual Report*, p. 21.

■ *A Probate Court* is funded by each of Alabama's sixty-seven counties (Birmingham and Bessemer in Jefferson County). Its jurisdiction is limited to the probate of wills, sale of property and settlement of estates by executors, administering estates of people who die without making a will (half of all Americans); guardianships over the insane, the incompetent, or minors; legal change of name; and adoption proceedings (unless heard in juvenile court). Other important functions are recording sales of property within the county, subdividing land, and indexing deeds and mortgages that are used to show clear title to buyers and sellers of real estate.

The probate judge has many duties, often participating in general county government by chairing the county commission. The probate judge is the only Alabama judge not required to be a licensed attorney, being partisanly elected for a six-year term by the county's voters. There is no limit on succession, and many have served for years. A·chief clerk is appointed who may perform the probate judge's duties in matters in which there is no contest. Most of Alabama's probate judges have been shifted to a salary system whereby the fees they collect go to the county treasury, instead of to the judge personally (still done in a few small rural counties). By legislative act, all salaried probate judges receive at least $52,500 annually, or $55,000 minimum if they preside over the county commission.

■ *A Municipal Court* can be established by each Alabama city that wants one, and about 270 have decided the revenue from fines collected exceeds the costs. They try infractions of municipal ordinances, which are punishable by up to six months' imprisonment (up to two years' probation) and/or fines up to $500, and they try violations of state law if the state misdemeanor has been made a municipal offense. Smaller Alabama towns not wanting a municipal court are served by the district court, which is required to hold sessions in each municipality of over 1,000 population.

Municipal court judges are required to be licensed attorneys and are appointed by majority vote of the city council for four-year terms if full-time, and two-year terms if part-time (an attorney may serve as municipal judge for several nearby towns). Salaries and filling of vacancies are decided by the municipal governing body.

■ *The District Court,* in each Alabama county, is the state trial court of limited jurisdiction, hearing cases without a jury. This being a court of record, the judge conducts preliminary hearings in criminal cases and adjudicates most prosecutions for misdemeanor offenses, local ordinance and traffic violations where a municipality does not have its own court. It has jurisdiction along with the circuit court to hear juvenile cases and

Figure 8.2 Municipal and district courts in Alabama do not have juries. (Courtesy of the Administrative Office of Courts, State of Alabama. Used by permission)

to receive guilty pleas in felony cases not punishable by death. It also shares concurrent jurisdiction with the circuit court in trying civil suits up to $5,000. Civil actions involving less than $1,500 (excluding interest and costs) are heard by the district court's small claims division, where citizens may present their own cases without an attorney. A free booklet explaining how to file a small claims case is available in the court clerk's office in each county.

The district court holds sessions at the county courthouse and in each town of over 1,000 population that does not have a municipal court. Depending on the caseload, one full-time judge or more may be partisanly elected for six-year terms without limit. Each must be a licensed attorney who has resided in the district for one year prior to the election and continues to live there while in office. Their salaries, set by the judicial compensation commission, are currently $71,500 per year, attracting local attorneys to run for the office.

Juvenile jurisdiction (for those under eighteen years old) is exercised by either the district court or the circuit court. Where there is only one district court judge, he or she will hear juvenile matters; otherwise the presiding (senior) circuit court judge will designate a district or circuit judge (the latter is termed a family court).

Juvenile court proceedings involve neglected or abused children, and cases in which a minor is charged with being delinquent or in need of supervision, or must be committed as being retarded or mentally ill. Cases may involve adults charged with contributing to the problem, termination of parental rights, paternity proceedings, or desertion and nonsupport. Juvenile court proceedings are confidential, but under Alabama law juveniles fourteen or older charged with serious crimes can be tried as adults in regular court.

■ *The Circuit Courts* are Alabama's courts of general jurisdiction, where jury trials occur in 4% of the criminal and 2% of the civil cases, so most are heard by the judge alone. They have original jurisdiction in domestic relations actions and civil suits where the amount in controversy exceeds $5,000, and they exercise concurrent jurisdiction with the district courts in civil controversies over $1,500 and in juvenile cases. All criminal prosecutions for all felony offenses are tried in circuit court, as well as cases appealed from municipal or district court.[2] Appeals to the circuit court may be heard with or without a jury, in a *de novo* (new) trial, all over again. Circuit courts have general supervisory authority over district, municipal, and probate courts.

The state is divided into forty circuits of one to five counties, with the court holding session in each. There are 125 circuit judges, with each circuit having one to twenty-four judges, depending on the caseload. (In circuits with multiple

Figure 8.3 The court (clockwise from left): The judge, witness, bailiff, jury, attorney addressing the bench, opposing counsel, court reporter. (Courtesy of the Administrative Office of Courts, State of Alabama. Used by permission)

Table 8.4
Alabama's Trial Courts: Record Caseloads

District Courts		Circuit Courts	
573,098 filings:		175,465 filings:	
Traffic cases	39%	Felony crimes	23%
Other Criminal	26%	Other Criminal	9%
Civil suits	6%	Civil suits	25%
Small claims	21%	Domestic relations	27%
Juvenile cases	4%	Juvenile cases	10%
Child support	4%	Child support	6%
	100%		100%

Source: *Alabama Judicial System 1992 Annual Report*, pp. 26, 30.

judges, a presiding judge is chosen—usually according to seniority—who is responsible for circuit management, although
each judge runs his or her own courtroom.) Circuit judges
must be licensed attorneys who have lived in the circuit for
one year prior to election and remain residents during their
term. They are partisanly elected by the voters of the circuit
for six-year terms, and most are routinely reelected (vacancies
are filled by appointment by the governor until the next general election). The state minimum salary for circuit judges is
currently $72,500 set by the judicial compensation commis-
sion, and they may also receive a county supplement of up to
40% of the state pay at the option of the county or counties
served.

There is an elected clerk of the circuit court in each county
(plus the Bessemer division in Jefferson County), who is responsible for court administration. The clerk must be a registered voter of the county, is partisanly elected for a six-year
term, and is currently paid $45,660. In some counties, a con-
stable can be elected from each precinct (beat) to serve court
papers for a fee, but the legislature is considering abolishing
this office.

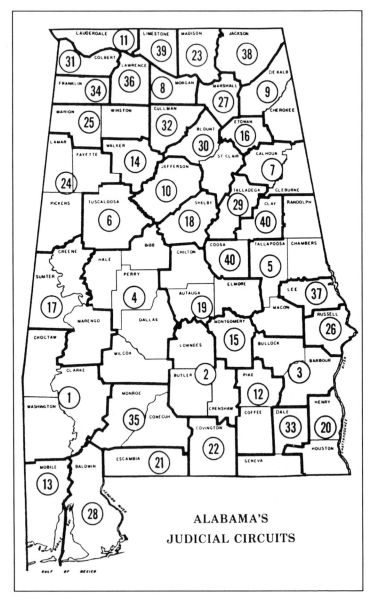

Figure 8.4 Alabama's judicial circuits. (Map courtesy of the Administrative Office of Courts. Used by permission)

The Judicial Process

The United States Constitution and our state constitutions guarantee "due process" in judicial proceedings. What are these procedures? Cases in the courts divide into two broad categories: civil suits between two parties, and criminal justice, where the government is prosecuting an individual for an alleged offense.

Civil suits are private litigation between individuals, such as *Smith v. Jones*, where Smith, the plaintiff, is suing Jones, the defendant. The normal civil procedure would be as follows: Smith would file a complaint in court alleging the wrong done to him by Jones. Served with the complaint and a summons to appear in court, Jones would have thirty days (fourteen days in district or small claims court) to file an answer. If the defendant does not respond, the court may still issue a default judgment against him. On the basis of the answer, the court might decide there is an insufficient case, or dismiss the complaint for lack of evidence. If no settlement is reached, however, the case will be put on the docket, or court calendar, for trial.

Attorneys for each party prepare their cases through discovery of all the pertinent elements through interrogatories (written questions answered under oath by the other side) and depositions (sworn statements by witnesses). To shorten trial time by focusing the contested issues, the judge may call a pretrial conference with the attorneys who stipulate the undisputed facts. Courtroom dramas featuring surprise disclosures are largely fictional. If no out-of-court settlement occurs, on the trial date the parties will appear in court and present their cases (the defendant may have filed a counterclaim or cross-claim against the original plaintiff). There is more discretion on the part of the judge in civil litigation, for often no jury is used since the parties are responsible for the court costs. The government is providing the courts as a service for private conflict resolution. The judgment of the court

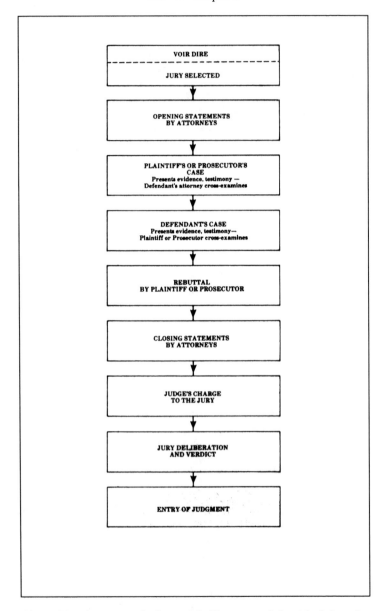

Figure 8.5 Anatomy of a jury trial. (Courtesy of the Administrative Office of Courts, State of Alabama)

may be appealed in certain circumstances, depending on the amount involved.

Criminal justice is the trial by the state of persons accused of breaking the law. The government prosecutes the accused on behalf of the people, and such a case would be styled *State of Alabama v. Jones*. There are three categories of criminal offenses under the laws of Alabama: *violations*, which carry a jail term of less than thirty days (such as public intoxication); *misdemeanors*, or minor crimes, carrying not more than a year's imprisonment (usually in city or county jails); and *felonies*, which carry a sentence of over a year, usually served in the state penitentiary (capital crimes are felonies with a possible death penalty).

The government employs attorneys to prosecute criminal cases on behalf of the people. This includes not only the state attorney general's office but also regional public prosecutors, called district attorneys in Alabama. For each of the forty judicial circuits, there is elected for a six-year term a full-time district attorney to prosecute the criminal cases in that circuit, and other circuits, if the state attorney general requests it. The "DA" is paid $71,500 per year ($1,000 less than the circuit judge) and may have assistants. Prosecutions in municipal courts for breaking city laws are among the duties of the city attorney.

Most crimes are not committed in front of law enforcement officers, where the result would be a direct arrest. Hence criminal charges are usually brought upon a complaint signed by a citizen (victim), police officer, or prosecutor acting upon probable cause that an illegal act was committed.

When a person is placed under arrest or detained for questioning, the "Miranda warning"[3] is given: (1) the individual has the right to remain silent, (2) anything said can and will be used in court, (3) the individual has the right to an attorney before and during questioning, and (4) if the suspect cannot afford an attorney, one will be appointed before any question-

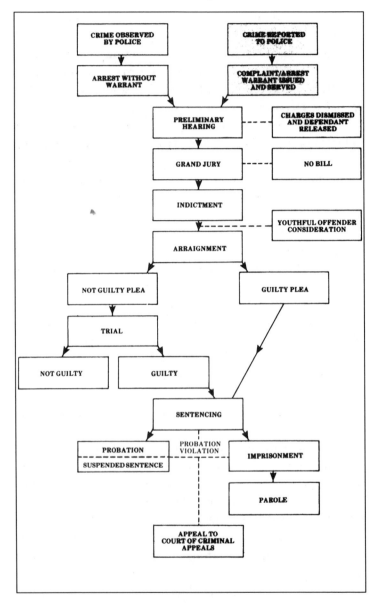

Figure 8.6 State felony case process. (Courtesy of the Administrative Office of Courts, State of Alabama)

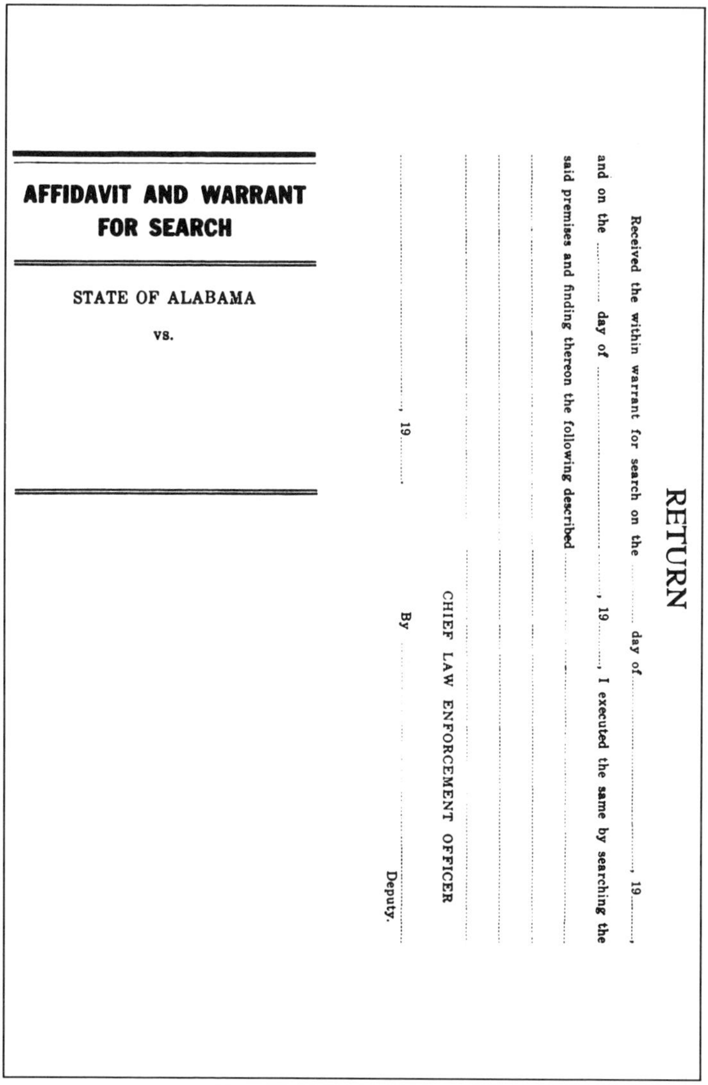

**AFFIDAVIT AND WARRANT
FOR SEARCH**

STATE OF ALABAMA

vs.

RETURN

Received the within warrant for search on the .... day of ...., 19......, I executed the same by searching the

and on the .... day of ...., 19......

said premises and finding thereon the following described

.... 19 ....

By ....
Deputy.

CHIEF LAW ENFORCEMENT OFFICER

Figure 8.7 An actual search warrant. On the first page the police officer swears there is probable cause for a search. The second page is served by the law enforcement officers. The third page is returned to the court, describing what was seized. Names have been deleted. (Courtesy of the Auburn City Attorney's Office)

State of Alabama

County of ....

Before me .... (Name and Title of Magistrate)

personally appeared ....

who being duly sworn, deposes and says that he has probable cause to believe and does believe that ....

....

....

....

....

....

....

Sworn to and subscribed before me this the   day of   19 ....

.... (Judge)

SEARCH WARRANT

The State of Alabama, County of ....

To any Sheriff, Deputy and/or Municipal Police:

Proof by affidavit haviny been made this day before me, by ....

....

....

....

....

....

You are hereby commanded to make immediate search on the person and premises of ....

....

....

....

for the following property ....

....

and if you find the same or any part thereof, to bring it forthwith before me, at my office at ....

.... Alabama.

Dated the .... day of .... 19...........

.... (Judge)

Figure 8.7   (continued)

STATE OF ALABAMA)
LEE COUNTY : **AFFIDAVIT FOR SEARCH WARRANT**
)

CITY OF AUBURN

VS.

_____ alias
   and
_____ alias

Before me, Richard D. Lane, Recorder Judge for the City of Auburn, Lee County, Alabama, personally appeared Detective Sergeant_____ of the Auburn Police Department, who being duly sworn, deposes and says as follows:

That he has reason to believe that on the person or persons of _____ alias, and _____ alias, or on the premises being occupied by _____ alias, and _____ alias, known as apartment'_____ located on _____, in Auburn, Lee County, Alabama, that there is now being kept, hidden, or concealed certain property, namely, Cannabis Sativa, Cannabis Indica, Cannabis Americana, Marijuana, and/or other compounds or mixtures containing Marijuana and other illicit narcotic drugs, a further description of which is unknown at this time, which are contrary to the Laws of Alabama.

And the facts tending to establish the foregoing grounds for issuance of a search warrant are as follows:

The undersigned Investigator has received information from a confidential reliable informant who has furnished the undersigned with information in the past which has proved to be reliable in the field of narcotics, and has led to the arrest and conviction of at least three (3) suspects in the past one year, that the said informant has been in the aforelisted residence on several occasions and has personally seen the vegetable material known as Marijuana kept on hand in a ready supply in the said residence by the aforelisted suspects. And that within the past fourteen (14) days, the informant has made a purchase from the aforelisted suspects at the aforelisted residence a vegetable matter which was alleged to be Marijuana and turned the same over to the undersigned who took the same to the State of Alabama Toxicology Department where it was analyzed and proved to be Marijuana.

Because of the aforelisted facts, the undersigned does believe that there is now being secreted in the aforelist residence illicit narcotics drugs which are contrary to the Laws of the State of Alabama, and there is probable cause for issuance of a search warrant.

Sergeant_____, Detective Division
Auburn Police Department

Sworn to and subscribed before me this the 1st day of February, 1974.

Richard D. Lane, Recorder Judge
City of Auburn, Alabama

Figure 8.7 (continued)

STATE OF ALABAMA)
              :
LEE COUNTY)

CITY OF AUBURN

    VS.

             _____ *alias*
      and
           _____ *alias*

                                 AFFIDAVIT

Before me, Richard D. Lane, Recorder Judge for the City of Auburn, Lee County, Alabama, personally appeared Detective Sergeant_____ for the Auburn Police Department, who being duly sworn, deposes and says that he has probable cause to believe and does believe that there is now being kept, hidden or concealed in the residence of_____ alias, and_____ alias, said residence being apartment_____ located on_____ in Auburn, Lee County, Alabama, Cannabis Sativa, Cannabis Indica, Cannabis Americana, Marijuana, and/or other compounds or mixtures containing Marijuana, and other illicit narcotic drugs, a further description of which is unknown at this time, which are contrary to the Laws of the State of Alabama.

                                   Sergeant   **Detective Division**
                                   Auburn Police Department

    Sworn to and subscribed before me this the **1st** *day of February, 1974.*

                                    Richard D. Lane
                                  Richard D. Lane, Recorder Judge
                                  City of Auburn, Alabama

- -

                      S E A R C H   W A R R A N T

STATE OF ALABAMA)
              :
LEE COUNTY)

CITY OF AUBURN

    VS.

             _____ *alias*
      and
           _____ *alias*

TO ANY SHERIFF, DEPUTY AND/OR MUNICIPAL POLICE OFFICER:

    Proof by affidavit having been made this day before me by Detective Sergeant_____ that he does believe and has been informed of certain facts that would cause a reasonable person to believe that Cannabis Sativa, Cannabis Indica, Cannabis Americana, Marijuana, and/or other compounds or mixtures containing Marijuana, and other illicit narcotic drugs, a further description of which is unknown at this time, are being kept, hidden or concealed in the residence of_____ alias and _____ alias, said residence being_____ located on_____ Auburn, Lee County, Alabama, which are contrary to the Laws of the State of Abalama. (See attached affidavit)

    You are hereby commanded to make an immediate search of the person or persons and premises of_____ alias and_____ alias, and/or all occupants of said residence,_____ located on_____ Auburn, Lee County, Alabama, for the following property: Cannabis Sativa, Cannabis Indica, Cannabis Americana, Marijuana, and/or other compounds or mixtures containing Marijuana, and other illicit narcotic drugs contrary to the Laws of the State of Alabama, and if you find same or any part thereof, to bring them forthwith before me at my office in Auburn, Lee County, Alabama.

    Dated the **1st** *day of February, 1974.*   *Richard D. Lane*

Figure 8.7   (continued)

Return of Search Warrant

I have executed the foregoing writ by searching the said residence at_____
_____, located on_____, in Auburn, Lee County, Alabama
and found therein_____ see attached list

dated the 2nd day of February, 1974 at 8:30 AM.

Sergeant_____, Detective Division
Auburn Police Department

I, Richard D. Lane, Recorder Judge for the City of Auburn, Alabama, do hereby certify
that the contraband confiscated in the search of the building or residence described
in the foregoing writ was brought before me this the 8TH day of February, 1974, and
that I ordered the same to be held in the custody of Sgt. _____ or to be released
to the Alabama Department of Toxicology at Auburn, Alabama, to be analyzed as evidence
in this case, and the contraband and analysis reports of same be presented to the
appropriate Court when so ordered by the Court.

Richard D. Lane, Recorder Judge
City of Auburn, Alabama

DESCRIPTION OF EVIDENCE AND RETURN ON THE WARRANT:

Sgt. _____
Detective Division
Auburn Police Department

Suspects: _____

INVENTORY OF CONTRABAND

1. 3 marijuana or hashish pipes
2. 1 set of diet scales
3. 1 skull ashtray containing 23 roaches
4. 1 match box containing marijuana residue
5. 1 match box containing germinated seeds
6. 1 plastic bag with two roaches
7. 1 large plastic bag containing marijuana
8. 1 paper sack containing marijuana
9. 8-1 oz. lids of marijuana in plastic baggies
10. 2-½ oz. lids of marijuana in plastic baggies
11. 1 homemade bamboo hash pipe.

Sgt. _____ Detective
Auburn Police Department

Figure 8.7 (continued)

ing. Any waiver of these constitutional rights must be voluntarily and knowingly done; any evidence illegally obtained cannot be used in court, under the "exclusionary rule."

Booking at the jail means recording the arrest (circumstances, time, place, nature of the crime, with names of witnesses or victims), photographing and fingerprinting to verify identity, and a computer check of any prior criminal record or outstanding (current) arrest warrants. Even if criminal charges are subsequently dropped, the person may have a record from the booking.

Alabama provides two methods of inquiry for determining whether a citizen who has been criminally accused should be tried or discharged: the preliminary hearing and the indictment by a grand jury. Their purpose is not to determine guilt or innocence, but whether there is enough evidence to require the accused to stand trial for the offense charged (thus providing scrutiny of overzealous police or prosecutors).

The preliminary hearing is held before a district or circuit judge, who listens to the evidence and either releases the accused from custody or "binds over" the person to the grand jury if reasonably suspect. If the latter is the case, bail may be set by the judge to ensure appearance. A misdemeanant may be released on personal recognizance—that is, a promise to appear in court. (A traffic ticket is often a voluntary forfeiture of bail—the driver pays a certain amount so as not to have to appear in court and by not showing up is presumed guilty and fined the money paid.) Those accused of felonies must put up a substantial amount to ensure their appearance: either their own money or property, or a bond, which is a sum loaned by a bail bond firm. The Alabama Supreme Court has recommended amounts ranging by offense to guide judges in setting bail. While excessive bail cannot be demanded, the judge has the prerogative of deciding whose bond is acceptable, since bail money often has to be borrowed. If bail cannot be raised or bond obtained, then the accused must remain in detention until trial.

The grand jury inquiry is a heritage from English law. In Alabama, a group of eighteen citizens chosen from the community decide whether there is probable cause to believe a crime was committed and that the accused probably committed it. The district attorney conducts investigations, obtains any necessary search warrants from a judge, presents information, and may call witnesses to testify confidentially. After its deliberations in secret, the grand jury may decide to return indictments, or "true bills," specifying the laws violated. The accused is then placed under arrest, or if already taken into custody, moved toward arraignment.

District attorneys, in conducting cases for the state, have wide discretionary powers. They may decide to "nol-pross" (*nolle prosequi*), or not prosecute the case if by doing so the interests of justice are better served. For example, charges against a minor accomplice might be dropped in exchange for testimony, since allowing the accomplice to "turn state's evidence" may incriminate more serious offenders. Or the defendant and the defense attorney may engage in "plea bargaining" with the prosecutor, whereby the accused will plead guilty to a lesser charge (breaking and entering) rather than demand a trial on a greater one (burglary). It can be argued that plea bargaining saves the state the time and expense of proving a difficult case but guarantees conviction of the guilty. Critics contend that the seriously guilty get off with minor punishment on a lesser charge, while frightened suspects are enticed to plead guilty even though a trial could prove them not guilty. The judge does not have to accept a bargained plea and may decide to try the case.

At formal arraignment, the defendant must plead guilty or not guilty to the charges presented by the prosecutor. A plea of not guilty by reason of insanity must be made at this point, or it is waived. The criminally insane may be committed to a

Figure 8.8 Grand jury indictment.

No. _____

THE STATE OF ALABAMA
LEE COUNTY

_____ Term, 19____

CIRCUIT COURT

THE STATE
vs
_____

_____

_____

INDICTMENT

_____

_____

_____

_____ No Prosecutor

_____ Judge Presiding

WITNESSES

_____

_____

_____

_____

Grand Jury No. _____

A TRUE BILL.—

_____ Foreman Grand Jury

Filed in open Court on the _____ day of _____, 19____

in the presence of the Grand Jury.

_____ Clerk

Presented to the presiding Judge in open Court by the Foreman of the Grand Jury, in the presence of _____ other Grand Jurors, and filed by order of Court this _____ day of _____, 19____

_____ Clerk

Bail fixed at $ _____

this _____ day of _____, 19____

_____ Judge Presiding

Sec. 15-8-70. Code 1975.

Service of Copy of Indictment and List of Jurors on Defendant in Capital Case. Sec. 15-16-180. Code 1975.

THE STATE OF ALABAMA

_____ COUNTY

Circuit Court. _____ Term, 19____

To the Sheriff of said County:

I hereby certify that this is a true and complete copy of the Indictment presented to the Court by the Grand Jury of said County.

against _____

charged with _____ together with all endorsements on said Indictment, and that the trial is set for _____ 19____, and you will serve this copy of Indictment on _____

or _____ his counsel.

Witness my hand, this _____, 19____

_____, Clerk

I hereby certify that I have received above stated copy of Indictment from the Circuit Court Clerk of said County, and served same

on _____

at _____ o'clock _____ .M., _____, 19____

_____, Sheriff

_____, D.S.

INDICTMENT

THE STATE OF ALABAMA, LEE COUNTY

Circuit Court, ————————————— Term, 19————

The Grand Jury of said County charge that before the finding of this Indictment ———————————

against the peace and dignity of the State of Alabama.

District Attorney of the 37th Judicial Circuit

Sec. 15-8-150, Code 1975.

Figure 8.8 (continued)

state hospital for observation and treatment. If the defendant pleads guilty with full understanding, representation by counsel, and procedural due process, then there is no trial or appeal. The judge sets the sentence unless the law broken prescribes jury sentencing and the violator demands it.

If there is a plea of not guilty, the defendant may be on bail until tried, and defense council engaged. Under United States Supreme Court rulings, an indigent defendant accused of a serious crime must be supplied with an attorney by the state. As part of their professional responsibilities, members of the bar are assigned these duties on a rotating basis by the courts. A list of local attorneys is kept by the judges, and appointed counsels are reimbursed for serving from the "fair trial tax" of seven dollars levied as part of court costs on all cases heard in Alabama. Larger Alabama counties have salaried public defenders whose job it is to represent indigents who cannot afford their own lawyers. A full-time public defender system, like the public prosecutor offices, has been adopted in some other states.

The case is put on the court calendar (docket) and a trial date set, unless a continuance is sought by either side for fuller preparation.

To qualify as an Alabama juror, a citizen must be nineteen or older; have resided in the county for a year; read, speak, and understand English; be physically and mentally capable; and not have lost his or her civil rights through criminal conviction (unless these were subsequently restored). Prospective names are randomly selected from the computerized drivers' license list and questionnaire mailed by the Administrative Office of Courts. A summons to appear at the courthouse is an important civic responsibility if a democratic system of justice is to be maintained. Alabama has abolished all exemptions for jury duty, and an excuse is granted only if service would create undue hardship. (State law requires employers to continue full-time employee pay during jury service.)

```
┌─────────────────────────────────────────────────────────────────┐
│                      GENERAL INFORMATION                          │
│                                                                   │
│  JURY SERVICE IS AN ESSENTIAL FUNCTION IN THE ADMINISTRATION OF   │
│  JUSTICE. IT IS YOUR OPPORTUNITY TO PARTICIPATE IN THE JUDICIAL   │
│  SYSTEM.                                                          │
│                                                                   │
│  -> READ THE SUMMONS TO DETERMINE THE DATE, TIME, AND PLACE YOU   │
│     ARE TO REPORT AND OTHER INSTRUCTIONS WHICH MAY BE INCLUDED.   │
│                                                                   │
│  -> TO QUALIFY FOR JURY SERVICE, A PERSON MUST:                   │
│       - Be a United States Citizen                                │
│       - Be a resident of the county named herein for 12 months    │
│         or longer.                                                │
│       - Be at least 19 years of age                              │
│       - Read, speak, and understand the English language          │
│       - Not have lost his right to vote as a result of a felony   │
│         conviction. (A person may serve if his right to vote has  │
│         been restored.)                                           │
│                                                                   │
│  IF YOU DO NOT MEET THESE QUALIFICATIONS, CALL THE PERSON AT THE  │
│  NUMBER LISTED IN THIS SUMMONS.                                   │
│                                                                   │
│  -> IF EMPLOYED, NOTIFY YOUR EMPLOYER IMMEDIATELY UPON RECEIPT    │
│     OF THIS SUMMONS.                                              │
│                                                                   │
│  -> EXCUSE FROM JURY SERVICE IS GRANTED ONLY IN CASES OF EXTREME  │
│     INCONVENIENCE, UNDUE HARDSHIP, OR PUBLIC NECESSITY. ANY       │
│     REQUEST TO BE EXCUSED PRIOR TO THE REPORTING DATE MUST BE     │
│     DIRECTED TO THE PERSON AT THE NUMBER LISTED IN THIS SUMMONS.  │
└─────────────────────────────────────────────────────────────────┘
```

Figure 8.9 Juror qualifications.

Grand jurors are randomly drawn from the qualified juror lists by a circuit judge, while prospective petit or trial jurors are examined ("voir dire") by the judge and attorneys to determine if they will be impartial in hearing the evidence. Both sides are allowed an equal number of peremptory challenges by which they can "strike" (exclude) jurors from a case; they also may "challenge for cause" jurors who have shown bias during questioning. Alabama trial juries usually number twelve, unless both sides agree to a smaller number. (Alternates may be chosen if a major trial would be interrupted by a juror's being suddenly excused for a family emergency or illness.) Since in civil cases jury expenses are charged to the parties, they may agree to a smaller number. Jurors in Alabama receive at least ten dollars per day, and service rarely exceeds five work days. During the trial, the jurors may be "sequestered," or kept at court expense overnight to prevent their being influenced, but usually the judge will simply caution them not to discuss the case with their family or friends so that they make up their own minds.

The jury (or judge, if both sides agree to try the case without a jury) renders a verdict at the conclusion of the trial. A civil case is decided according to a "preponderance of the evidence" presented, while in a criminal case the state must prove the accused "guilty beyond a reasonable doubt." Not guilty means the defendant is acquitted and released, unless the state asks for a retrial on new charges. After weighing the guilt or innocence of the accused, the jury may be unable to agree. In the case of a "hung jury" the judge may declare a mistrial, and the prosecutor has to decide whether to try the case all over again. Under Alabama law, if the jury verdict is guilty, the jury recommends the penalty for the most serious crimes committed against persons, but the judge decides the sentence provided by law.

The judge has broad powers in sentencing, considering both aggravating factors and mitigating circumstances. The criminal may be ordered to pay restitution or services to the victim. The judge may suspend the fine or sentence upon conditions of probation under supervisors of the Alabama Board of Pardons and Paroles, although probation cannot be granted where the sentence is for ten or more years. Imprisonment may be in a county jail for less than a year, or else in the state correctional institutions listed in Chapter 7.

A criminal defendant may appeal a conviction. A successful appeal may result in release or in a new trial. Even if committed to a penal institution the prisoner may be paroled or conditionally released before the sentence expires. Probationers and parolees are supervised by the Alabama Board of Pardons and Paroles, whose caseworkers seek to rehabilitate offenders and return them to society. Former felons must petition the board for restoration of civil rights such as the right to vote, to serve on juries, and to bear firearms in the state, showing evidence of good behavior.

Appeals can be made by either side in a civil case, and sometimes both sides appeal. In a criminal case, only the defendant found guilty can appeal, since if the defendant was found innocent, trial again on the same charge would be unconstitutional double jeopardy. Under Alabama law the appellant has forty-two days from the date of civil judgment or criminal sentence to file a written brief claiming error in trial procedure or in substantive law as interpreted by the judge. (In Alabama, as in other states, a death sentence carries an automatic right of appeal to the highest court.) The responding party, the appellee, files an answering brief, and either side may request oral argument before the appellate court. Since questions of law (not fact) are at issue, appellate courts consist only of judges. They may (1) affirm the trial court's ruling, (2) modify the earlier judgment, (3) reverse the decision and remand (return) the case for further proceedings, or (4) reverse and render—that is, set aside the decision and make another instead (see Tables 8.1, 8.2, 8.3). In Alabama, the losing side has fourteen days to petition an appellate court for rehearing, until at the Alabama Supreme Court all remedies have been exhausted in the state's courts.

Alabamians and Their Courts

In the past decade, Alabama has greatly improved its court system, but several issues remain.

More suits than ever before are being filed in Alabama's courts. While criminal defendants are constitutionally entitled to speedy trials, civil cases may become backlogged. "Justice delayed is justice denied" because witnesses may become unavailable, evidence disappears, and congestion means trials are continued to later dates. The Alabama Supreme Court has adopted the following time standards: adult custody or bail set, or juvenile detention hearing, within seventy-two hours of arrest; preliminary hearings within six months; child support actions within twelve months; domestic relations cases in eighteen months; district court misdemeanors and traffic violations within six months and small claims within nine months; misdemeanors within nine months and felonies within twelve months in circuit court; and civil cases settled after filing or tried in district court within fifteen months or within thirty months in circuit court.[4] While exceeding these times does not affect legal actions, such standards enable the public to measure the judges running for reelection.

Financing Alabama's courts costs more than $85 million per year, and there is public concern over costs, particularly judicial retirement. To attract able attorneys to the bench, salaries have been raised by a five-member judicial compensation commission,[5] unless the legislature disapproves. While court fees have been raised substantially (see *Code* 12-19-2), fines and forfeitures cannot make Alabama's courts self-supporting, although less than two percent of the state budget goes to the judicial branch.

While all Alabama judges (except municipal ones) are partisanly elected for six-year terms, most initially are appointed by the Alabama governor to fill vacancies. Unlike in some states with a "merit plan," where gubernatorial choice is limited to those judicially qualified, Alabama governors have been criticized for appointing political supporters or their relatives to the bench.[6]

Since it is rare for an incumbent judge to be defeated for reelection, Alabama has successfully devised a method for removing unfit judges. The 1973 judicial article created a Judicial Inquiry Commission of seven members, consisting of one appellate judge appointed by the Supreme Court, two circuit judges appointed by the Circuit Judges Association, two attorneys appointed by the state bar, and two nonlawyer citizens appointed by the governor. It has authority to conduct confidential investigations and to receive or initiate complaints against any Alabama judge. If merited, it files a complaint with the Court of the Judiciary, consisting of five members with four-year terms: one appellate judge selected by the Supreme Court, two circuit judges selected by the Circuit Judges Association, and two attorneys selected by the state bar. This *ad hoc* court has the authority, after a public hearing, to (1) retire judges who are mentally or physically unable to perform their duties, (2) censure judges, (3) suspend judges with or without pay for failure to perform their duties, misconduct in office, or violation of a canon of judicial ethics, or (4) remove them from office. The judge may appeal to the Alabama Supreme Court, which, in the twenty years since this procedure replaced impeachment, has upheld the findings in the twenty-five cases decided.

The Alabama legislature is considering whether to limit the amount of campaign donations that attorneys can give to judicial candidates or incumbent judges. Since Alabama does not currently limit either punitive damages or the percentage that an attorney can collect from a client who wins, court reform is a continuing battle between business or medical defendants and trial lawyers, who contribute to various judicial candidates. For such reasons, some other states use an appointive merit system to fill positions on the bench.

Alabama has accomplished much in recent years in creating a uniform court system with consistent jurisdictions, rules of procedure, and continuing training of both attorneys and judges. While the courtroom is not a happy place—people are there because they feel wronged or are charged with an offense—Alabamians can feel increased confidence that justice is being done.

Notes

1. To afford the public opportunity to observe the Alabama Supreme Court, it may hear oral arguments elsewhere, usually in Mobile and at the law schools in Birmingham and Tuscaloosa.

2. Decisions by courts of limited jurisdiction can be directly appealed to the intermediate appellate courts and are only rarely allowed by law or rule.
3. Required by a famous 1966 United States Supreme Court decision: *Miranda v. Arizona*, 384 U.S. 436 (1966).
4. Order of the Alabama Supreme Court, effective October 1, 1990.
5. Appointed for four-year terms by the governor, the lieutenant governor, the speaker, and two by the state bar, members cannot hold other public or party office.
6. Alabama antinepotism statutes do not cover executive appointments to the judicial or legislative branches.

For Further Reading

Alabama appellate decisions are published in both the *Alabama Reporter* and the *Southern Reporter,* found in law libraries.
Administrative Office of Courts. *Alabama Courts Come to Order*; *Alabama Judicial System* Annual Reports; *Alabama Juror's Handbook*; *Guide to Alabama Court Procedures.*
Code of Alabama, 1975. Title 12: Courts; Title 13A: Criminal Code; Title 15: Criminal Procedure; Rules of the Alabama Supreme Court.

NINE

Alabama Local Government

Counties: Aiding the State

Virtually all American states are divided into counties, or their equivalent.[1] Alabama has sixty-seven counties, names and dates of organization of which are listed in Appendix A. The governing county commissions consist of three to nine members elected for four-year terms (except for Barbour and Bullock counties, where local acts authorize six-year terms). Their terms begin on the seventh day after their election in November. Any vacancies are usually filled by gubernatorial appointment until the next election. Commission members may be removed only by impeachment proceedings held in the circuit court of the county. State law sets a minimum salary for county commissioners at $14,600 annually ($18,600 for chairman) in the fifty-three counties where the duties are considered part-time, and at least $25,000 per year ($30,000 for chairman) in the fourteen counties where commissioners are required by law to serve full-time. Local legislation may prescribe greater amounts, so there is considerable variation in compensation.

Meetings of the county commission are still presided over by the probate judge in eighteen counties, but the trend in recent years has been for the voters to elect a countywide chairperson, or else the commissioners appoint a chair from

Figure 9.1 Alabama county seats.

among themselves, often on a rotating basis, so that all preside during part of their terms (Table 9.1). The major difference is that the probate judge cannot vote unless there is a tie vote between the commissioners, but the elected or appointed chairman votes like the other members. Due to court suits and settlements, more counties have elected their commissioners from districts to ensure minority representation (from majority African-American district[s]), and for all members to chair the commission in rotation. Chilton County uses cumulative voting, where voters receive the same number of votes as seats being elected (seven), which they can divide among any candidate(s) they want, and which has the political effect of electing, if enough voters cast all their votes for one person, a minority candidate (even if voters are geographically dispersed, where a majority African-American district cannot be drawn). Proponents of increasing the number of districts would contend that it has resulted in the district election of more African Americans and Republicans, while critics say that it results in a politics of favoring districts over consideration of the county or city as a whole.[2]

Important duties of the county commissioners include financial control through approving all appropriations, authorizing purchases, and levying a general tax for county government and any special taxes for purposes specified by the Code of Alabama. Commissioners are custodians of all county property and allocate office space to be used by the various departments. The commission is responsible for the general health and welfare of the county through providing care for the indigent, supporting medical facilities, enforcing sanitary regulations, and appointing members to many county boards responsible for human resources (welfare), public housing, and hospitals.

Counties may also operate utilities, airports, and waste disposal and recreational facilities, sometimes on a regional basis with other jurisdictions. While delivery of services may be ad-

Table 9.1
Alabama County Commissions

County	Number of commissioners	Chair elected: E appointed: A rotated: R Probate Judge	Registered voters (as of Nov. 1992 election)	
			Whites	Blacks
1. Autauga	5	Chair: A	17,301	3,816
2. Baldwin	7	Chair: R	57,281	5,826
3. Barbour	7	Chair: A	10,375	6,834
4. Bibb	5	Chair: R	6,955	1,516
5. Blount	4	Probate Judge	24,494	352
6. Bullock	4	Chair: E	2,322	4,193
7. Butler	4	Probate Judge	6,865	3,902
8. Calhoun	5	Chair: R	54,365	10,350
9. Chambers	6	Chair: A	17,233	7,461
10. Cherokee	4	Probate Judge	11,649	750
11. Chilton	7	Chair: R	19,340	2,571
12. Choctaw	4	Probate Judge	4,681	2,962
13. Clarke	5	Chair: R	10,177	6,220
14. Clay	5	Chair: R	6,607	1,208
15. Cleburne	4	Probate Judge	8,319	492
16. Coffee	7	Chair: A	19,447	3,394
17. Colbert	6	Chair: R	19,954	3,298
18. Conecuh	5	Chair: R	6,155	4,044
19. Coosa	5	Probate Judge	4,779	2,122
20. Covington	4	Chair: E	24,190	3,381
21. Crenshaw	5	Chair: A	6,573	2,036
22. Cullman	2	Chair: E	41,101	296
23. Dale	4	Probate Judge	22,007	3,525
24. Dallas	5	Chair: A	17,075	19,606
25. DeKalb	4	Chair: E	20,102	1,122
26. Elmore	5	Chair: A	24,770	5,326
27. Escambia	5	Chair: A	12,669	3,293
28. Etowah	6	Chair: R	53,618	7,724
29. Fayette	6	Chair: R	10,455	1,368
30. Franklin	4	Probate Judge	18,281	745
31. Geneva	4	Probate Judge	14,169	1,717
32. Greene	5	Chair: A	1,571	5,282
33. Hale	4	Probate Judge	total 9,768	
34. Henry	5	Probate Judge	6,080	3,199
35. Houston	4	Chair: E	27,599	5,985
36. Jackson	4	Chair: E	22,036	903
37. Jefferson	5	Chair: A	265,727	112,398
38. Lamar	4	Probate Judge	9,883	1,297
39. Lauderdale	4	Probate Judge	34,867	2,745
40. Lawrence	5	Chair: R	15,250	2,667
41. Lee	5	Probate Judge	46,712	10,182
42. Limestone	4	Chair: E	27,736	2,685
43. Lowndes	5	Chair: A	2,437	5,937

Table 9.1 Continued

County	Number of commissioners	Chair elected: E appointed: A rotated: R Probate Judge	Registered voters (as of Nov. 1992 election)	
			Whites	Blacks
44. Macon	4	Chair: E	1,943	10,581
45. Madison	6	Chair: E	115,228	23,818
46. Marengo	5	Chair: A	9,718	8,898
47. Marion	5	Chair: A	18,694	425
48. Marshall	4	Chair: E	43,406	554
49. Mobile	3	Chair: R	total 212,078	
50. Monroe	4	Probate Judge	9,177	5,174
51. Montgomery	5	Chair: A	68,349	38,161
52. Morgan	4	Chair: E	56,606	4,651
53. Perry	5	Chair: A	3,369	5,575
54. Pickens	5	Chair: R	7,919	5,049
55. Pike	6	Chair: A	12,151	5,829
56. Randolph	5	Chair: R	8,811	2,507
57. Russell	7	Chair: R	11,066	6,142
58. St. Clair	4	Chair: E	24,728	3,776
59. Shelby	9	Chair: R	65,026	4,547
60. Sumter	6	Chair: R	3,204	6,923
61. Talladega	5	Probate Judge	24,858	8,449
62. Tallapoosa	5	Chair: R	20,830	6,426
63. Tuscaloosa	4	Probate Judge	62,645	16,278
64. Walker	4	Chair: E	39,457	2,559
65. Washington	5	Probate Judge	7,070	2,286
66. Wilcox	6	Chair: A	total 10,811	
67. Winston	2	Chair: E	16,601	48
		total active	1,664,063	443,386
		"other race"	24,126	
		State total active voters:	2,364,232	

Sources: Association of County Commissions of Alabama; active voter figures as reported by counties to the state director of voter registration.

ministered by the state, counties may have to contribute to the funding of such "mandated" programs. The county commissioners designate the roads and bridges to be constructed or repaired. In thirty-eight counties, highway administration is centralized in a unit system where the commissioners act in concert and jointly make decisions that are carried out by a full-time county engineer. The state will pay 70% of this registered professional engineer's salary. In the remaining coun-

Table 9.2

Methods of Electing County Commissioners

Method	Counties with staggered terms	Counties with concurrent terms
1. Runs countywide with district residency requirement	Blount Bullock Cherokee Morgan	Covington DeKalb Franklin Jackson Marshall St. Clair Tallapoosa
2. Runs countywide with no district residency requirement	Cleburne Cullman	Chilton
3. Elected by district with residency requirement	Bibb Chambers Choctaw Clarke Dale Escambia Etowah Fayette Geneva Hale Henry Lamar Lauderdale Lee Limestone Lowndes Macon Marengo Monroe Perry Talladega Washington Wilcox	Autauga Baldwin Barbour Butler Calhoun Coffee Colbert Conecuh Coosa Crenshaw Dallas Elmore Greene Houston Jefferson Lawrence Madison Marion Mobile Montgomery Pickens Pike Randolph Russell Shelby Sumter Tuscaloosa Walker
4. Nominated by district and elected countywide	Clay Winston	

Source: Association of County Commissions of Alabama.

ties, each commissioner supervises an independent work crew and equipment operating in that district of the county. Road funds are divided among all the members of the commission, each of whom decides the work to be done and hires the work crew. Larger road- and bridge-building projects may be bidded out to private contractors.

Besides the commissioners, there are several other elective Alabama county officials: the probate judge, sheriff, coroner, members of the board of education, tax assessor, and tax collector (the latter two offices are increasingly being combined into that of revenue commissioner). Some counties elect a superintendent of education as well as a school board. Each of these separately elected officials has a mandate from the people, so that the county commissioners can only exert coordinating financial control and persuasion.

The probate judge is a central courthouse figure elected for a six-year term beginning the first Monday after the second Tuesday in January. A probate judge must be an Alabama citizen who has resided in the county for one year. State law sets a $52,500 per year minimum ($55,000 if chairman) for the sixty probate judges on salary; the remaining seven in smaller rural counties collect fees and commissions on their transactions (up to a $75,000 maximum set by the state). The probate judge issues licenses (except in a dozen counties) for marriages, driving, automobile tags, businesses, professions, and certain occupations, plus recording deeds, mortgages, certificates of incorporation, and other legal documents, upon which a fee is charged. However, if the county commission does not appropriate office expenses, the judge personally pays such help. (Licenses are issued by license commissioners in Calhoun, Clarke, Dallas, Houston, Lauderdale, Limestone, Madison, Mobile, Morgan, Russell, Shelby, and Tuscaloosa counties. They are elected by the voters or appointed by the county commission and paid the salaries shown in Table 9.3.)

As the title implies, the judge probates (validates) wills and

Table 9.3
Minimum Annual Salaries for County Tax Assessors, Tax
Collectors, Revenue Commissioners and License
Commissioners (*Code of Alabama*, 40-6A-2, as of 1993)

County population	Annual salary
Less than 25,000	$32,500
25,000 to 75,000	$37,500
75,000 to 197,000	$40,000
197,000 or more	$42,500

administers estates of those who die without wills. Related to this function is jurisdiction over guardianships, adoptions, and legal determination of insanity. The probate judge is responsible for election administration, compiling lists of the registered voters and having ballots printed. He or she serves as the county's main recordkeeper and submits numerous reports required by state law. Many probate judges have held the office for years. Probate judges may be removed from office by Judicial Inquiry Commission and Court of the Judiciary proceedings[3] (see Chapter 8), upon criminal conviction, or upon being declared insane; vacancies are filled by the governor until the next election.

The sheriff, by virtue of his law enforcement powers, has traditionally been regarded as a powerful figure in southern counties. In Alabama the term of office is four years, and (since the passage of a 1938 amendment allowing it) most have been reelected to successive terms. The sheriff is a constitutional officer in Alabama and has state sovereign immunity as a member of the executive branch. State law provides that sheriffs be paid at least $35,000 per year, and some receive more, or an expense allowance, depending upon local legislative acts. The sheriff is responsible for executing court orders and maintaining a county jail for prisoners, according to the standards set by state law. The sheriff preserves order at elections and maintains security of ballots.

The coroner investigates cases of violent or unusual death to determine the category under Alabama law: homicides, suicides, accidents, natural causes, and unknown causes. An inquest may be held to rule on the cause of death not occurring under medical care, or experts from the state Department of Forensic Sciences may be called in to determine if crime was involved. The coroner is elected to a four-year term. One survey showed that thirty-eight of the sixty-four coroners worked in the funeral business.[4] Jefferson, Montgomery, and Mobile counties have appointed qualified physicians as medical examiners, which is the nationwide trend. In another heritage from English common law, the coroner assumes the duties of sheriff when that office is vacant or the sheriff is unable to act. Coroners are paid varying salaries or expenses per case.

County tax assessors and tax collectors are elected for six-year terms. They may be paid more than the state minimum salary (Table 9.3), and only a couple of counties remain on the fee system. The tax assessor determines the fair market value of property (both real—estate—property and personal property such as vehicles or boats). That is multiplied by the following assessment ratios in Alabama to give the assessed value:

owner-occupied residential, agricultural, and forest property, or historic building	10%
private autos and trucks for personal use	15%
all property of utilities	30%
all property not otherwise classified (such as commercial vehicles)	20%

Fractional assessment reduces fluctuation in judgments of market value.

Since assessment is a matter of judgment, this office is politically sensitive, and expertise in appraising is an important qualification for candidates. When their property was assessed at market value, many Alabamians protested, leading the legislature to increase the homestead exemption and tax agricultural and forest land at its current use rather than according to the potential value of the property.

Until reassessment, many citizens are unaware that the amount of their tax bills is equal to the tax rate times the assessed value. Even if taxes are not raised, citizens may have to pay more because the assessor has reappraised their property upward as inflation raises its market value. Each Alabama county has a board of equalization that takes the assessor's figures, inspects the property, and sets assessed value, which the citizen can appeal at a hearing. The board is composed of three members who have been county residents for at least five years. (The county assessor, who is not a member, acts as secretary.) At least nine names are proposed by the cities, county board of education, and county commissioners, with the state commissioner of revenue then selecting three persons who are appointed by the governor. They are paid by the state and local jurisdictions according to the number of days they work and the assessed valuation.

The tax collector maintains a roll of all taxable property in the county. Upon receiving the assessment figures from the assessor, the tax collector applies the tax rate set by the legislative body (state legislature, county commission, or city governing body), and computes everyone's tax bill. Real (estate) property taxes in Alabama are due October 1, and personal property taxes by December 31; taxes must be paid on automobiles before license tags are renewed. Taxes not paid by December 31 for the year become delinquent, and the property may be attached and sold at public auction. The tax assessing and collecting functions have been consolidated in the office of revenue commissioner in more than thirty counties: Autauga, Bibb, Blount, Bullock, Chambers, Cherokee,

Clarke, Clay, Cleburne, Coffee, Coosa, Covington, Crenshaw, Cullman, Dale, Elmore, Etowah, Fayette, Geneva, Henry, Houston, Jackson, Lauderdale, Limestone, Macon, Marengo, Mobile, Morgan, Pickens, Randolph, Russell, St. Clair, Talladega, and Walker. Revenue commissioners are generally elected for six-year terms, but specific details depend upon the constitutional amendment or local legislation creating the office, which can increase the state compensation listed in Table 9.3.

Alabama counties face many challenges in providing more services than ever before. County commissions are responsible for local government services outside the municipalities, some of which are withdrawing services from their "police jurisdiction." The original county functions of roads, hospitals, elections, courts and jails, and tax assessment and collection have been expanded to more urban services and regulation, such as the legislature recently giving larger Alabama counties authority to adopt building codes. The few part-time officials that were needed for a small rural county are finding that the county commission must meet every week and direct a career force of employees with a budget of millions of dollars. An experienced Alabama county commissioner has wryly commented:

> The Commissioner of today—if he really wants to do his job adequately—must be an expert, or at least knowledgeable, in the fields of recreation, garbage, roads, sewage, people, water, poverty, welfare, pensions, insurance, buildings, purchases, budgets, finance, law enforcement, courts, elections, education, taxes, health, hospitals, airports, planning, civil defense, parks, playgrounds, history, agriculture, housing, pollution, integration, libraries, street lighting, street sweeping, cemeteries, conventions, regional councils, advertising, industry, commerce, museums, forestry, marinas, fishing lakes, computers, tax exemptions, microfilming, state government, federal government, city government, intergovernmental relations, wom-

en's lib, 18-year olds, juvenile delinquency, drugs—and, if he
has time, it also helps to know the field of politics.[5]

Our Town: Alabama's 440 Municipalities

Alabama municipalities range from Birmingham with
266,000 inhabitants to Oak Hill, population 28. Each of these
municipalities, whether classified under Alabama law as a
"city" over 2,000 people, or as a smaller "town," has its own
government, as opposed to a simple "community" settlement.
As discussed in Chapter 2, the Alabama legislature established eight classifications of municipalities based on the
1970 census:

> Class 1 cities: over 300,000 population
> Class 2 cities: 175,000–299,999
> Class 3 cities: 100,000–174,999
> Class 4 cities: 50,000–99,999
> Class 5 cities: 25,000–49,999
> Class 6 cities: 12,000–24,999
> Class 7 cities: 6,000–11,999
> Class 8 cities: cities and towns of under 6,000 population

Birmingham has lost population, but remains the state's
Class 1 city, while new cities are classed when they are established or gain population. The legislature may pass general
laws applying only to a single class, which produces variations
on the following description of municipal government.

How is a new municipality formed? Alabama law requires a
minimum population of 300, with 150 qualified electors peti-
tioning the county probate judge.[6] No land may be included
in the proposed municipality unless 60% of the property owners sign the petition. Upon receiving a valid petition, the
judge advertises an election to be held within thirty days, and
if a majority of votes cast are in favor, an order is issued de-

Figure 9.2 Incorporated places in Alabama. (Source: Alabama League of Municipalities, U.S. Department of Commerce)

claring the town or city incorporated. The municipality then possesses such corporate powers as to sue and be sued, make contracts, own property, and have perpetual succession: there will always be a "City of X," although the elected officers may change. However, cities do "die" occasionally in Alabama, either through nonuse of powers (failure to elect a chief executive officer, collect taxes for three years, or keep the streets in proper condition) or if three-fourths of the qualified voters favor dissolution.

Governmental powers exercised by the municipality cover a wide scope of regulatory activities. The "general police power" includes not only law enforcement, but licensing, regulation of commerce, abatement of nuisances and other measures for public safety, health, and well-being. Land usage is controlled through zoning regulations, building codes, and inspections. Fire protection is among the oldest civic responsi-

Figure 9.3 Environmental testing of underground storage tanks near a residential area. (Courtesy of the Alabama Department of Environmental Management. Used by permission)

bilities, and the size of the city fire department and its water supply are important factors in setting fire insurance premiums. The city constructs numerous public works, such as streets, curbs, gutters, sidewalks, lighting, traffic lights, storm sewers, and drainage systems. Recreational programs have been expanded from public parks to lakes, swimming pools, golf courses, sports stadiums, and playing fields. Cultural opportunities include municipal operation of libraries, art galleries, museums, and civic auditoriums, all of which are designed to improve life in the city.

Alabama cities exercise proprietary powers in operating municipal utilities, such as electric, gas, water, and sewer services. The municipality may produce and sell the service itself, or may buy the commodity wholesale and retail it to customers through a city-operated distribution system. Alabama cities can also operate transportation activities; they run most of the state's licensed airports, bus lines, or "on-demand" vans. Municipal ownership is frequently supported on the grounds that public control is necessary since private enterprise cannot operate the needed service at a profit. Other cities have "privatized" certain services to private companies under franchise (which can last up to thirty years in Alabama).

The structure of municipal administration in Alabama takes two main forms: the mayor-council and the city manager. (The city commission form became extinct in Alabama during the 1970s and 1980s, as it has been abandoned nationally. While the United States Supreme Court in *City of Mobile v. Bolden* (1980)[7] held that at-large elections [by place] are constitutional as long as discrimination is not intended, the remaining Alabama commission-governed cities, faced with litigation, voted to abandon the system in favor of a mayor and council election by districts.)

Ninety-five percent of Alabama's cities and towns use the mayor-council form of government. Under Alabama law, mu-

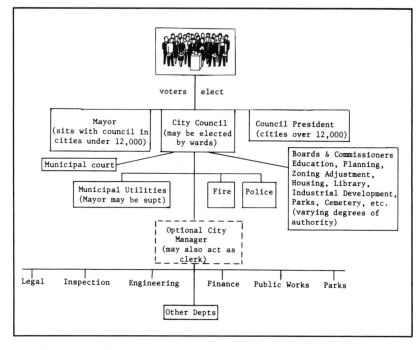

Figure 9.4 The mayor-council form of municipal government in Alabama.

nicipalities of under 12,000 have a five-member council that is presided over by a mayor who appoints council committees and may vote on proposals, although lacking veto power. The council decides whether its members will be elected "at large" from the whole city or by geographical districts (wards). If districts are used, they must be of equal population size under United States Supreme Court apportionment decisions. In Alabama and six other southern states, any electoral reorganization affecting representation must be approved by the United States Department of Justice under the federal Voting Rights Act.

In municipalities of over 12,000 population, a president of

the city council is elected at large to preside over a council of between five and fourteen members. They can be elected at large or by ward, but if there are seven wards or less, two are elected from each district. This arrangement can be varied by local desire and population class: for example, in cities of over 50,000, the council may not consist of more than twenty members or wards. The president of the council can vote on all questions (with few exceptions under local acts), chooses council committees, and acts as mayor in case of vacancy, disability, or absence from the office. The mayor in Alabama cities of over 12,000 thus does not sit or vote with the council, but does have the power to veto ordinances and resolutions, and to item-veto bills setting municipal salaries, all of which can be overridden by a two-thirds vote of the council. If the mayor does not sign or veto the act, it becomes effective ten days after passage by the council.

The mayor, the president of the council, and its members (called aldermen in Alabama law, but popularly referred to as council members or councillors) must be qualified electors of the municipality and residents of the ward they represent during their term of office. They are elected concurrently (with some exceptions by local act) for four-year terms on the second Tuesday in July (1992, 1996, etc.). If no candidate receives a majority, a runoff election between the two with the most votes is held the third Tuesday thereafter. Municipal officials' terms usually begin the first Monday in October. In cities of under 300,000 (including Birmingham since the 1980 census), political parties are forbidden to hold primaries to select a party nominee for municipal office so that elections are on a nonpartisan ballot. While compensation is not specified by state law, council members are commonly paid on a flat monthly basis, or compensated for each meeting attended, or reimbursed for expenses. These are usually nominal sums for the civic duty involved. The mayor's salary is set by the council at least six months before the election, and elected officials' salaries cannot be reduced during their terms of office.

Alabama city councils must meet in public session twice each month, and special sessions are held to consider certain topics upon written request by two members or the mayor. The council may also meet informally, but can transact official actions only at public meetings. A municipal law is called an ordinance and must be passed by a majority of the council's membership. If the mayor sits with the council (in a city of under 12,000), and his or her vote produces a tie, the mayor is required to vote again to break it. When a council president presides and his or her vote produces a tie, the measure does not pass. A major portion of the council's work is conducted through committees, customarily chaired by a council member, although the mayor may participate by invitation. Allowing familiarity through functional specialization, typical committees might work in the areas of public safety, public works, sanitation, finance, and utilities. While the council committees oversee these areas and make policy recommendations to the council, Alabama law designates the mayor as "chief executive," giving general supervision over municipal administration. The mayor may remove any nonelective city official for good cause, but if the appointment was shared with the council, a majority of its membership must agree.

The Alabama legislature passed the council manager act of 1991 providing[8] that any municipality except a class 1 city may elect a seven-member council by single member districts (and a mayor at large) for a four-year term. A majority vote of the whole council appoints a city manager who has executive and administrative qualifications and experience and who serves at the council's pleasure (removal also takes four votes). The manager is responsible to the council for the proper administration of all affairs of the municipality and can appoint or remove (subject to any civil service or merit system law) any department head or employee, but *not* the members or employees of a dozen specified boards: library, recreation, utility, school, hospital or medical clinic, airport, housing, industrial development, plumber or electrician, planning, or zoning. The manager enforces all laws and ordinances, prepares the budget, and performs other duties prescribed by the council. Although it needs to be emphasized that the elected officials retain complete responsibility for adopting municipal policies as cities develop, more technical information is needed for making decisions, and increased use of professional administrators can be expected. While previously a few Alabama municipalities have hired managers, this law provides that the mayor and council members will deal with municipal employees only through the city manager, except for purposes of inquiry.

There are several other municipal officials besides the governing body. The *clerk* is appointed by the municipal governing body and may also be designated as city treasurer. Duties include maintaining minutes of the council or commission meetings, recording ordinances passed, keeping other required city records, and election preparations. If financial administration is involved, accounting, license collection, and preparation of the municipal payroll become major responsibilities of the clerk.

The *city attorney* is appointed by the governing body and may be a lawyer in private practice hired part-time on retainer. The attorney provides legal advice to the municipality, defends it in lawsuits, and reviews (if not actually writing) proposed ordinances and contracts to assure their validity for the city. The city attorney may also act in court as the prosecuting attorney of those who break city laws.

There may be a number of *independent municipal boards or commissions*, with responsibility for certain operations. The degree of autonomy varies according to the need for a separate legal entity for bonding or contracting purposes, the function of the board, and the interest of the people involved. City school boards are well known; other examples are municipal water, library, cemetery, industrial development, and public housing boards. They are usually composed of unpaid citizens appointed by the municipal governing body. Motives for service include civic betterment (library), related tasks (a church deacon on the cemetery board), knowledge in area (those with realty interests are often found on zoning adjustment or planning commissions), or better service with lower rates (business owners on the utilities board). The effectiveness of such bodies obviously depends upon their membership, which is usually appointed for lengthy, overlapping terms. While this gives stability and independence, citizens should guard against allowing private interests to dominate the boards.

The size of the city's work force indicates the degree of organization. Small towns may get by with a city clerk and a few workers in the field, whereas large cities have departments by function (e.g., engineering) and specialized job tasks (civil engineer). The larger Alabama cities have career merit systems, with tests sometimes given in conjunction with the county. The quality of service received from the city obviously depends on the qualifications of those who perform it. Municipalities need dedicated personnel with advanced training or college degrees in a surprising variety of fields.

Special Districts: Providing Services

There are over 400 special districts in Alabama that provide such services as utilities, housing and community development, soil and water conservation, fire protection, hospitals, airports, marinas, and other functions. Unlike "independent" special districts in many other states, which have directly elected governing boards and can levy taxes on their own, most "dependent" Alabama authorities are appointed by the state, county, or municipal elected officials and are financed by appropriations or fees for their services. Formed under state law (often with federal encouragement and financial assistance), special districts can cross other governmental boundaries to provide service and can borrow money when counties and municipalities have constitutional debt limits. There has been political controversy over whether low-income housing, hospitals, and utility services can best be provided by private enterprise or by the public sector through special districts in Alabama.

Local Government Finance

Local government revenues come from four main sources:

1. Locally raised revenues such as taxes, fines, fees, and assessments. Alabama counties and cities have only the taxation powers authorized by the state constitution or legislature.
2. State-shared revenues, such as a percentage of the 6% tax on financial institutions' profits, the state-collected gasoline tax (16 cents per gallon), and taxes and profits from the Alcoholic Beverage Commission stores.[9] In the early 1990s, the state annually distributed more than $30 million to the cities and $200 million to the counties.
3. Grants-in-aid of a particular function, such as highways, made by the state or federal government. Money is typically distributed by a formula based on need (a subjective perception subject to legislative changes).
4. Legislative appropriations for specified local projects or programs, sometimes criticized as "pork" or "fat" in government spending by those who are not recipients. Alabama budgets have typically contained long lists of local appropriations.

Local government revenues in Alabama are derived as follows:

1. General property tax. The property tax has been a major support of local government because it is an *ad valorem* tax levied according to assessed value. It provides a steady source of income by levying a general rate on all tangible property upon which a lien can be placed in case of nonpayment. Its major problems are that it is a slower-growing revenue producer in times of prosperity and that the tax is not related to service demanded: if the land is used as a subdivision it is taxed equally with undeveloped land worth the same amount, yet the government spends money on fire and police protection for the residents. There may be sizable differences in community wealth measured in assessed valuation, presenting equalization problems between local jurisdictions' taxes. For these reasons, there has been a historical trend away from the general property tax and a greater reliance on intergovernmental payments from the state or national governments.

2. Sales taxes are also *ad valorem* levies at a certain percentage of the total price and may be either general or specific excises on liquor, cigarettes, gasoline, etc. Besides sharing in the general state sales tax proceeds, more than sixty Alabama counties and 300 municipalities levy special sales and use taxes of 1% to 3%. In addition, there may be local sales excises on commodities such as gasoline and cigarettes, which are usually designated for roads or schools. Retail sales taxes can thus be "piggybacked"—an extra percentage levied by local jurisdictions—but collected at the same time, and since such taxes are not exacted in one lump sum, people are not as aware of paying them. The main disadvantage is that a general levy is regressive (poorer people pay a larger proportion of their income), particularly if necessities such as food are included.

3. Privilege licenses are taxes or fees levied for conducting a business, profession, or occupation. They may be an annual flat rate or a sliding scale. An increasingly used mu-

nicipal revenue source is the "occupational license tax" levied on all who work in the city based upon earnings, in effect operating as a municipal income tax. Under state law, business licenses can be imposed on the police jurisdiction at one-half the rate prevailing inside the city limits. Entertainment taxes on admission tickets and hotel/motel occupancy taxes are being tried around Alabama. While these selective privilege licenses have proved productive revenue sources, their imposition at the discretion of local governing bodies has met public resistance.

4. User fees are service charges according to benefits received for garbage collection, building inspection, public cemeteries, and recreation such as swimming pools. A major source of these are the profits from municipally operated utilities such as water, electricity, and gas. While usually charges are set high enough to cover only the costs of providing the service, in certain Alabama cities utility profits are the largest source of municipal revenue.

5. Other local government revenues come from nontax sources such as court fines and forfeitures. Special assessments may be levied for capital improvements: for example, to put in sidewalks, the government may charge the property owners along the street, who have a period (often ten years) in which to pay off their share of the cost in installments.

While public demand for services has increased, many revenue sources have remained relatively inelastic to the capital expenditures required, so that many jurisdictions have resorted to borrowing. Borrowing usually occurs for large capital improvements, or for unanticipated emergencies. In Alabama, counties are normally limited in their indebtedness to 5% of their assessed valuation, and cities to 20% of the assessed value of property within their limits. There are, however, numerous local exceptions,[10] and several types of debt are not included in the restriction, such as short-term notes (due within one year) issued in anticipation of taxes. Bonds, as a promise to pay, require a popular referendum where a majority of voters approve.[11] Whether the bond issue passes is influenced by public attitudes about going into debt, the project involved (do we need this facility?), interest rates (which will add to the long-term cost), whether previous debt is reaching the limit set by the state, and current economic conditions.

Many local jurisdictions have sought to avoid the constitutional debt limitations by forming special boards (e.g., a county hospital board) or public authorities (for housing) that can borrow without having the liability count against the parent government. Bondholders may feel more secure with a separate entity that will safeguard revenues for debt repayment rather than having these go into the local treasury's general fund. The need to borrow may be reduced through better financial planning, including allocation of funds through a budget. A budget divides expenditures into current operating expenses and capital outlays (i.e., a long-term plan for expensive physical improvements).

These are the steps in the budgetary process: officials of each department plan their work for the coming fiscal year (October 1 to September 30 in Alabama) and submit estimates of the cost. Fixed expenditures (such as retirement or debt repayment obligations) are calculated, and estimates of revenues for the coming year made. Preparation of the budget document balances needs and resources, often in public hearings. The final budget, including setting of tax rates, is then adopted by the city or county governing body. Purchases must be authorized, and the warrants issued in payment usually are signed by two designated officials. Contracts over $5,000 by Alabama agencies must be made in open competitive bidding to the lowest responsible bidder ("professional services," such as for attorneys or architects, are exempt, leading to alleged favoritism on occasion). Alabama law requires that a statement of each county's (but not all cities') receipts, expenditures, and indebtedness be published in a general circulation newspaper, and auditors from the state Department of Examiners of Public Accounts periodically review each county's records.

Matching financial resources to needs presents challenges to every public official. Alabama local government is big business: even a small rural county can have a monthly payroll of over $250,000. Alabama's counties employ 15,000 full-time employees; municipalities 35,000; school districts 70,000; and other special districts (hospitals, fire protection, utilities, etc.) 15,000 workers. Major local expenditures are for schools, police and fire protection, public works, sanitation, and employee benefits. Citizens have to decide the level of local government services they desire and are willing to pay for.

Notes

1. Connecticut and Rhode Island have abolished counties; Alaska has "boroughs," Louisiana has "parishes," and some metropolitan areas have consolidated city-county government.
2. The U.S. Supreme Court declined in 1992 to extend coverage of the federal Voting Rights Act to governmental reorganization in two Alabama counties where, when African Americans were elected as county commissioners, the white incumbents set up a common road fund by majority vote or adopted a unit road system. See *Presley v. Etowah County Commission* and *Mack et al. v. Russell County Commission*, 112 S. Ct. 820 (1992), decided 6 to 3.
3. A probate judge who chairs a county commission is removed by judicial inquiry proceedings rather than by impeachment: *Ex parte Hahn*, 592 So. 2d 577 (Ala. 1991).
4. Joe Simmons, "Officials Say Lay Coroners Lacking Expertise," *Montgomery Advertiser*, October 17, 1982, 1.
5. Speech by James Record at Auburn University, March 11, 1971.
6. To discourage further incorporations in Jefferson County, any proposed new municipality has to have at least 10,000 people

and be over three miles away from an existing one. See *Code of Alabama*, 11-41-1.

7. 446 U.S. (1980). The court was deeply divided, 6 to 3. Mobile now elects its council by districts.

8. See *Code of Alabama*, 11-43A-1 to 115, for details.

9. Counties or cities lucky enough to strike oil or gas share 10% of the production privilege tax.

10. From constitutional amendments or statutory legislation.

11. Refinancing bonds (of a previous issue) and assessment bonds (for public improvement) do not require an election.

For Further Reading

Alabama local government laws on counties and municipalities are found in Title 11 of the *Code of Alabama*.

Alabama League of Municipalities, 535 Adams St., Montgomery, publishes *Handbooks for Mayors and Council Members* and a magazine.

Association of County Commissions of Alabama, 100 N. Jackson St., Montgomery, publishes a directory listing addresses, meeting times, county commissioners, and telephone numbers and also publishes a magazine, *The County Commissioner.*

Alabama County Finance Manual. Auburn University: Center for Governmental Services, 1990.

Dean, John. *The Making of a Black Mayor: A Study of Campaign Organization, Strategies, and Techniques in Pritchard, Alabama.* Washington, D.C.: Joint Center for Political Studies, 1973.

Handbook for Alabama County Commissioners. 7th ed. Tuscaloosa: Alabama Law Institute, 1993.

Handbook for Alabama Probate Judges. 5th ed. Tuscaloosa: Alabama Law Institute, 1989.

Handbook for Alabama Tax Assessors, Tax Collectors, License Commissioners, and Revenue Commissioners. 4th ed. Tuscaloosa: Alabama Law Institute, 1990.

International City Management Association. *Municipal Year Book (Year)* gives some Alabama city information from annual surveys.

U.S. Bureau of the Census. *County and City Data Book*, and periodic city and county publications on employment and finances.

TEN

Challenges for Alabama's Citizens

In the previous chapters, we have examined the structure and scope of government in Alabama. As citizens, taxpayers, and voters, what are some of the major issue areas confronting us?

The Red and the Black: Financing Government

As purchasers of goods and providers of services, governments are affected by inflation as much as are individual pocketbooks. Just like people, governments have entered into long-term financial commitments to provide facilities and hire a career work force. Inflation spirals current spending and makes long-range financial planning difficult because of the complexity of computing the costs of public improvements. Recession not only cuts Alabamians from the workforce, but cuts the tax bases of their governments.

■ *Revenues.* Where does the money come from? Figure 10.1 shows Alabama's major revenue sources. Taxes contribute about half, with sales and gross receipt taxes about a quarter, followed by income and property taxes, and forty lesser ones. Interest earnings, licenses, and fees ranging from college tuition (and auxiliary enterprises such as dormitories or cafeterias) to university hospital patients make up one-sixth of the budget that the state raises. Federal categorical grants (for

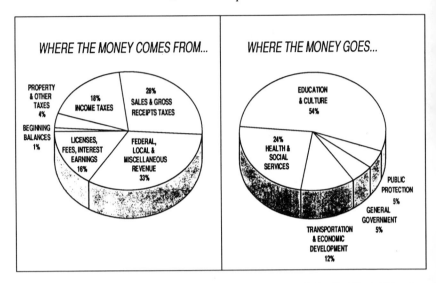

Figure 10.1 Alabama's state budget, 1991. (Courtesy of the Public Affairs Research Council of Alabama. Used by permission)

purposes ranging from education to highways), some money reimbursed for services by local governments, and miscellaneous revenues constitute the remaining third.

The tax burden is ordinarily distributed according to the principles of ability to pay and benefit received. Tax incidence can be neutral, progressive, or regressive. A neutral tax would treat everyone exactly the same, but human civilization has yet to develop the perfect tax; so total taxes in a democracy presumably tend toward equality ("fairness"). A progressive tax is higher upon those with greater means to pay, while a regressive tax takes a greater proportion from those with lesser resources. A tax levied at a flat rate (such as a 4% state sales tax) may actually have a regressive incidence, because while a millionaire may buy more (and pay a greater tax total), the flat amount will tax a greater *proportion* of a poor person's disposable income. A number of state studies have concluded that Alabama's current tax system tends to have a regressive impact, which helps explain the political aversion to taxes, even when renamed "revenue enhancements." State limitation on taxation may derive from constitutional restrictions or legislative limits on local taxation. These can take the forms of exclusion of certain tax sources (exemptions) or restrictions on the amount (rate) that can be levied.

■ *Expenditures.* Alabama currently spends about $5 billion per year, mostly on education, welfare, and highways. Alabama is different from other states, however, in "earmarking" or designating 90% of its money for specified purposes through constitutional provisions or state law. Some taxes are paid into public trust funds and can only be used for certain purposes (such as education or retirement), while other expenditures are mandated as the state's matching share to participate in federally funded programs.

Table 10.1
Alabama Appropriations (FY 1992–93)

Purpose	Percentage
Education	53.0
Medicaid	9.0
Public Health	3.0
Mental Health	3.0
Human Resources	3.0
Corrections	3.0
Highways	8.0
Judicial	2.0
Legislature	0.5
Debt repayment	1.5
Other functions	14.0
	100.0

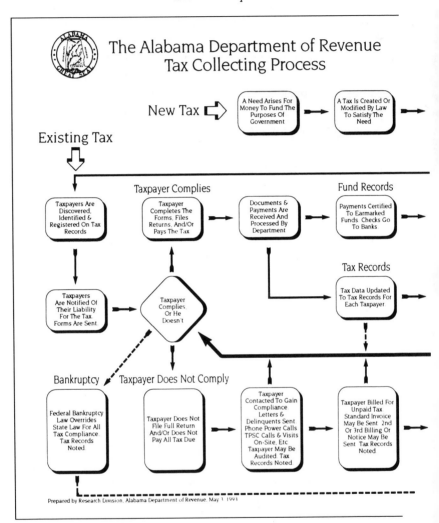

Figure 10.2   The tax collecting process. (Diagram courtesy of the Alabama Department of Revenue)

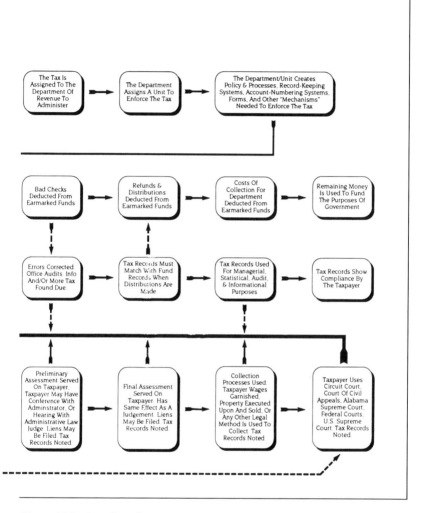

Figure 10.2 (continued)

No matter what candidates promise in their campaigns, any governor or legislature has discretion over only 10% of the Alabama state budget. Popular distrust of politicians at allocating money means the state has two major budgets, the Special Education Trust Fund, which constitutionally receives the largest amount from Alabama's taxes, and the general fund, which finances all other functions of state government. As the earmarked or designated taxes flow into each budget at separate rates, depending upon economic conditions, either budget in recent years has fallen behind the amounts appropriated, so there have been percentage cutbacks (called "proration" in Alabama). While states cannot run a deficit like the federal government, such spending cutbacks in midyear, suspending programs or laying off employees, are causing Alabamians to reconsider their governmental fiscal system.

Public demand for services has increased expenditures faster than revenues have grown to meet them, so that governments have resorted to borrowing. The state debt is now $4 billion, or about $1,000 for each Alabamian. More than half this debt is in revenue bonds, which are paid off with revenues specifically pledged toward their retirement. The rest of the debt is in general obligation bonds, for which the "full faith and credit" of the government is obligated for repayment. These are considered more secure and hence bear a lower interest rate than revenue bonds (or those secured by a mortgage), although general obligation bonding requires a referendum vote by the electorate. At the present time, most bonds are issued in serial form, with a certain portion of the debt due each year whereby both principal and interest are repaid to the registered owner or else coupons are detached from the bond and redeemed. Financial obligations of state and local governments are generally exempt from federal income taxes, thus bearing a lower rate of interest than commercial borrowing and being an attractive investment to those in the higher income brackets. A typical bond advertisement listing

Interest exempt, in the opinion of Bond Counsel, from Federal Income Taxes.

NEW ISSUE   Moody's Rating: Aa

$30,000,000

Alabama Public School
and College Authority

6% Capital Improvement Bonds, Series J

Dated: June 1, 1974   Due: June 1, 1975-89

Principal and semi-annual interest (December 1 and June 1) payable at State Treasurer's Office, Montgomery, Alabama, or at the Union Bank & Trust Company, Montgomery, Alabama, or at the First National City Bank, New York, N.Y. Coupon Bonds in the denomination of $5,000 each, registrable as to both principal and interest.

Bonds maturing 1985-1989 will be callable as a whole or in part in inverse numerical order on any interest payment date on or after June 1, 1984 at par & accrued interest plus a premium of ½ of 1% for each six months between the redemption date and the maturity date, but no premium may exceed one year's interest on, or be less than ½ of 1%.

AMOUNTS, MATURITIES AND YIELDS OR PRICES

Amount	Maturity	Yield	Amount	Maturity	Yield or Price
$5,200,000	1975-78	5.25%	$1,000,000	1984	5.60%
200,000	1979	5.30	1,200,000	1985	5.70
300,000	1980	5.35	1,400,000	1986	5.80
300,000	1981	5.40	5,700,000	1987	5.90
600,000	1982	5.45	6,700,000	1988	5.95
800,000	1983	5.50	6,600,000	1989	100

(Accrued interest to be added)

These Bonds are offered when, as and if issued and received by us and subject to approval of legality by Bradley, Arant, Rose & White, Birmingham, Alabama.

W. H. Morton & Co.
(Div. of American Express Co.)

Salomon Brothers

Merrill Lynch, Pierce, Fenner & Smith
Incorporated

Weeden & Co.
Incorporated

Bear, Stearns & Co.

Donaldson, Lufkin & Jenrette
Securities Corporation

Loewi & Co.   Thomson & McKinnon Auchincloss Kohlmeyer Inc.
Incorporated
May 15, 1974

Figure 10.3   Typical notice of a government bond offering.

the state's credit rating of Aa, the amount of debt to be repaid each year, and the securities brokers where such bonds could be purchased in $5,000 denominations is shown in Figure 10.3. Who gets government's bond business is also an issue: by competitive bid or by political influence.

The State of Alabama is also a major institutional investor, in managing pension funds for state employees, teachers, judges, and law enforcement officers. While there are separate pension boards composed of state officials and representatives elected by the participants, management has been centralized in the Retirement Systems of Alabama. The RSA has built several state office buildings in the capitol complex for leasing income, but resisted occasional state attempts to borrow ("raid") its funds at low interest, instead investing both within and outside Alabama.

Since state and local governments must operate on a balanced budget, tax rates and service levels must be carefully weighed—subject to upset by unexpected emergencies. When confronted by such financial decisions, citizens and elected representatives should ask: Is it needed? How much money will it cost? Is it necessary now? Answering these fundamentals will help in determining spending priorities.

In 1991, Alabama ranked forty-fourth in per capita tax burden: $964 per person, lower than the national average of $1,235. Alabamians will have to ask what proportion of their financial resources should be devoted to public spending—not simply how much it costs the taxpayers, but what government will do when it gets the money.

Cultivating Democracy at the Grass Roots

Such questions are based on trust between people and their government. Democracy is based on the premise that government will be responsive to the people's will. But voter turnout in state and local elections is usually low. Local officials say one of the most frustrating experiences is to conduct a public hearing on an important decision—a zoning plan, adopting a budget, setting the tax rate— and have only three or four members of the public show up. Even if the state legislative committee, county commission, or city hearing room is packed, do these citizens represent the majority of public sentiment? Or are they simply a vociferous minority? It is politically embarrassing, as well as discouraging, for officials to make a decision and find they have stirred up a hornet's nest. Effective self-government requires continuing participation from constituents. American state and local government, as contrasted to centralized systems found elsewhere, demands officials who are selected by, are close to, and know the problems of the community. Through approving the services to be rendered, choosing persons to administer them, and checking on their performance in office, the vital democratic processes of participation, discussion, and political education are visible to both officeholder and citizen.

Streamlining Government Operations

How can government in Alabama be an effective servant for the people? In judging governmental performance, perhaps we too often examine structure rather than responsiveness. Checks and balances and diversity in forms of government are important mechanisms, but should help rather than hinder the machinery of governing. Alabamians are constantly faced with revising the state constitution, having a reapportioned state legislature, deciding how to finance government, and examining the operations of local governments. All of these changes require understanding by citizens as to purpose and goals.

Career Opportunities in State and Local Government

Government is one of the largest employers in Alabama: more than 38,000 full-time state employees, 15,000 county

employees, 35,000 municipal employees, 40,000 schoolteach-
ers, and 30,000 support personnel were employed in the early
1990s. Housing, hospital, and other special districts had an
additional 15,000 full-time employees. Virtually every occupational skill found in private enterprise is also needed in
public service. As state and local governments expand their
services, vocational and technical skills are needed, as well as
college degrees in many fields. Although no one gets rich in a
public service career, the recent graduate interested in steady
employment and salary, not to mention health and retirement
benefits comparable to most found in private business, should
explore the opportunities available in government employment.

Governmental Policy Choices: What Will Alabama Be in the Future?

The successive decisions taken by our state and local governments perhaps have more influence upon our day-to-day
lives than many others. The decisions made today will affect
not only our quality of life, but that of future Alabamians as
well. Yet perhaps the most difficult aspect of deciding public
policy is that there are no absolutely right or wrong answers.
If there were, political campaigns would hardly be necessary
to show us both sides of the question. Rather than clear-cut
black and white issues, we are faced by a variety of alternatives
in a gray area with uncertain effects for the future. The problems of public choice are more difficult than our personal decisions simply because everyone else is involved. Whatever op-
tions are chosen in Alabama, it can be concluded that the
future of state and local governments will depend upon the
interest taken by the citizens they serve.

Appendixes

APPENDIX A
Alabama Counties

County	Auto Tag Key No.	1990 Census Population	Date Originally Created	Origin of Name	County Seat
Jefferson	1	651,535	1819	Pres. Thomas Jefferson of Virginia	Birmingham
Mobile	2	378,643	1812	Maubila Indians	Mobile
Montgomery	3	209,085	1816	Lt. L. P. Montgomery of Tennessee	Montgomery
Autauga	4	34,222	1818	Indian village	Prattville
Baldwin	5	98,280	1809	Sen. Abraham Baldwin of Georgia	Bay Minette
Barbour	6	25,417	1832	Gov. James Barbour of Virginia	Clayton
Bibb	7	16,576	1818	Gov. William Bibb of Alabama	Centreville
Blount	8	39,248	1818	Gov. Willie G. Blount of Tennessee	Oneonta

County	No.	Population	Year	Named for	County Seat
Bullock	9	11,042	1866	Col. Edward C. Bullock of Alabama	Union Springs
Butler	10	21,892	1819	Capt. William Butler of Creek Wars	Greenville
Calhoun	11	116,034	1832	Sen. John C. Calhoun of South Carolina	Anniston
Chambers	12	36,876	1832	Sen. Henry C. Chambers of Alabama	LaFayette
Cherokee	13	19,543	1836	Indian tribe	Centre
Chilton	14	32,458	1868	Judge William P. Chilton of Alabama	Clanton
Choctaw	15	16,018	1847	Indian tribe	Butler
Clarke	16	27,240	1812	Gov. John Clarke of Georgia	Grove Hill
Clay	17	13,252	1866	Sen. Henry Clay of Kentucky	Ashland
Cleburne	18	12,730	1866	Gen. Patrick R. Cleburne of Arkansas	Heflin
Coffee	19	40,240	1841	Gen. John Coffee of Alabama	Elba

County	Auto Tag Key No.	1990 Census Population	Date Originally Created	Origin of Name	County Seat
Colbert	20	51,666	1867	George and Levi Colbert, chiefs of Chickasaw Nation	Tuscumbia
Conecuh	21	14,054	1818	Indian name	Evergreen
Coosa	22	11,063	1832	Indian village	Rockford
Covington	23	36,478	1822	Gen. Leonard W. Covington of Maryland	Andalusia
Crenshaw	24	13,635	1866	Judge Anderson Crenshaw of Alabama	Luverne
Cullman	25	67,613	1877	Johann Cullman, immigration promoter	Cullman
Dale	26	49,633	1824	Gen. Samuel Dale of Alabama	Ozark
Dallas	27	48,130	1818	A. J. Dallas, U.S. Secretary of the Treasury	Selma
DeKalb	28	54,651	1836	Gen. Baron DeKalb of the American Revolution	Ft. Payne

County	No.	Named for	Date	Population	County Seat
Elmore	29	Gen. John A. Elmore of Alabama	1866	49,210	Wetumpka
Escambia	30	Indian name	1868	35,518	Brewton
Etowah	31	Cherokee Indian name	1866	99,840	Gadsden
Fayette	32	Gen. Marquis de Lafayette of the American Revolution	1824	17,962	Fayette
Franklin	33	Benjamin Franklin of Pennsylvania	1818	27,814	Russellville
Geneva	34	Geneva, Switzerland	1868	23,647	Geneva
Greene	35	Gen. Nathanael Greene of Georgia	1819	10,153	Eutaw
Hale	36	Col. Stephen F. Hale of Alabama	1867	15,418	Greensboro
Henry	37	Gov. Patrick Henry of Virginia	1819	15,374	Abbeville
Houston	38	Gov. George S. Houston of Alabama	1903	81,331	Dothan
Jackson	39	Gen. Andrew Jackson of Tennessee	1819	47,796	Scottsboro

County	Auto Tag Key No.	1990 Census Population	Date Originally Created	Origin of Name	County Seat
Lamar	40	15,715	1867	Sen. L. Q. C. Lamar of Mississippi	Vernon
Lauderdale	41	79,661	1818	Col. James Lauderdale of Tennessee	Florence
Lawrence	42	31,513	1818	Capt. James Lawrence of Vermont, U.S.N.	Moulton
Lee	43	87,146	1866	Gen. Robert E. Lee of Virginia	Opelika
Limestone	44	54,135	1818	Limestone Creek	Athens
Lowndes	45	12,658	1830	Congressman William Lowndes of South Carolina	Hayneville
Macon	46	24,928	1832	Sen. Nathaniel Macon of North Carolina	Tuskegee
Madison	47	238,912	1808	Pres. James Madison of Virginia	Huntsville
Marengo	48	23,084	1818	A Napoleonic battlefield	Linden

County	No.	Population	Year	Named for	County Seat
Marion	49	29,830	1818	Gen. Francis Marion of South Carolina	Hamilton
Marshall	50	70,832	1836	Chief Justice John Marshall of Virginia	Guntersville
Monroe	51	23,968	1815	Pres. James Monroe of Virginia	Monroeville
Morgan	52	100,043	1818	Gen. Daniel Morgan of Virginia	Decatur
Perry	53	12,759	1819	Commodore Oliver H. Perry, U.S.N.	Marion
Pickens	54	20,699	1820	Gen. Andrew Pickens of South Carolina	Carrollton
Pike	55	27,595	1822	Gen. Zebulon M. Pike, explorer	Troy
Randolph	56	19,881	1832	Sen. John Randolph of Virginia	Wedowee
Russell	57	46,860	1832	Col. Gilbert C. Russell of Alabama	Phenix City
Shelby	58	99,358	1818	Gov. Isaac Shelby of Kentucky	Columbiana

County	Auto Tag Key No.	1990 Census Population	Date Originally Created	Origin of Name	County Seat
St. Clair	59	50,009	1818	Gen. Arthur St. Clair of Pennsylvania	Ashville
Sumter	60	16,174	1832	Gen. Thomas Sumter of South Carolina	Livingston
Talladega	61	74,107	1832	Creek Indian village	Talladega
Tallapoosa	62	39,826	1832	Indian name	Dadeville
Tuscaloosa	63	150,522	1818	Indian chief	Tuscaloosa
Walker	64	67,670	1823	Sen. John W. Walker of Alabama	Jasper
Washington	65	16,694	1800	Pres. George Washington of Virginia	Chatom
Wilcox	66	13,568	1819	Lt. James M. Wilcox of Creek Wars	Camden
Winston	67	22,053	1850	Gov. John Winston of Alabama	Double Springs

APPENDIX B
Governors of the State of Alabama

Name	County of Origin	Party	Dates in Office	Background
1. William Wyatt Bibb	Autauga	Dem.	1819–1820*	Territorial governor
2. Thomas Bibb	Limestone	Dem.	1820–1821	President of state senate, brother of W. W. Bibb
3. Israel Pickens	Greene	Dem.	1821–1825	U.S. representative
4. John Murphy	Monroe	Dem.	1825–1829	State senator
5. Gabriel Moore	Madison	Dem.	1829–1831***	U.S. representative
6. Samuel B. Moore	Jackson	Dem.	1831	President of state senate, no relation to G. Moore
7. John Gayle	Greene	Dem.	1831–1835	Speaker, state house of representatives
8. Clement Comer Clay	Madison	Dem.	1835–1837***	U.S. representative
9. Hugh McVay	Lauderdale	Dem.	1837	President of state senate
10. Arthur Pendleton Bagby	Monroe	Dem.	1837–1841	Speaker, state house of representatives
11. Benjamin Fitzpatrick	Autauga	Dem.	1841–1845	Planter

	Name	County	Party	Years	Office
12.	Joshua Lanier Martin	Tuscaloosa	Dem.	1845–1847	State judge
13.	Reuben Chapman	Madison	Dem.	1847–1849	U.S. representative
14.	Henry Watkins Collier	Tuscaloosa	Dem.	1849–1853	Chief justice, Alabama Supreme Court
15.	John Anthony Winston	Sumter	Dem.	1853–1857	State senator
16.	Andrew Barry Moore	Perry	Dem.	1857–1861	Circuit judge
17.	John Gill Shorter	Barbour	Dem.	1861–1863	Circuit judge
18.	Thomas Hill Watts	Montgomery	Dem.	1863–1865	Confederate attorney general
19.	Lewis Eliphalet Parsons	Talladega	Dem.	1865	Provisional governor
20.	Robert Miller Patton	Lauderdale	Dem.	1865–1867	Subordinate to Swayne
21.	Maj. Gen. Wager Swayne	Montgomery		1867–1868	Military governor
22.	William Hugh Smith	Randolph	Rep.	1868–1870	Union loyalist
23.	Robert Burns Lindsay	Colbert	Dem.	1870–1872	State senator
24.	David Peter Lewis	Madison	Rep.	1872–1874	Lawyer

Name	County of Origin	Party	Dates in Office	Background
25. George Smith Houston	Limestone	Dem.	1874–1878	Lawyer
26. Rufus Willis Cobb	Shelby	Dem.	1878–1882	State senator
27. Edward Asbury O'Neal	Lauderdale	Dem.	1882–1886	Lawyer
28. Thomas Jefferson Seay	Hale	Dem.	1886–1890	State senator
29. Thomas Goode Jones	Montgomery	Dem.	1890–1894	Speaker, state house of representatives
30. William Calvin Oates	Henry	Dem.	1894–1896	U.S. representative
31. Joseph Forney Johnston	Jefferson	Dem.	1896–1900	Lawyer and banker
32. William James Samford	Lee	Dem.	1900–1901*	State senator
33. William Dorsey Jelks	Barbour	Dem.	1900** 1901–1907	President of state senate
34. Russell M. Cunningham	Jefferson	Dem.	1904–1905**	Lieutenant governor

	County	Party	Years	Occupation
35. Braxton Bragg Comer	Jefferson	Dem.	1907–1911	President, railroad commission
36. Emmet O'Neal	Lauderdale	Dem.	1911–1915	Lawyer, pres. Alabama Bar Association
37. Charles Henderson	Pike	Dem.	1915–1919	President, railroad commission
38. Thomas Erby Kilby	Calhoun	Dem.	1919–1923	Lieutenant governor
39. William W. Brandon	Tuscaloosa	Dem.	1923–1927	Probate judge
40. David Bibb Graves	Montgomery	Dem.	1927–1931, 1935–1939	Lawyer
41. Benjamin Meek Miller	Wilcox	Dem.	1931–1935	Justice, Alabama Supreme Court
42. Frank Murray Dixon	Jefferson	Dem.	1939–1943	Lawyer
43. Chauncey Sparks	Barbour	Dem.	1943–1947	Lawyer
44. James Elisha Folsom	Cullman	Dem.	1947–1951, 1955–1959	Insurance executive
45. Gordon Persons	Montgomery	Dem.	1951–1955	President, Public Service Commission
46. John Malcolm Patterson	Russell	Dem.	1959–1963	Alabama attorney general

Name	County of Origin	Party	Dates in Office	Background
47. George Corley Wallace	Barbour	Dem.	1963–1967 1971–1979 1983–1987	Circuit judge
48. Lurleen Wallace	Barbour	Dem.	1967–1968*	Wife of G. C. Wallace
49. Albert Preston Brewer	Morgan	Dem.	1968–1971	Lieutenant governor
50. Jere Beasley	Barbour	Dem.	1972**	Lieutenant governor
51. Forest "Fob" James, Jr.	Lee	Dem.	1979–1983	Manufacturer
52. H. Guy Hunt	Cullman	Rep.	1987–1993	Probate judge
53. James Folsom, Jr.	Cullman	Dem.	1993–	Lieutenant governor

*   Died in office
**   Acting governor
*** Resigned governorship to become United States senator

APPENDIX C

The Reed Buskey House and Senate Plan Court District Arrangement (Nesting)

Senate	House
1	1, 2, 3
2	4, 5, 6
3	7, 8, 9
4	10, 11, 12
5	13, 14, 15
6	16, 17, 18
7	19, 20, 21
8	22, 23, 24
9	25, 26, 27
10	28, 29, 30

| 11 | Talladega County, Coosa County and part of Elmore County (all of 31, part of 32, all of 33, and part of 35) |
| 12 | Calhoun County (part of 32, all of 34, part of 35, and all of 36) |

Senate	House
13	37, 38, 39
14	40, 41, 42
15	43, 44, 45
16	46, 47, 48
17	49, 50, 51
18	52, 53, 54
19	55, 56, 57
20	58, 59, 50
21	61, 62, 63
22	64, 65, 66
23	67, 68, 69
24	70, 71, 72
25	73, 74, 75
26	76, 77, 78
27	79, 80, 81
28	82, 83, 84
29	85, 86, 87
30	88, 89, 90
31	91, 92, 93
32	94, 95, 96
33	97, 98, 99
34	100, 101, 102
35	103, 104, 105

Index

Absentee ballot, 46–47
Adjustment, Board of, 135
Adjutant general, 120–21
Administration, 98–99, 174–75, 180, 236
Administration, gubernatorial. *See* Governor
Administrative Office of Courts, 210
Adoptions, 157, 191
Advertising, political, 62, 74
Aeronautics, Department of, 143–44
African Americans. *See* Black political participation
Agreements, interjurisdictional, 35
Agriculture, 8, 12, 141
Agriculture and Industries, Commissioner of, 27, 44, 136–37, 141–43
AIDS, 155, 168
Alabama, state statistics, 1, 10–11
Alabama, University of, 148–49
Alabama Administrative Monthly, 96
Alabama Bar Association, 184
Alabama Cooperative Extension Service, 137
Alabama Democratic Conference, 75, 129
Alabama Development Office, 10, 145
Alabama Education Association, 131
Alabama Law Institute, 96
Alabama League of Municipalities, 37
Alabama Public Television, 112

Alabama River, 1
Alabama Territory, 5
Alcoholic Beverage Control Board, 164, 166, 237
ALERT (Alabama legislative computer terminal), 100–102, 114, 183
Amendments, constitutional, 27–29, 110, 119
Apportionment, legislative. *See* Reapportionment
Appropriations, 245
Aquaculture, 8
Archives, state, 179
Arraignment, 207
Assessment, 225–26, 239; special assessments, 239
Attorney, city, 199, 235
Attorney General, state, 22, 133–34
Auburn University, 137, 149
Auditor, state, 44, 136
Authorities, public, 162, 240

Bail, 206–7
Ballots, 46, 49, 52, 135
Bank, state, 19
Banking, State Department of, 144–45
Bar Association, Alabama, 184
Baxley, William J., 129–30
Beasley, Jere, 128–29
"Beat" (precincts), 45, 52, 195
Bibb, William Wyatt, 5
Bid, competitive, 240, 250

Bill format, 100. *See also* Legislation
Birmingham, 128, 169, 171, 228, 233
Black, Hugo, 34
"Black Belt," 1, 5, 18, 25, 26, 128
Black political participation, 7, 22–23, 25–26, 33, 51, 57, 87, 95, 128–29, 188, 219
Boards, municipal, 235–36. *See also titles of specific boards*
Boats, 146
Bonds, 24, 38, 53, 240, 248
Boswell Amendment, 26
"Bourbons," 23, 25–26
Bracket bills, 34
Brewer, Albert, 127–29
Buck's Pocket, 5
Budget, local, 240, 250
Budget, state, 99, 110, 112, 120, 250
Budget isolation resolution (BIR), 110
Bureaucracy, 180

Cabinet, governor's, 173
Cahaba, 18
Calendar, legislative, 103–4, 112
Campaign finance, 60–74
Candidates, 51–52
Capital punishment, 199
Capitol, state, 18
Capstone Poll, 54
Carpetbaggers, 22–24
Cater Act, 37
Caucus, 49
Census, 5, 7, 15, 31, 53, 87
Certiorari, 35, 185
Challenge, election, 48
Chattahoochee River, 2
Children's services, 153, 157, 191, 193
Circuit Court, 190, 193–95
Cities. *See* Municipalities
City commission, 231
City manager, 234–35
Civil rights, 25, 212
Civil suits, 197, 214
Classification, 34, 173, 228
Clay, Clement C., 19
Clemency powers, 122
Clerk, city, 45, 235

Clerk of the House, 93, 102
Code of Alabama, 102, 152, 183, 219
Commission, city, 231
Commission, county, 219–23, 227
Committees, legislative, 91, 93–94, 98, 100, 102–3, 112
Community power, 58
Compacts, interstate, 38
Comptroller of Public Accounts, 19
Confederacy, 20, 22–23, 25
Conference committee, 107
Congress, U.S., 17, 20, 22–23, 43, 183
Conservation and Natural Resources Department, 146, 166
Constables, 195
Constitutional conventions, 29, 115 (n. 9)
Constitution of Alabama: 1819, 17–21; 1861, 20–21; 1865, 21–22; 1868, 22–23; 1875, 23–25; 1901, 25–29, 95–96, 110
Constitution, U.S., 17, 26–27, 29, 37, 39, 183, 197
Constitutionality, 29, 100, 133–34
Consumer protection, 134, 137, 138, 146
Contracts, 35, 133, 230
Coosa River, 1, 148
Coroner, 225
Corporate powers, 32
Corporations, 135
Corrections, Department of, 168
Council, city, 232–34
Council President, 232–33
Councils of Governments, 36
Counties, 5, 33, 191, 217–33, 241; Association of County Commissions, 37
County commission, 219–23, 227
Courts, Alabama, 184–91
Creek Indians, 2
Crime, 166–67
"Cross-over" voting, 52, 130
Cullman County, 34
Cumulative voting, 219
Curfew, 172
Current use, 226

Death penalty, 199

Debate, legislative, 104
Debt, 19, 21, 23–25, 28, 32, 135, 237, 239–40, 248, 250
Declaration of Rights, Alabama, 95
Democratic Party, 14, 25, 49, 52, 58
Demopolis, 2
De Soto expedition, 1
Development authorities, 148
Dillon's Rule, 33
Disasters, natural, 172
District Attorney, 199, 207
Divorce (dissolution of marriage), 31, 189
Docks, state, 162
Dodd, Donald B., 14
Dothan, 8

"Earmarking" (designated) revenues, 129, 245, 248
Education, 14, 23, 27, 137, 149–50
Education, Board of, 23, 137, 151
Educational Television Commission, 151
Elections: dates, 51–52, 132, 233; hours, 48–49; at large, 231–32; by place, 49, 231; primaries, 49, 51–52; runoff, 51–52; special, 134
Emergency powers, 172
Employees, government, 143, 175, 251–52
Engineer, county, 221
Engrossment, 104, 115 (n. 6)
Enrollment, 107
Equalization, Board of, 226
Ethics Commission, 113, 135
Examiners of Public Accounts, 97, 133, 136, 241
Exemption, property, 23
Exclusionary rule, 206
Executive amendment, 108, 119
Expenditures, state, 245, 248. *See also* Budget
Extradition, 31, 122, 133

Farmers. *See* Agriculture
Federalism, 37
Fees, user, 239
Fee system, 223
Felony, 91, 169, 190, 193–95, 199–200, 206

Finance, State Department of, 122, 136
Fire Marshal, 144
Fire protection, 230–31, 241
Fiscal note, 97
Fitzpatrick, Benjamin, 21
Flea markets, 34
Florida, 2
Folmar, Emory, 129
Folsom, James E. 123–24, 128
Folsom, James Jr., 131
Forensic Sciences, Department of, 225
Forest products, 8
Forestry Commission, 148
Franchise. *See* Suffrage
Franchises, municipal, 231
Fraternal societies, 49
Full faith and credit clause, 30

Geologist, state, 148
Georgia, 5
Gerrymandering, 25
"Goat Hill," 18–19
Gomillion v. Lightfoot, 33
Governor, 19, 28, 44, 107, 117–22, 145, 169, 173, 185, 214
Graddick, Charles, 130
Grandfather clause, 26
Grand jury, 207, 211
Grants-in-aid, 37, 145, 237
Gulf Marine Fisheries Commission, 39
Gulf Shores, 118

Habeas corpus writ, 190
Health, public, 152–53
Health, State Department of, 14, 153
Hearing, public, 103, 112, 251
Highways, 159–62, 221, 223
Home rule, 34, 96
Homestead, 23; exemption, 226
Horseshoe Bend, 2
Housing, public, 219
Hubbert, Paul, 131
Human Resources, Department of, 123, 157
Hunt, Guy, 130–31
Hunting license, 146
Huntsville, 17, 18, 36

Immigration, 12. *See also* Migration
Impeachment, 90, 99, 132–33, 215, 217
Income, personal, 8, 10, 11
Incorporation, 228–30
Indians, 2, 5, 7
Indictment, 206, 208, 209
Industrial Relations, Department of, 14, 22, 158
Industries, 8, 145
Inflation, 243
Injunction, 35
Insanity, 43, 132, 153, 156, 191, 193, 207, 210
Insurance, 144
Interest groups, 37, 75, 99, 123
Item veto, 107–8, 119–20, 233

Jackson, Andrew, 2, 49
James, Forest, Jr. ("Fob"), 29, 128–29
Jefferson County, 35, 241 (n. 6)
Johnson, Andrew, 21–23
Judges, 19, 188–95, 212, 214–15
Judicial Inquiry Commission, 214, 224
Juries, 19, 190, 207, 210, 211
Juvenile court, 193

Labor, Department of, 158–59
Law enforcement, 166–67, 199
Laws. *See* Legislation
Legislation: general, 96, 100, 183, 228; local, 27, 34–35, 96, 109, 112, 217; private, 27, 96, 109; special, 27, 34, 96, 109
Legislative Council, 96, 99, 133
Legislative courtesy, 109–10
"Legislative days," 88
Legislative Fiscal Office, 96–97
Legislative Reference Service, 96, 99
Legislators, 19, 87, 90, 93, 95, 113–14
Legislature, 19, 22, 24, 27, 34, 87–115
Lieutenant Governor, 22–23, 27, 91, 96, 132–33
Lobbyists, 75–84, 113. *See also* Interest groups
Louisiana Territory, 2

McCorquodale, Joe, 129
McMillan, George D. H., Jr., 129
Madison County, 36
Mandamus, 35, 190
Mandates, 221, 245
Martial law, 125, 172
Mass meeting, 49, 52
Mayor, 231–34
Media, news, 57–58, 60, 74, 112, 114, 119
Medicaid and Medicare, 144, 153, 157
Medical examiners, 146
Mental Health and Mental Retardation, Department of, 153, 155
Merit (career personnel) system, 120, 173
Metropolitan Statistical Areas, 12–13
Migration, 7, 12, 14
Militia, state. *See* National Guard
Mining, 148
Minorities. *See* Black political participation
Miranda warning, 199
Misdemeanors, 199
Mississippi, 2, 5
Mobile, 2, 129, 162, 169
Mobile v. Bolden, 231
Montgomery, 18, 169
Municipalities, 33–34, 191, 228–36, 241; Alabama League of, 37

National Guard, 120–21, 171–72
Native Americans. *See* Indians
Natural resources, 8, 148
Newspapers. *See* Media, news
Nominations, 49, 51–52
Nonpartisanship, 58, 233
Nonresidents, 30

Occupational licensing, 145–47, 239
Oil and gas, 8, 29, 129, 148
Opinion, legal, 133–34, 185
Opinion, public, 60, 119
Ordinances, local, 183, 192, 233–34

PACs (political action committees), 60, 75, 84, 135
Pardons and Paroles, Board of, 122, 169, 212

Parks, state, 146
Parsons, Lewis E., 21
Parties, political, 51, 58. *See also* Democratic Party, Republican Party
Patronage, political, 120–21, 173
Patterson, John M., 125
Pensions and Security, Department of. *See* Human Resources
Peremptory challenge, 211
Perpetual succession, 32, 230
Personnel (government employees), 143, 175, 251–52
Phenix City, 35, 125
Place system, 49
Plantations, 5, 18, 29
Plea bargaining, 207
Plurality, 51
Police, 166–67, 199
Police jurisdiction, 32, 167, 227, 239
Political action committees (PACs), 60, 75, 84, 135
Poll list, 45
Poll tax, 26
Poll workers, 53
Population, 5, 7
Populists, 25–26
"Pork" in spending, 237
Poultry promotion, 8
Precincts, 45, 52, 195
Preemption, 35
Prefiling, 102
Preliminary hearing, 206
President pro tempore, 119
Press secretary, 121
Prisons, 167–69
Privatization, 231
Privileges and immunities clause, 30
Probate Judge, 45, 52, 191, 217, 219, 223–24
Probation, 169–70
Property tax, 225–26, 238
Proprietary powers, 231
Proration, 112, 248
Prosecutor, 22, 133, 207. *See also* District Attorney
Public defender, 210
Public Safety, Department of, 166
Public Service Commission, 138–39, 185, 189. *See also* Utilities

Punitive damages, 215

Quorum, 88, 90, 104

Railroads, 27, 139
Ratification, 23, 28, 29
Readings, of bills, 101, 103–4
Reapportionment, 87, 123, 125, 232
Recess, legislative, 115 (n. 7)
Recession, economic, 8, 19, 243
Reconstruction, 22–23
Referendum, 240
Registration, voting, 43–46
Repealer clause, 100
Representatives, state. *See* Legislators
Republican Party, 14, 22–23, 25, 49, 52, 57, 91, 95, 128, 130
Residency requirements, 23, 26, 43, 132, 138, 233
Resolution: joint or simple, 102, 108–9, 119, 185; local, 233
Restitution, 212
Retirement systems, Alabama, 136, 250
Revenue Commissioner, 226–27
Revenue sharing, 237
Reynolds v. Sims, 87 (n. 1)
Right to work law, 8

Salaries. *See titles of specific offices*
Sales tax, 238
Saving clause, 115 (n. 5)
Scalawags, 22
School boards, 33, 151–52, 241
School financing, 149–50
School superintendents, 152
Search warrant, 201–5
Secession, 20–21
Secretary of State, 19, 52
Secretary of the Senate, 93, 102, 134–35
Securities Commission, 145
Segregation, 22, 27, 29, 149
Selma, 167
Senators, state. *See* Legislators
Senators, U.S., 25
Seniority, 91
Sessions, legislative, 27, 88, 90
Severability clause, 100

Sharecroppers, 15
Sheriff, 19, 53, 166, 224–25
Slaves, 19, 21
Small claims, 193
Speaker of the House, 91, 96, 119, 133
Special districts, 33, 236–37, 241
Statehouse, 114
"Stopping the clock," 112
Suffrage, 19, 22–23, 25–26, 43
Sunset laws, 99
Supreme Court, Alabama, 29, 34, 130, 133, 184–85, 187–88, 206, 213–15
Supreme Court, U.S., 33, 185
Swayne, Wager, 22

Talladega, 149
Tallapoosa River, 2
Tax Assessor, 225–26
Taxation, 23, 32, 160, 164, 237, 243–47, 250
Tax Collector, 226
Television. *See* Media, news
Tennessee and Tombigbee rivers and Waterway, 39
Tenure commission, 152, 189
Textbooks, 137
Trademarks, 49, 135
Transportation, Department of, 159–62
Treasurer, city, 235
Treasurer, state, 19, 25, 135–36
Trial jury, 19, 190, 210–11
Troopers, state, 122, 166
Trucks, 160, 162
Trust funds, 29, 129, 150, 245, 248
Tuscaloosa, 1, 18, 156
Tuskegee University, 149

Unanimous consent, 103

Unemployment, 8, 10, 158
Uniform state laws, 39
Unions, 8, 46, 74, 159
Universities, 148–49
User fees, 239
Utilities, 138, 219, 231, 234, 236–37; Public Service Commission and, 138–39, 185, 189

Vacancies in office, 120. *See also titles of specific offices*
Veterinarian, state, 143
Veto, 107–8, 119, 233
Vine and Olive Colony, 2
Vital Statistics, 5, 14, 153–54
Voir dire, 211
Voting. *See* Suffrage
Voting machines, 46, 52
Voting registration, 43–45
Voting Rights Act, 87, 232, 241 (n. 2)
Voting turnout, 53, 250–51

Walker, John W., 17
Wallace, George C., 37, 125–29
Wallace, George, Jr., 131–32, 135
Wallace, Lurleen Burns, 126–27
Wards, 232
Warrant, arrest, 206
Warrant, payment, 135–36, 240
Waste, toxic, 30, 153
Welfare, public, 157–58, 219
Wildlife refuges, 146
Winston County, 21
Wiregrass, 5, 26, 123
Women, political participation, 7, 23, 26, 95, 188
Write-in candidates, 49, 52

Youth Services, Department of, 38, 152, 169, 171

Zoning, 230, 236, 251